The Just Right Home

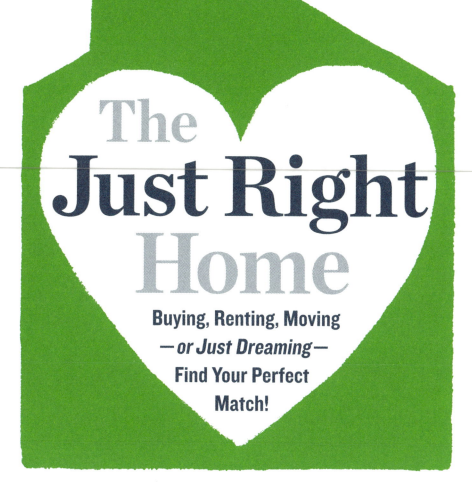

The Just Right Home

Buying, Renting, Moving
—or Just Dreaming—
Find Your Perfect
Match!

MARIANNE CUSATO

with Daniel DiClerico

WORKMAN PUBLISHING · NEW YORK

To my parents, Marcy and Dave Cusato

Library of Congress Cataloging-in-Publication Data is available.

ISBN 978-0-7611-6891-1

Cover and interior design by Jean-Marc Troadec
Photo credits on page 371.

Workman books are available at special discounts when purchased in bulk for premiums and sales promotions as well as for fund-raising or educational use. Special editions or book excerpts also can be created to specification. For details, contact the Special Sales Director at the address below, or send an email to specialmarkets@workman.com.

Workman Publishing Company, Inc.
225 Varick Street
New York, NY 10014-4381
workman.com

Printed in United States of America

First printing March 2013

10 9 8 7 6 5 4 3 2 1

Acknowledgments

First and foremost, many thanks to our editor, Mary Ellen O'Neill, whose expertise and knowledge combined with her endless enthusiasm has made this process an absolute pleasure. Every author should be so lucky! Thanks also to Peter Workman and the entire team at Workman Publishing for making this book possible. Special thanks to my agent, Gail Ross, for believing in our idea and helping us sell the concept.

Thank you to Linda Stephen for her insightful edits and suggestions, always turned around with lightning speed; Jonathan Smoke and Hanley Wood Market Intelligence for ongoing access to housing market data and research; Craig Savage and Mark LaLiberte for their building science insights; Monica Quigley for her help with the real estate worksheet; Jacqueline Thomas for her research assistance; and all of those who shared their Words of Wisdom.

This book stands on the shoulders of many great thought leaders, like Suze Orman, Richard Florida, and Robert Shiller. But especially Andres Duany and Elizabeth Plater-Zyberk, both of whose mentorship have been central to my professional career.

Thank you to my coauthor, Daniel DiClerico. Always a pleasure to work with, Dan truly was the secret weapon required to make this book happen.

And finally, I would like to thank Irina Woelfle for inspiring many of the core ideas in this book and working with us along the way to make sure that we stayed on target.

Contents

Part 3: Deciding and Moving In

Appendices

Introduction

Am I living in the right place? You don't have to be planning a move to ask this question. I think about it daily, and I suspect it's on your mind too. I wonder if my career is stable enough so that I can keep up my current lifestyle. I want to ignore the possibility of another economic dip, but the hard reality is that it could happen. Then there are the social questions. I am single, but would like to change that eventually. Would moving increase my odds of finding the right someone?

Moving today means more than changing addresses. It is an opportunity to assess how you really want to live. The formulas that once guided our life decisions are being questioned, opening the door for you to create your own formula and live a more fulfilling life. Where you live is much more than the structure you live in. Where you live is tied to your community, your job, your family, your health, and your personal finances. This book explores the factors beyond home that affect your quality of life. The goal is to help you consider all of the variables so you can make the best decisions possible, whether you're taking stock of your current situation or planning a move to someplace new.

When the house of cards fell in the mid-2000s, more than a mortgage meltdown was revealed. The fundamental formula that guides the lifestyle of the American middle class also came into question. First graduate from college and get a job in the city. Then get married and buy a house in the 'burbs. Later have kids and buy a larger house farther out in the 'burbs. Retire and buy a smaller house someplace warm. Live happily ever after.

What happens if you followed the formula, but the formula let you down? For many, keeping up with the Joneses was a pursuit with diminishing returns. It might have felt great at first, but it eventually revealed a dismal quality of life, with long hours in the car, half-furnished homes, and overextended credit. The silver lining of the bad economy is that we have a chance to hit the reset button, to stop and think about what really matters in our lives, and to ask ourselves what will provide true, lasting value rather than a quick fix.

The inevitable housing collapse has revealed new values. Once upon a time, if you didn't fit the formula, you might have still done what you thought you "should" do. Or perhaps what was easiest, even if it wasn't what you really wanted for your life. Unfortunately, in this pursuit of what we thought we "should" be doing, a lot of people ended up very unhappy, making decisions that were doomed to fail.

Today, your choices are yours, and your future is yours. If you are worried that you aren't in the right place, if you are concerned that you can't sustain your current lifestyle, now is the time to truly assess your realities and make the tough decisions. Don't wait until it is too late to make a move.

When the good times were rolling, free credit and cheap gas enabled a system of conspicuous consumption where housing was an easy-to-attain status symbol. Our life decisions didn't feel like they had much consequence. Of course, anyone in an upside-down mortgage (owing more than the house is worth) knows that was never the case. Today's economic instability, both globally and in our personal finances, weighs heavily on all decisions we make about where and how we live. It is no longer a given that we can earn as much in the future as we have in the past, or that the job with benefits (vacation, health insurance, and a 401K) you planned your life around will remain. It is no longer given that the value of a home you purchase today will increase tomorrow. What is a given is that today you have an opportunity to make thoughtful and meaningful decisions about the type of life you want to live.

So what is your American Dream? Where is Home Sweet Home for you? How can you avoid turning your home into a golden noose? The old formula was set up like a treadmill that you couldn't get off. The more money you made, the more you spent. The more you spent, the more you needed to make. Despite all of our riches, when did we stop to live? The American Dream used to be a cottage with a white picket fence. Over time, it morphed into the Garage Mahal on a cul-de-sac. The American Dream is evolving again. The question is, Where is it going? That is up to you. We all have the image of our perfect "dream home," perhaps a villa in the South of France or an estate in wine country. But we also have the realities of daily life. One of my key goals is to help you articulate your actual needs (not just wants) and to offer ideas that will help you find a home that is livable, lovable, and within your means.

My original title for this book was *The Autopsy of the McMansion*. At the height of the housing boom, roughly 2 million new homes were being built each year. Most of these homes were larger than needed, isolated from everything, and more expensive than their owners could afford, yet they were endearing to millions. My idea was to examine how these homes evolved and to explore the next chapter for the "American Dream Home." I was told this was a great topic for a magazine article, but not a book. My advisers were right. I was missing the big picture. While new-home starts (that's industry-speak for the number of new homes being built) dropped to as low as 300,000, more than 37 million people switch addresses in any given year and millions more sit on the sidelines contemplating a move. To serve the needs of those 37 million (plus) people, this book needed to help navigate the landscape and explore personal realities to help them, and you, find the right home—a home that is more than a structure, or to paraphrase a song from my college days, "not (just) the place you live, but the place you belong."

The original book idea lives on, woven into the pages you are about to read, because to move forward we must first understand where we have been. You can read it from front to back, back to front, or in any order you like. Some sections may not apply to you, whereas others will be central to your journey. As you read, remember that one size doesn't fit all, so take what you want and leave the rest. Most important, understand that you can have something other than the default setting.

In a sense, the Great Recession is perhaps best renamed the Great Opportunity. If you feel you are not in the right place in life, it is never too late to correct your course. If you are young and starting out, wondering what you "should" do next, follow your gut. If the conventional formula works for you, go for it and don't look back. But if it doesn't, don't worry.

Wherever you are in life, be true to yourself about your realities so you can keep your priorities in check. Listen to your heart, but follow your gut. And always live within—or even a bit below—your means. My hope is that this book will help you understand all of your options and assess your true needs, so that you will be able to make informed and educated decisions about where and how you want to live. And in the end, live the life you want to live on your own terms.

Part 1: Preparing

Chapter 1

Are You Thinking About Moving?

I f you've picked up this book, it means you're in the process of moving, considering a move, or perhaps weighing whether your current living situation is sustainable. Whatever the case, you're likely to hear plenty of conflicting reports as you start talking to friends, families, and professionals: Housing will never be the same; it will lead the recovery. It's a buyer's market; it's a renter's market. It's better to wait out the storm; it's better to cut your losses and make a change. There are bargains everywhere; it's never been easier to lose your shirt.

The fact of the matter is that all of these statements are true to some degree. That's because we all have our own realities and individual paths to finding a fulfilling life. The best of times for person X might be the worst of times for person Y. My point here is not to complicate an already confusing time. Rather, I want to make the case that with something as big and variable as determining how and where to live, the only factors that really count are the ones that matter to you.

Your personal and family needs are more important than market forces. The goal of this book is to help you sort through what you see and hear in the news, what you've been told by professionals, and the societal pressures that tell you what you "should" do, to enable you to make your own decisions, decisions that will meet your long-term goals and balance all of your needs.

Let's start by taking stock of your current realities. Ask yourself these questions, answering as honestly as possible. Take a moment to reflect on each answer, and if you feel it would be helpful, jot down thoughts and notes in a journal. Keep this list of questions, and your answers, in mind as you read this book and especially as you plan your search and make your final decisions about where to live.

QUIZ: ASSESSING YOURSELF

Current and Future Lifestyle

1. Where are you in your life today? (Consider your age, career, family, finances, health, and general level of contentment.)
2. What changes do you see in your life in the coming years?
3. How might these changes affect your housing needs?
4. How does where you live support your personal goals, financial goals, physical goals, and family's needs?

Personal Economics

1. Can you afford your current lifestyle?
2. Will you be able to continue to afford your lifestyle in the future?
3. How secure is your job and your career?
4. If you lost your job, could you afford to keep up your current lifestyle? If not, do you have a contingency plan in place?

Family Needs

1. Do you have aging parents who will or might need care?
2. Do you have kids? If they are grown, might they need to move home? If they are young, does your current living setup allow them to thrive?

In the last few decades, our society has lost sight of the importance of where and how we live. Facebook is considered a community, filled with friends we never see, some of whom we've never even met. In a time when we've never been so "connected" with a virtual community, we've never been more isolated and disconnected from our homes and our physical communities. Since the bubble burst, millions of Americans have been left trapped, living in far-reaching exurbs, in homes that are beyond their means and don't even meet their needs. Your home should meet your needs and desires, but it should also be financially and environmentally sustainable.

Regardless of where you are in the process of planning or just considering a move, the goal of this book is to help you make the most informed decisions possible. Now is the time to really assess your current course to determine if you are on the right path or would benefit from making some changes. This book is your guide.

Redefining the Formula for Finding a Home

In the old economy (pre-2008, that is), homeownership was seen as a rite of passage that everyone aspired to and most people attained. "If you own your own home, you're realizing the American dream," George W. Bush declared in 2002. Back then, nearly 70 percent of Americans owned their homes, up from the roughly 45 percent who did so a century earlier. Bush was hardly the first U.S. president to pound the pulpit in support of Americans buying more houses. As

> **The bubble years changed everything. Instead of homes providing a long-term investment, they became a means of making a quick buck.**

far back as Herbert Hoover in the 1920s, homeownership was idealized as a moral imperative for the nation, one that would spur civic-minded citizenry, safer neighborhoods, better schools, and financial stability for all.

Once upon a time, those ideals often held up, largely because most people committed to a thirty-year fixed rate mortgage, which they paid off just before retirement, providing cheap digs in their old age. But the bubble years changed everything. Instead of homes providing a long-term investment, they became a means of making a quick buck. At the height of the craziness, a significant number of homes were purchased with the express intent to "flip" the property and move on to something bigger and better. Under this paradigm, resale value ruled the day. What you wanted was less important than what some prospective buyer down the line would supposedly demand.

We live in a very different world today. Since the music stopped, millions have defaulted on their mortgages, millions more are underwater (owing more than the property is worth), and credit is all but frozen. As bad as things seem in a down economy, we always recover.

Home Defined

The word *home* has many meanings, from habitat to headquarters, though it's most commonly used to describe one's place of residence. Home is where you hang your hat, as the saying goes. That's how I'm using the word *home* in this book, though I want to point out that a place of residence can take many forms. It might be a single-family house, but it could also be a condo, town house, mother-in-law flat, apartment, or other building type.

But we'll never return to the bubble years. The numbers just don't add up, not now that lending practices have come back down to earth and homeowners are no longer able to treat their homes like ATMs.

Today we have new formulas. Homeownership is once again a commitment. As a result, renting is now a viable, even preferable, option for many. And for those who are prepared for and able to make the commitment to buy, resale value is giving way to live-in value as the main criterion for buying a house.

Lessons for Maximizing Your Live-In Value

What is the live-in value of your home? Live-in value is the measure of how well a home balances your needs, budget, and desires. It's a simple concept that was lost during the *Flip This House* frenzy of recent years. Not everyone's live-in value is the same. The overarching goal of this book is to help you come up with your own definition, from the most livable city and neighborhood to the home that best nurtures your wants and needs. Before we narrow the scope, here are three lessons to keep in mind:

Lesson One: Forget everything you've ever been told about where you should live.

That might sound extreme, but it's true. I travel around the country frequently, giving presentations about smart design for homes and communities. More often than not, the response I get is some version of "I wish I had heard you speak before I bought my last house." And it doesn't come just from first-time or otherwise inexperienced home buyers. People upgrading to their second or third homes were just as likely to get caught up in the recent housing bubble, and their homes are now golden handcuffs.

Builders I meet will often say, "I agree with what you're saying, and I'd love to build and live in a community like you're describing. But I could never sell it to my buyers." At the same time, I hear homeowners say how much they love the idea of living in a neighborhood with sidewalks and a mix of housing sizes, but that builders aren't able to build like that anymore. In this sense, the current housing crisis might better be described as a hostage crisis. Everybody—from developer to builder to real estate agent to home buyer—was held hostage to what he or she thought everybody else wanted.

This is why it's so important to understand that one size does not fit all when it comes to finding your right home and community. The path to finding your right home lies in determining what works for *you*. Not the next person who will own your home, not your parents who purchased their first place just out of college, not your friends who got a great "deal" on a foreclosure. Take in all of the information around you, but don't take it as your own—unless it works for you.

Lesson Two: Long-term satisfaction comes from substance, not sizzle.

A home is, first and foremost, a roof over your head. But it provides more than mere shelter. I meet a lot of people who are unhappy with where they live. Within five minutes of speaking with them, it's obvious they didn't properly weigh all the pros and cons of the property before making the investment. Think about the last car you bought. Chances are you inquired about the fuel economy, right? Now consider your last home purchase or rental. Did you ask about its annual heating and cooling costs? Probably not. We're just not conditioned to think about our homes with that level of detail, which is pretty crazy given that it's often the single biggest purchase we'll make in our lives.

There's a great passage from David Brooks's thought-provoking 2011 book *The Social Animal: The Hidden Sources of Love, Character, and Achievement*. Talking about the control our unconscious mind has on how we shop, Brooks writes, "Even people shopping for major purchases don't know what they want. Realtors have a phrase, 'Buyers lie,' because the house many describe at the beginning of their search is nothing like the one they actually prefer and buy." He goes on to note, "Builders know that many home decisions are made in the first seconds upon walking in the door. A California builder, Capital Pacific Homes, structured its high-end spec houses so that upon entering, the customer would see the Pacific Ocean through the windows on the main floor, and then the pool through an open stairway leading to the lower level. The instant view of the water on both levels helped sell these $10 million homes. Later cogitation was much less important."

Brooks is right about how quickly decisions are made, and in the example he cites, the ocean view isn't actually a bad thing. Indeed, connection to the outdoors is one of the design rules of thumb you're going to read about in this book. But builders' efforts to sway buyers aren't always so genuine, which is another reason why they'll often pour so much of their budget into the front façade of the house and ignore the sides and back. That's why I would tweak Brooks's argument and say that later cogitation, although less important to the initial decision of whether to buy or not, is absolutely critical when it comes to determining long-term satisfaction. An ocean view will certainly make a dramatic first impression, but the principles outlined in this book will ensure happiness for years to come.

Lesson Three: Be honest with yourself while balancing your priorities.

Okay, so here's the hardest pill to swallow. Finding your dream home on the ideal block in the perfect city is probably a long shot. Compromise is a fact of life, especially when it comes to choosing where to live. The goal of this book is to minimize your compromises as much as possible so that they don't take away from your happiness. Not to get all *Kumbaya* on you, but the right home should nurture your soul.

Compromise and balance require a foundation of honesty and truth. If you are not true to yourself about your needs for today and in the future, as well as your financial realities, it will be very difficult to make the right move.

When considering a move, you are vulnerable to two dangerous emotions: *fear* of making a mistake and *embarrassment* of not being able to afford more. These emotions have led a lot of good people to make really bad choices.

This point is especially important if you are assessing whether or not your current situation is financially sustainable. It is far worse to deny that you are struggling and let everything slide away than it is to make the necessary changes while you still have options on the table.

Fight the fear factor by arming yourself with knowledge and an understanding of your needs and options. As hard as it might be, honesty is the best cure for embarrassment. It is easy for our eyes to be bigger than our stomachs, so to speak, when looking for a home. And quite difficult to admit to your real estate agent, your spouse, or for that matter, yourself, that you can't afford certain things. Suze Orman has a fantastic phrase: "Stand in your truth." She defines it as being "painfully honest, clear-eyed stocktaking of your personal finances as well as your dreams for the future."

As you go through this book, your specific needs will come into sharper focus. You may end up with a list that has ten or twenty items on it. Make sure you stay grounded in your truth at all times. The challenge will be targeting the three or four that you can't live without. That doesn't mean you have to give up on the rest. But those core must-haves will be what you formulate your search around.

Have You Been Sold a Bill of Goods?

Location, location, location! We've all heard the phrase; it's ingrained in society. With the mere mention of a housing search to a group of friends, it's sure to roll off someone's tongue. But what if this phrase and a handful of others central to the sales of homes have been sending us down the wrong path?

Have you heard these common real estate phrases?

- "I know that you were looking in the $×× range, but if you can swing a little more, look how much more you can get."

- "Let me tell you about the house. First, it is ×× square feet and has granite counters."

- "It doesn't matter if *you* want _____ [insert any number of items here]; you will need it to resell. After all, the best time to start thinking about selling your home is before you buy. In a couple of years, you can sell for a profit and move on."

And of course,

• "Location, location, location!"

Translation: "Spend more than you can afford, on a house that you don't really want, which can't meet your needs over time, and although the 'location' is great, it might not be anywhere near anything you do on a daily basis. But don't worry: You can sell it in a flash and move on whenever you want."

Have you purchased a home with one or more of these phrases in mind? If you have, you're not alone. You are also probably not in an ideal housing situation. Here is what to look for next time around:

Real Estate Mantra Redux

• "Proximity, proximity, proximity." Proximity trumps location. Where your home is located is important, but only in relation to a bigger picture. The ideal location takes into account the proximity and travel time between your daily needs.

• "Live within, or below, your means." Watch out for the "upsell." This is sometimes the bitterest pill to swallow, but it is crucial to your long-term sustainability.

• "All square feet are not created equal. How do you want to live in the house?" Size doesn't matter, but what you do with that size does matter.

• "Buy the home you want to live in." Not a home you move in only to resell. In today's world you are not guaranteed to sell your home

A Real Divide

Like square feet, not all real estate professionals are created equal. As in any profession, there are professionals committed to helping you find your best value and those who lean heavily on old defaults to get a sale. In chapter 19 we outline the questions you need to ask to help you find the best possible fit.

whenever you want, and you will be lucky to sell it for a profit. And, you might just find that when you focus on the elements that create the best live-in value for you and your family, it often ends up translating to a higher resale value down the road.

Make sure that you always keep your requirements and realities in mind when making a move. *Your live-in value will be greatly reduced if you end up with an overextended mortgage, overpriced rent, or unexpected commuting costs that eat up a third of your household budget.*

The Decision Balancing Act: Function, Cost, and Delight

If you've ever tried to sustain a great-tasting diet on a budget, then you have wrestled with the Decision Balancing Act. Who hasn't stood in the grocery store staring down the aisles, trying to figure out which foods simultaneously taste great, won't break the bank, and aren't too fattening or unhealthful? The world would be a better place if eating a dozen doughnuts for $3 didn't turn us all diabetic and obese. And if only those vitamin-rich canned vegetables that cost a dollar didn't taste like tin. These analogies represent function, cost, and delight—the three requirements to look for in every purchasing decision, but for our purposes, especially in deciding where you'll live.

For most things, housing included, successfully satisfying one of these categories is easy. Balancing two is doable with a little work. But true success comes only when function, cost, and delight are all addressed in equal ways—and this is where the real work starts. When looking for a new place to live, constantly ask yourself how the three elements of the Decision Balancing Act balance out. And if you're looking for a home with a spouse or partner, or older children who understand and appreciate the importance of the move, make sure all points of view are heard.

Function First question: Does the home fit your life—now and in the future? So many home-finding decisions are influenced by where you are in life, especially these days when people are marrying later (if at all), delaying retirement (albeit not by choice), and living longer (a good thing!). This life phase adjustment has affected the traditional model of home buying. Time was, people married in their twenties and bought a starter home, often in or near the city; had a few kids and upgraded to a larger home, usually in the suburbs; then downsized to a smaller home or town house, typically somewhere warm, to live out their retirement years. A fair number of folks still follow that path. But many of us, myself included, are looking for a different formula. This might mean going from owning back to renting, or moving from the suburbs back into the city. As you start to consider function, don't be ruled by old formulas that don't always apply to the new world.

> **When your community offers amenities, the pressure is released from your home to have to provide them too.**

Next: Is the home near places that meet your daily needs? As noted previously, let's replace "location, location, location" with "proximity, proximity, proximity." What's the difference? Location tells you where something is, whereas proximity indicates its closeness to other objects. Once upon a time, when neighborhoods were designed with a balance of homes, jobs, shopping, schools, and recreation, we were able to meet our needs with a five-minute walk. Nowadays, you might be looking at a forty-five-minute, traffic-choked drive to pick up a quart of milk. The farther homes get from stores and other amenities, the more we depend on the home to meet all of our needs—and thus at the height of the boom, home theaters, cafés, hair salons, and other public amenities found their way into average homes, illustrating the deep divide between home and community. Ideally, your community offers not only connection to getting your daily needs met, but also civic assets in reasonable proximity to your home. When your community offers amenities, the pressure is released from your home to have to provide them too.

The Story Behind the Story: Planned Obsolescence

Planned obsolescence is all around us. Just take your cell phone. Either you have the uncontrollable need to upgrade every time a newer version is released. Or you hold out and after not too long, the batteries start to die, reception fizzles, and cracks show on the display. The practice started in the 1920s and '30s, when mass production was coming online in the United States. Manufacturers found that they were producing products faster than consumers needed to replace them. To avoid slowing down production, they decided to design products to fail sooner.

The term *planned obsolescence* was coined by the American industrial designer Brooks Stevens in 1954, who defined it as meaning "instilling in the buyer the desire to own something a little newer, a little better, a little sooner than is necessary." In her compelling 2010 documentary *The Light Bulb Conspiracy,* Spanish filmmaker Cosima Dannoritzer explores the topic by looking at some of the earliest examples of the practice—light-bulbs and nylons. (Did you know that at one time nylons were designed so strongly that they could tow a truck? That was until sales dropped because women didn't need to replace their hose. The issue was resolved when the product engineers designed them to fail.)

General Motors introduced planned obsolescence to the auto industry in the early 1920s. At the time, the Ford Model T dominated the market and represented 50 percent of cars sold nationwide. GM couldn't compete on price or performance with the Model T, so they decided to compete with

Last but not least: Is the house well built and easy to maintain? There is a huge range in the quality of housing construction in this country. Let's take something as basic as insulation. Most homes, including many in regions that experience frigid winters, don't have sufficient insulation in their attics to prevent cold air from getting inside. If you're buying a new home, existing or newly built, and you're able to include this one efficiency upgrade, you could conceivably lower your energy bills by a few hundred bucks every year. (More on this in Chapter 17.)

revolving style. They introduced new lines of cars every year, designed to phase out the ones from earlier years. These cars did not have to run as well as the Model T, because the goal was to get people to replace them every three years. What was once a major purchase now became a discardable item. The practice was so successful that by 1927, Ford shut down production of the Model T and shifted to GM's sales model.

Planned obsolescence is great business for everyone but the buyer. It is ingrained in our society that new must be better and the sooner you can upgrade the better, so we open up our wallets, even when they are empty. This phenomenon is at the heart of the housing collapse. Homeowners everywhere were encouraged to buy something a little newer, a little better, a little sooner than they needed.

One of the biggest reasons I wanted to write this book was to help reverse this perception. Although a home's systems, appliances, and overall style will need periodic upgrading and sprucing up, the home itself is an investment, one that affects not only your finances but also the environment. It is more than a little annoying to have to buy a new printer every couple of years, but nothing compared with how outrageous it is to think about a home as an expendable item that you live in for a few years before upgrading to the next shinier model. Take care not to fall into this trap.

Cost You'll read a lot about cost in this book, but here's my bottom-line position. If you can't sustain the type of lifestyle you want and need because your monthly housing and transportation costs are too high, you are living beyond your means. That includes being able to make adequate contributions to your retirement savings so that your future lifestyle won't be negatively affected by your current living situation. I meet too many people who are unwilling or unable to take a long view of their housing situation. At best, they end up having to sacrifice things that are truly meaningful, whether it's summer camp for the kids or crucial home improvements. At worst, their onetime dream home ends in the nightmare of foreclosure, ruining their financial stability for years to come.

Delight This is the "fun part," which for some people can translate into "nonessential." Don't make this mistake. Your home may work for you, and you may be able to afford the monthly payments, but if you don't feel that little pleasure every time you pull onto your street or walk through the front door, Home Sweet Home will eventually become a source of frustration. I liken it to being in a relationship with someone you're not all that crazy about. You might be able to go through the motions for a while, but sooner or later the cracks in your affection will show. A home may be inanimate, but your relationship to it should be growing and evolving all the time.

Getting Personal: Life Phase and Demographics

THE EFFECT OF DEMOGRAPHICS ON HOUSING IN THE UNITED STATES

Nationwide, we are starting to see a dramatic shift in where and what type of housing is being built. This is influenced by a variety of factors, including land cost, economic activity, and even weather conditions. One of the greatest factors affecting housing today is shifting demographics. Two cohorts of the population currently account for roughly half of all Americans: baby boomers, born between 1946 and 1964, and echo boomers (aka millennials or Gen Y), born between 1982 and 1999. Both groups are starting to change life phase en masse. As echo boomers head off to college and into the workforce, the boomers are left at home in the empty nest.

Large numbers of people in both of these demographic groups are starting to turn away from large homes on big lots in favor of compact communities where you don't need to hop in the car to buy a cup of coffee. In the case of the baby boomers, their child-rearing days are coming to a close, so they're often looking to downsize to homes in walkable neighborhoods close to stores. Echo boomers, meanwhile, grew up in (or at least near) the big house at the end of the cul-de-sac having to drive to school or to see friends at the mall. However, they are increasingly driving less and looking for ways to live in an area where they can walk, bike, or use public transportation for shopping, restaurants, and schools.

> **" The house that might have been your choice at one time may be different from your choices today and in the future. "**

That doesn't mean the American suburb is going to turn into a ghost town. There are still plenty of people who want to live there, including many from the roughly 50-million-strong Gen X generation (born between 1965 and 1982) who are in their prime child-rearing years. Nonetheless, these demographic changes combined with increasing demand (and costs) for energy worldwide will have a lasting effect on where and how we build homes. Arthur C. Nelson of the University of Utah has estimated that there will be 22 million unwanted large-lot suburban homes by 2025.

What does all of this mean for you? Although the specific details will depend on where you are in your life, the overarching theme to remember is that housing formulas are no longer a given. The house that might have been your choice at one time may be different from your choices today and in the future. As you read this book, keep an open mind to new things. You might be surprised where you end up.

What is your life phase?

If you are a single twentysomething just starting out in your career, the right home for you may look very different from that of a married couple with kids. Although many of the same principles apply to all life phases, some details will inevitably vary. As you will hear me say throughout the book, one size does not fit all. Throughout the book you will find sections dedicated to assessing needs by life phase. Here are the six main stages of life:

> ## DISIDULS—New housing for a new era of marriage
>
> Think you've heard everything? Some builders are now designing homes for a new market segment, "divorced spouses in a dual living situation" or DISIDULS. The homes designed with double master suites target couples who have divorced but want to stay together for the kids or are financially unable to split.

Young Adults (Millennials or Gen Y) You are in your early twenties and just starting out in the world. Having recently graduated from high school or college, you are either working on entering the workforce or are early in your career. Unless you are in the 1 percent, you'll most likely have limited financial means at this stage of your life. This is the time to start establishing yourself in life and career.

Single Professionals and DINKs (Double Income, No Kids) This is a growing group that spans the widest age bracket as more and more people are waiting to get married and start families. You might be in your late twenties but could be in your fifties. You are established in your career. You are single or married without kids. If you are in this group, you probably have a little more financial flexibility.

Young Families You are anywhere from your mid- to late twenties to your forties and have one or more young children. You are probably married, but might also be single or divorced. You are probably strapped for both space and cash. The needs of the family are taking priority over your individual needs. This will change how you assess and balance your wants and needs for life decisions and housing.

Established Families You are established in your career and with your family. A good number of you are Gen-Xers in your late thirties and early forties, but many of you are in your fifties from the last wave of boomers. As with those in the young families category, you could be married, but you might also be single or divorced. You will be taking a hard look at your financial future as the prospects of college and retirement start dawning on the horizon.

Empty-Nesters Your kids have flown the coop. They might be college students or young adults. You might have financial considerations relating to college expenses and could be looking at the possibility of retirement. You may be thinking about downsizing into a smaller home or looking at multigenerational housing options, as you have the potential for both boomerang kids coming back home and elderly parents needing a place to live.

> " The key to finding happiness in where you live is to follow your gut, be honest about your realities, and, in some cases, learn how to settle in style. "

Elderhood You are established in your retirement. As the life expectancy rate in the United States continues to improve—it was seventy-nine in 2010, up from seventy in 1970—your group will only get bigger. You will need to be thinking about aging in place, defined as the ability to live in one's home and community safely, independently, and comfortably, regardless of age, income, or ability level. It's made possible by features in the home, such as a master bedroom on the first floor, wider doors, and grab bars in the bathrooms, as well as the home's proximity to health care services and your ability to get around if you are unable to drive.

KEEPING YOURSELF IN CHECK

Balancing Act

Making your right move requires first understanding all of the options, then assessing your wants and needs, and finally balancing all of this information with your actual realities. This book presents a lot of information, suggestions, and variables. You might find yourself a little overwhelmed at times. At the end of each chapter, I have included a section to help keep you grounded in your search. The key to finding happiness in where you live is to follow your gut, be honest about your realities, and in some cases, learn how to settle in style.

Gut Check

Every time I listen to my gut—or instinct—events turn out in my favor. Any time I ignore it, I regret it. Sometimes it seems to be telling me to do something unconventional. Sometimes my gut tells me to do something that appears to create larger problems, perhaps by disappointing or upsetting others. In these cases, I have been known to ignore it, assuming that this will be best in the long run. I always regret these decisions.

Your instinct is a powerful barometer. Mine is my compass. It tells me what to do, even when I don't want to hear it. Making a move is a big deal. It can affect every aspect of your life. Don't dismiss how you feel because it isn't what everyone else is doing. My gut has never let me down, but I have let myself down a few times by ignoring it.

Reality Check

Now, having said all of that about following your instincts, make sure you don't lose sight of your realities. If you are married and have kids, you will also have to incorporate the needs and wants of others into the equation. Who makes the compromise when you and your spouse have different desires? My advice is to be as honest as possible at all times with yourself and your loved ones—and to consider not just price per square foot for a house or apartment but the effect the location of the home will have on your life: commuting time to work or school, exercise opportunities, chats with neighbors, and so on. It might be hard in the short term, but in the long run, your planning will pay dividends.

CHAPTER CHEAT SHEET

Key points to remember

- Watch out for real estate jargon like "location, location, location" and "You need it to resell." Remember, in today's world, proximity trumps location, and live-in value trumps resale value.

- Assess your actual needs, not your perceived needs or the need to keep up with the Joneses.

- Trade-offs are inevitable when searching for a home. Being honest with yourself about your budget and your needs will help you balance the pros and cons of all your options to find the home that is the best fit for you and your family.

Questions to keep in mind

- Does your existing or prospective new home meet your balancing act by meeting your needs (function), budget (cost), and desires (delight)?

- Are you being realistic about your realities?

- Have you clearly expressed your feelings and positions to your spouse, partner, or anyone else who will be part of the home-finding process?

Chapter 2

Moving, Staying, Renting, Owning, Buying, Building? Ahh!

**M**oving into a new home has always been an exhilarating process. Think of the image of the beaming bride and groom crossing the threshold of their home for the first time. Exciting stuff. Of course, these days you don't have to wait for wedding bells to buy your first home. In fact, single women have been the fastest-growing segment of the real estate market, representing about 20 percent of all buyers. Single men add another 10 percent.

The formula for moving has changed in other ways. Perhaps most fundamentally, it's no longer gospel that everyone should make owning a home their top priority. For those lucky enough to have their financial house in perfect order, ownership still makes sense as a long-term investment. But since the bottom of the economy officially dropped out in September 2008, fewer people can make that claim. Hence the dip in rental vacancy rates that's taking place in many cities as more people either delay purchasing a home or go from owning back to renting. Nationwide, it fell below 10 percent in late 2011 for the first time in years, all the way to 7 percent in the West. Following the economic rule of supply and demand, as vacancy rates have gone down, rental rates have increased.

There's plenty of volatility in new housing as well. Although housing starts haven't ground to a complete halt, they're well off their millennial high—2006, when a whopping 2.2 million new homes were built. In 2011, that number was around 300,000. Not great figures for an already beleaguered industry, but not insignificant either. After all, that's a lot of potential new places for you to live.

What's also significant is the type of housing that's being built today versus ten or even five years ago. For one thing, single-family residences are shrinking. After peaking in 2002 at 2,277 median square feet, with much of that girth going to McMansions and other megahouses, the average home is now down around 2,100 square feet. We're also building a lot more multifamily housing units, from town houses to high-rise apartment complexes, to serve the growing number of people who want to live closer to city centers.

WORDS OF WISDOM

"We wanted to move back to New York from Philadelphia, but couldn't sell our house without taking a huge hit. So we decided to rent it out and also rent in New York. The amount we charge more than covers the mortgage, so we come out ahead every month." Mark and Cristi P., New York, NY

"When we moved to Austin, a city we didn't know well, we thought about buying a house right away. Even though it's more expensive to rent, I'm really glad we didn't buy. We thought we knew the neighborhood we wanted to live in, but it turns out that there are others that are better for us. If we had bought ahead of time, we likely would have spent a lot of time and money selling it in a year or two." Steve S., Austin, TX

One final change: the makeup of the household itself, as more boomerang kids move back in with Mom and Dad, and aging parents take residence in a bedroom or the granny flat out back. In 1980, there were 28 million multigenerational households in the United States, according to the Pew Research Center. By 2008, that number was up to 49 million. Between 2007 and 2008 alone, 2.6 million more households went multigenerational, largely because of financial straits brought on by the recession. One national survey in 2011 found that 30 percent of households were doubling up.

Essentially, the entire landscape of American housing is in a state of total flux, and that's calling into question some of the most basic questions of all: Should you move or stay put? Rent or own? Buy existing or build new? Your life phase, financial realities, and current housing situation will greatly influence how you answer these questions, starting with the first and biggest: Should you stay or should you go?

Moving Versus Staying

Is the indecision killing you, like in the old punk-rock anthem by the Clash? "If I go there will be trouble . . . but if I stay there will be double." Relax. This is not a lose-lose proposition. You just need to think through the options in a logical and honest fashion to figure out which one is right for you. Whatever you decide, it doesn't have to be your one and only home until the end of time, though I do want you to take a long view here, especially if you're thinking about buying. The days of revolving-door homeownership are long gone—and with good riddance, since that kind of model could never be sustained.

Organize your thought process around two key questions:

- What is the reason behind the move, and in particular is it being driven by you or by some external force?
- Can you afford to move without making too many compromises? This means calculating the actual costs of moving, the possibility of selling an existing home, and any expenses associated with the new place.

The weight of these two considerations will vary, depending on your specific situation. For example, some people have enormous stability in their financial and personal life, so they might have the luxury to think about moving for years before taking the plunge, whereas others are forced to do so virtually overnight by life circumstances beyond their control. Similarly, the person who is underwater on his or her mortgage will have to think a lot harder about the finances of moving than someone who owns their home outright. The important thing is that you come at the decision from all angles.

WHY ARE YOU MOVING? IDENTIFYING THE DIFFERENT TYPES OF MOVES

If you are trying to decide whether to stay or to move, the first step is to clearly establish your reason for moving. I like to put moves in three different categories.

Mandatory Moves

These might take the form of a job loss or transfer to a new city, a divorce or change in relationship status, or the loss of a home because of a natural disaster, such as a flood or hurricane. More often than not, this type of move comes with little warning and a large dose of emotional upheaval. One of the most stressful things in life is not knowing where your home will be in the near future.

In nearly every mandatory move, an external factor is at play, usually with a fairly firm deadline. That makes for a real pressure cooker, which is when mistakes are most common. Although you need to act fast, it's critical that you not jump in without making sure it is the right fit. More often than not, when I meet people who paid too much for their home, or commute way too far to work, or live with a substandard house, it's because they took the first thing that came along when they were stressed out from dealing with other issues in their lives.

And so, if you are moving in the midst of emotional turmoil, or you're relocating to a new city on short notice, I strongly recommend that you rent first before buying. You might look for a flexible short-term rental home, perhaps even one that is furnished. The key is not to jump into a purchase that you will regret and may not be able to unload easily. If you currently own, the pressure will also be on to sell your existing home. If you are underwater or unable to sell, you might consider renting out your current house rather than taking too much of a loss in price.

The Inoculating Move

In a growing trend, some people are starting to purchase substantially less home than they can afford. Worried about global markets and general economic uncertainties, uninterested in being overextended just to impress friends or keep up appearances, many are looking to inoculate themselves financially for the future. Consider this: It is not necessarily in your long-term best interest to get a mortgage for the full amount your banker approves. After all, it is in your bank's best interest to give you the maximum loan that you will be able to repay.

Mandatory moves also might arise from losing your house to foreclosure or in a short sale. Although this is never easy, you can help yourself out by making your current living situation last for as long as possible. Because of the backlog in the courts, many people in foreclosure are often able to stay in their homes for a year or more without making payments while the process works itself out. Maximize this time and save as much as possible while you plan for your next move. Often when your time is up in the house, you will be given very little notice, so have a plan in place to make the smoothest move possible.

Need-Based Moves

Like mandatory moves, need-based moves are driven by external forces, but you have more control over them. For example, maybe you're married and planning to start a family, meaning you'll need more space in the next year or so. Or perhaps you're at the end of the family-rearing stage, empty-nested and looking to downsize. In these situations, a move is needed, but you won't be under the same pressure of a mandatory move. As a result, if you're in a position to buy, you can take advantage of this time to get your finances in order and find a new home that's the right fit for you. You don't want to dawdle, but make sure to give yourself sufficient time to get it right. You will be surprised at how long you can make do if you are actively looking and planning to make a change. If you have to sell your existing home, remember to keep a reality check on current prices in your market so that your expectations remain in check.

Desire-Based Moves

In theory, this type of move should be the easiest of all, since you're not dealing with external pressures. Maybe you just feel like a change of scenery or a fresh start in a new city. And yet, the freedom to go anywhere at anytime can have a paralyzing effect on some people. If you're easily spoiled for choice, consider renting instead of buying, since it carries less commitment.

Time and money are on your side with a desire-based move. You can move fast or take it slowly, and you will have the ability to call

Why People Move

Listed below are the top reasons for moving according to a recent American Housing Survey conducted by the U.S. Census Bureau.

To establish household	10%
To be closer to work/school	9.3%
New job/transfer	9.3%
Needed a larger home or apartment	8.8%
Wanted a better home	6.8%
Wanted lower rent or maintenance	5.3%
Married, widowed, divorced, or separated	5.2%
Change from renter to owner or owner to renter	4.6%

the shots to get the best possible deals and find the best possible fit. But try not to take these luxuries for granted. Use the time to understand your finances, save as much money as possible, and assess your housing needs. If you have the mobility to move freely, fast is fine, but just make sure the numbers all work and the housing is right for you before you jump in headfirst.

CAN YOU AFFORD TO MOVE WITHOUT TOO MUCH COMPROMISE?

This question is particularly important if you have to sell an existing home. The first point I need to make here might be a little hard to hear, and that is that *your house is not worth what you want it to be worth—it's worth what someone else is willing to pay for it*. Of course, you will receive lowball offers, pass on these, but take a very careful look at what you are asking. Is it a 2005 price or today's price?

Look for comparable sales data for homes in your neighborhood. These "comps," which are available online through the Multiple Listings Service, should be from the last six months and for homes with the same basic features to ensure their accuracy. Websites like zillow.com and trulia.com also provide comparable sales data.

Don't live in a desirable market? If you don't want to slash the price of your home drastically, you'll need to make it as attractive as possible. Consider the condition of your home. There are often some fairly inexpensive projects you can do to stage and tidy up its appearance inside and out, such as adding potted plants by the front door and a fresh coat of neutral paint inside. But the bones of the home are still the bones of the home, so you need to be realistic about the condition when assessing your price and marketability.

Accepting the Condition of Your Mortgage

Ideally your mortgage is in good standing with the bank, and the amount you have put into the house and owe is less than or equal to the value of the home. But this is often not the case. Indeed, during the worst days of the housing crisis, more than one in five mortgage holders were underwater, with the percentages going way up in hard-hit states like Arizona, California, Florida, and Nevada.

So what should the value of your home really be?

We know the bubble burst, and that prices are still way down from their 2006 highs. But have they hit rock bottom, or could we be headed for a double dip? Ask five different economists and you're likely to get five different answers (at least!). But if I had to trust one economist over the rest, I'd go with Robert Shiller, the Yale professor and cocreator of the Case-Shiller Home Price Index. He predicted the burst of the housing bubble in the second edition of his book *Irrational Exuberance,* published in 2005. In the book, Shiller talks about how radically overvalued home prices became starting in the mid-1990s (see chart on next page). He also argues that home prices, when adjusted for inflation, have produced modest returns, nowhere near the 10 and 12 percent that many people came to expect during the housing boom.

So what does that all mean for the future? Even experts as prescient as Shiller can't say for certain where the U.S. housing market is headed, which is why it's best to take a very conservative view of home values, assuming that at best you'll see an annual return of around 3 percent. If your home goes up in value more, all the better. But you never want to be in a position where you're relying on artificial market forces.

I'll come back to Case-Shiller in Chapter 5, where I talk in more detail about determining the true value of a home. That includes the how-to for analyzing comparable properties in the neighborhood, as well as a primer on calculating compound interest.

If your house is underwater, you're left with three options: staying put, doing a short sale, or letting the house go into foreclosure. The first question to ask yourself here is, Can you afford the monthly payments? If you can afford your monthly payments and you are not facing the external factors of a mandatory move, it might be best to stay in your home. While it is unlikely that we will see the high values of the years just before the bubble burst, prices should start to come up again in the coming years and you may be able to get closer to even financially before moving a move. If not, you might be able to lower your monthly payments by refinancing, though

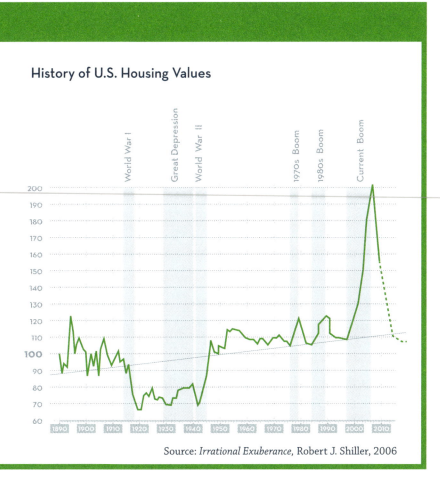

History of U.S. Housing Values

Source: *Irrational Exuberance*, Robert J. Shiller, 2006

keep in mind that it doesn't make sense over the long haul to extend the term of your loan. Also, refinancing carries fees, typically 1 or 2 percent of the total loan. Another option is to take advantage of the federal loan modification programs, which can lower your monthly payments by around 30 percent. Go to makinghomeaffordable.gov for more details.

If there's simply no way you can afford to stay in your home, you need to come up with an exit strategy. There are two basic options: short sale or foreclosure. In a short sale, the bank or mortgage holder lets you sell the home for less than the balance on your mortgage without requiring you to make up the difference. Banks are often willing to go along because the process is less complicated than a foreclosure, but you need to demonstrate true financial need, such as a job loss.

In a foreclosure, the bank takes back the home and you walk away. As simple and liberating as that sounds, it can often be a grueling ordeal that takes months and months to work out. The matter could even end up in court, depending on your state's laws. More important, foreclosures mean a big hit on your credit score. You can build your credit back up over time, but it will likely be five to seven years before a bank will even think about giving you another mortgage. So you need to be prepared for the prospect of long-term renting. Also, beware that an important tax break ended in 2012. Starting in 2013, if you sell your home in a short sale, you will have to pay taxes on the amount of money you lost.

TIMING THE SALE OF YOUR HOME

If your mortgage is in good standing, your only hurdle will be selling your home. This may take longer in a down economy. In a hot market, the average "days on market" for many homes will be less than a month, whereas in a slow market homes can languish for months and even years.

If you have to move for reasons outside your control and you can't sell your home, consider renting it out until you can sell it. Though this will force you into a landlord role, it will alleviate some of the pressure of balancing the purchase of a new home with the sale and closing of your current home. If the purchase of your next house depends solely on the sale of your current house, consider an intermediate period of renting between sale and purchase. It can be heartbreaking to have the perfect home lined up at the perfect price

> **Fast Fact** Homeownership rates worldwide: In France it's 57 percent, in Germany it's 46 percent, and in Switzerland it's just 37 percent, according to a 2011 report in *The Wall Street Journal*. In the United States, the rate is around 66 percent.

and lose it because something goes wrong with your existing house sale. If you have excellent financial standing, you might also consider getting a swing loan from the bank to cover the down payment on your new home while your existing home is still on the market. Of course, this means you'll basically be carrying two mortgages until the existing house sells, so swing loans are not without their risks.

Renting or Owning

MORE THAN MATH: THE PROS AND CONS OF RENTING VERSUS OWNING

Renting used to have a bit of a second-class reputation in this country. Those who had the means owned their homes. Those who didn't rented. Although politicians and policy experts stopped short of calling renting un-American, many actively endorsed an ownership society, for example by lobbying for tax incentives that benefit homeowners. But this paradigm started to shift course in the latter half of the 2000s. Between 2007 and 2010, household growth (that is, the number of new owner-occupied homes that were created) averaged just 500,000 per year, less than half the 1.2 million annual pace averaged between 2000 and 2007. By 2012, the homeownership rate (that is, the percentage of Americans who own their home versus rent it) was down to 65.4 percent, almost 5 percent below its 2004 peak, and the lowest level since 1997.

There are several reasons for the decline in homeownership in the United States. First and foremost, young adults are putting off purchasing their first home until the economy stabilizes. Some are waiting for the market to finally bottom out, and others are locked out by the frozen credit market. According to the 2011 Hanley Wood Housing 360 national survey, the top reason for not owning a home among renters was "I cannot afford the down payment on a home" (57 percent), followed by "It costs too much to maintain a home" (45 percent) and "I cannot afford the monthly mortgage payments" (39 percent). In fact, the under-thirty-five cohort saw its homeownership rate sink to a mere 38 percent in 2011. Meanwhile, the growth in foreign-born households has slowed considerably.

And many of the millions of Americans who lost their homes to foreclosure wouldn't choose to own again even if their ransacked savings and tarnished credit scores allowed it, according to a study by Harvard University's Joint Center for Housing Studies.

So what do these trend lines and statistics mean to you? Only that you should give serious consideration to both owning and renting. Here are the key considerations to keep in mind.

KEY CONSIDERATIONS

What is your seven-year plan? The old rule of thumb was that if you planned to be in your next home for fewer than five years, it made sense to rent. You might consider this as a starting point if you are deciding between renting or buying, but the truth is you may need to be in the home for seven years or longer before owning makes more sense than renting. That's because it's still too early in the housing recovery to know if the rate of appreciation will cover the costs of selling your home.

At the very least, you'll fork over 6 percent of the sale price to the real estate agent. Transfer taxes to the county and state or flip taxes to the cooperative or homeowners' association could cost you another 1 or 2 percent. Then there's the unexpected repairs you may have to make after the inspection, as well as the obvious moving costs. All of a sudden, your selling costs could be up around 10 percent. In some markets, home values will certainly go up that much in five years. But in others, renting remains a much safer bet, especially since there's no guarantee that you'll be able to sell your home in a timely manner. See page 35 for more details on crunching the numbers of renting versus owning with the help of an online calculator. I go over all the costs associated with owning a home in more detail in Chapter 3.

Do you have financial discipline? Wealth creation is a big part of the debate between owning versus renting. The pro-ownership camp argues that owing a home is an excellent long-term savings strategy that beats throwing away your money on rent. You slowly build up equity in your home, and once the mortgage is finally paid off, you

NYT's Rent Versus Own Calculator

The Internet is crawling with buy-versus-rent calculators, but the one I like the best is on *The New York Times* website (nytimes .com/interactive/business/buy-rent-calculator). It gives you a projected break-even date based on your current rent, the price of the prospective home, and the type of mortgage you're seeking. For example, if you currently pay $1,000 in rent and are looking to buy a $200,000 home with a thirty-year fixed-rate mortgage at 5 percent interest, you'll break even after six years. When you plug in your own calculations, assume that home prices and rents will rise at an annual rate of 3 or 4 percent.

have a place to live for free, not counting taxes, maintenance, and utilities. Proponents of renting counter that the vast sum of money you spend on mortgage interest, property taxes, maintenance, and the like could be better put toward other investments.

Which side is right? It depends on the current market conditions, but a 2011 study looked back over the previous thirty years and found that, on average, people who rented during that time were better off financially than those who owned. There's a huge caveat to the finding, however, which is that the positive result of renting "is strongly dependent upon fiscally disciplined individuals that, without fail, reinvest residual savings from renting." In other words, if you're able to take the money you're not spending on mortgage interest and put it into your retirement account, renting could pay off in the long run. But if that money will go to new shoes and fancy restaurants, you're better off with the forced savings plan that homeownership entails. You need to take a long, hard look at your habits (not to mention your investment portfolio) before making this decision.

How settled are you in your job and career? The get-up-and-go flexibility of renting can be conducive to job success. Historically, this has been true only for younger people just starting out in their careers, which is why renter demographics have traditionally

Owning makes you fat and renting makes your kids dumb. Really?

There's no shortage of research money spent on trying to understand the benefits of renting versus owning. But the more of these studies you read, the less clear the benefits become. Take the 2009 paper by a real-estate professor at the University of Pennsylvania's Wharton School, which concluded that, compared with renters, "the average homeowner consistently derives more pain (but no more joy) from their house and home." Ouch! As if that's not bad enough, the study also found that the average female homeowner is twelve pounds heavier than her renting counterpart. (That gives new meaning to the South Beach Diet, what with the high number of renters in this tony, well-toned Miami enclave!)

On the other hand, if you want to find the health benefits of homeownership, you don't have to look far. In 2010, the National Association of Realtors (NAR) compiled a bunch of academic studies supporting the positive effect owning a home has on personal health. In one, homeowners reported higher self-esteem and happiness than renters—emotional benefits that translate into superior physical health.

The NAR paper cuts even deeper than physical health to the issue that hits home for any parent: their child's education. "Consistent findings show that homeownership does make a significant impact on educational achievement" was the conclusion. What? If you choose to rent, your kid might not get into an Ivy League college? Of course not! And I don't mean to poke fun at the science behind these academic studies. But when the media gets its hands on them, the headline is often distilled to a single, hyperbolic message. "Homeownership is painful!" "Renting makes you skinny!" That's why, as you weigh the benefits of renting versus owning, I want you to filter out these surveys and studies and concentrate on the only focus group that matters: you and whoever else will be sharing your next home.

skewed younger—people in their twenties are twice as likely to move as people thirty to thirty-four years old and 3.5 times more likely than people who are forty-five to fifty-four. But in a down job market, workers of all ages benefit from being unfettered by mortgage payments, maintenance requirements, and the like. As Richard Florida asserts in *The Great Reset*, his 2010 treatise on how attitudes about living and working have changed since the Great Recession, "older manufacturing firms, jobs, and industries are being destroyed and new industries, occupations, and firms are being created. . . . In today's economy and the economy of the future, geographic mobility is required to match workers and their skills to appropriate jobs." And so, if there's a strong possibility that you'll need to change locations for a new job in the next five or so years, you should consider renting.

> **Having freedom of mobility is a real luxury, especially in this economy. But feeling settled and stationary is pretty nice too. Give thought to which one fits your life best when deciding to rent or own.**

Mobility Versus Stability Being a renter myself, I love having the flexibility to pick up and go whenever I please. I make use of it often, having changed zip codes seven times in the last fourteen years. I've moved for my career, I've moved to be in a better neighborhood, and I've moved because I just felt like a change. I love this freedom. Plus, when something major goes wrong with the property, say the roof leaks or the broiler goes kaput, I'm not on the hook for the repair.

Having said that, I also recognize the drawbacks of renting. Even if I want to stay in an apartment, my landlord might decide to sell, and that will leave me looking for a new place to live. There is a certain calm that comes with knowing where you'll be a year down the road, not to mention five or ten years. Some people cherish this stability, the pride of ownership, and the ability to make changes to their home. Having freedom of mobility is a real luxury, especially in this economy. But feeling settled and stationary is pretty nice too. Give thought to which one fits your life best when deciding whether to rent or own.

IDENTIFYING YOUR CITY'S RENT RATIO

You've probably heard the expression "All real estate is local." That's especially true when the ratio of renters to owners is in flux. Between 2004 and 2010, the number of renters in the United States surged by 3.9 million, driving vacancy rates down and prices up. By 2009, one quarter of all renters were spending more than half their income on rent and utilities, and another quarter were spending between 30 and 50 percent. The volatility and price hikes have been greater in some places than others. That's why you need to check the metrics in your part of the country. Rent ratio is the most useful tool. It's defined as the ratio of the purchase price of a home divided by the annual cost of renting a similar home. For example, if a two-bedroom house costs $250,000, and the annual rent for a similar home is $12,000 ($1,000 per month), then the rent ratio for that market is roughly 21 ($250,000 ÷ $12,000 = 20.8).

Most experts put the rent ratio tipping point somewhere between 15 and 20. The higher the rent ratio number, the more home prices will need to go up to justify the cost of buying. Given current economic conditions, you should take a more conservative view, looking for a rent ratio closer to 15 than 20. If the ratio is below 15, buying is preferable, whereas if it's above 20, you should definitely consider renting.

Here are a couple of examples building on the one above:

Home price of $350,000 versus rent of $1,000/month, $350,000 ÷ $12,000 = 29.1 (Renting is a better value.)

Home price of $250,000 versus rent of $1,600 a month, $250,000 ÷ $17,000 = 14.7 (Owning is a better value.)

Rent Ratios by City

Rent ratio compares the cost of renting versus owning a comparable property in a given city. As you can see from this sampling of metro areas (defined as a city's urban center and its surrounding jurisdictions, including its suburbs), there's a lot of volatility across the nation. Rent ratios will likely vary again from neighborhood to neighborhood within each city.

Metro Area	Ratio	Metro Area	Ratio
East Bay, Calif.	35.9	Chicago	16.6
Honolulu	34.4	New Orleans	16.2
San Jose, Calif.	32.7	Philadelphia	16.1
San Francisco	27.9	Houston	15.9
Seattle	27.3	Miami	15.6
Charlotte, N.C.	27	Los Angeles	15.4
New York (Manhattan)	26.7	Kansas City, Kan.	15.3
Portland, Ore.	25.9	*National average*	15.1
Nashville	24	Indianapolis	15.1
Denver	22.6	St. Louis	14.6
San Diego	22.1	Las Vegas	14.3
Milwaukee	21.4	Atlanta	14.3
Austin, Texas	20.5	Orlando, Fla.	14.1
Memphis	19.3	Dallas–Fort Worth	13.8
Boston	18.4	Phoenix	13.3
Oklahoma City	18.2	Detroit	12.4
Columbus, Ohio	17.6	Cleveland	11.7
Salt Lake City	17.6	Pittsburgh	11.4

Source: Moody's Analytics

SURVEYING THE HOUSING STOCK

Your decision to rent or buy will probably influence the type of home you choose. But don't fall back on the old stereotypes of what a rental property looks like versus an owner-occupied residence. Contrary to what many people believe, not all rentals take the form of cramped apartments in bustling urban centers occupied by a bunch of twentysomethings. In fact, more than half of the nearly 40 million Americans who rent live in suburban or nonmetropolitan areas. And half of all rental units are in small structures, including single-family homes, whereas only a quarter or so are in large apartment buildings.

Conversely, not all owner-occupied residences take the form of freestanding houses on tree-lined suburban streets. Instead, more than 10 million Americans live in an attached structure, such as a town house, or some type of multifamily structure, be it a brownstone or a high-rise apartment building. Given that so much of the new construction that has happened since the economic downturn is in the multifamily market, this trend is only going to intensify. We're also going to see more and more homeowners living in or near central cities, as opposed to only in the suburbs. New York City offers an extreme example of this. In the early 1990s, only 15 percent of the region's building permits were issued for residential projects. A decade later, the figure was up around 50 percent. You need only walk around Lower Manhattan, which has been the city's fastest-growing neighborhood, to feel the transformation from 9-to-5 financial hub to upscale, residential enclave with twenty-four-hour activity. Other cities are experiencing the same phenomenon. For residential building permits issued between the late 1990s and late 2000s, Chicago went from 7 to 27 percent, Portland, Oregon, from 9 to 26 percent, and Atlanta from 4 to 14 percent.

WHAT ARE THE ALTERNATIVES TO HOUSES?

If you're not into raking leaves and patching roofs, you might look past the single, detached house to a condo, co-op, or town house. Low maintenance is the biggest asset with this type of housing, especially for retired buyers and renters or for those whose busy schedules don't afford time for upkeep and repairs. These homes also tend to be in or near urban centers, which means greater amenities, more access to mass transportation, and deeper cultural enrichment. On the downside, they'll never be as private or independent as a freestanding house, and outdoor space is a luxury, not a guarantee.

Chapter 10 provides a detailed look at the various types of residential buildings, but here's a quick overview of three main alternatives to freestanding houses:

Types	Pros	Cons
Condo	• Monthly fees tend to be lower than co-ops. • Financing is easier to obtain. • Down payments are smaller. • Subletting is generally allowed. • Resale has fewer hurdles.	• Initial sale price is usually higher. • Monthly fees aren't tax deductible. • You have no control over your choice of neighbors.
Co-op	• Lower initial sale price. • Sense of community is stronger than with a condo. • Monthly fees are tax deductible. • Less speculation means co-ops tend to hold their value better than condos or town houses.	• Close scrutiny from co-op board during approval process. • Subletting is not allowed or is greatly restricted. • You may be charged a "flip tax" if you sell the property within a set period, e.g., one to three years.
Town House	• You'll have a private entrance. • No noise from neighbors above or below you. • Outdoor space is often an option.	• Heating costs are not usually included in monthly fees. • Shared walls can lead to noise from neighbors on either side. • Association bylaws limit exterior changes, such as changing the color of the front door.

Whether you go the condo, co-op, or town house route, it's vital to ensure that the building or homeowners' association is being managed effectively. Always ask about the size of the cash reserve, which is used to cover ongoing maintenance and upgrades. While you're on the subject of improvements, inquire about the long-term repair plan. Natural disasters and the like are a fact of life, but the folks in charge should be budgeting for foreseeable projects, such as a boiler replacement or repainting a building's brick exterior. Last but not least, try to speak with current residents or those who have recently lived there. They'll be able to tell you better than anyone if your prospective new home is a pleasant and predictable place to live.

Buy Existing or Build New?

Custom building a home offers more freedom and control than buying an existing home. Plus we're in the middle of a prolonged construction downturn, so you shouldn't have trouble finding a high-quality builder and design team. But it's a time-consuming process that involves a lot of moving parts, which could drive you crazy if you're not well organized with some tolerance for chaos.

Buying an existing home is a far easier proposition, and offers the added benefit of coming with a fixed cost and timeline for purchase. But, unless you plan to gut the place before you move in, you will have to accept the design and finishes as is. Between those two extremes, there are several additional options, each with its own list of pros and cons. The following chart provides an at-a-glance comparison of all the choices you have for buying a new home.

> **Fast Fact** In the 1950s, approximately eight in ten households were headed by a married couple. Today, that figure is down below five in ten, meaning that more than half are headed by a single person. At the same time, multigenerational living is on the rise. That's affecting the nation's housing stock, for example with more apartment buildings being constructed, especially since the housing bubble burst.

Pros and Cons of Buying Existing vs. Building New

Options	Pros	Cons
Purchase an existing home	• Quickest way to buy a home. • Location and price options are virtually endless. • Older homes can be full of character, and they're often in established neighborhoods.	• Difficult to customize. • Likely to cost more to operate per month than a new home. • Some fixing up will likely be required.
Build in a tract development	• Fast, affordable way to have a semicustomized home. • New construction can mean all the modern conveniences.	• Often in areas of sprawl that tend to be dependent on cars. • Neighborhoods and yards tend to be devoid of mature trees and landscaping.
Build a modular home	• Fast, affordable way to have a semicustomized home. • Usually not tied to a sprawl-based community. • Factory-built homes can be more sustainable and energy efficient.	• You still need to get proper permits and access to sewer lines and utilities. • Not all modular companies produce attractive homes, especially those with the old double-wide design. • Financing options can be fewer than with a traditional home.
Build a custom home	• You get to choose every detail, down to the finish and paint colors. • Custom homes can be extremely green, especially if you find a builder through the U.S. Green Building Council.	• Costs the most and takes the longest amount of time. • The home won't be time tested, so any problems with the construction or design will be yours to discover.

Three questions to ask a potential neighbor that won't make you look ridiculous

I f you're not the gregarious type, approaching a total stranger to ask about their neighborhood can be a little awkward. Try to be as friendly as possible and state your intentions up front with an opening line like, "Excuse me, I really like this neighborhood and would love to move here. Do you mind if I ask you a few questions?" Ideally that will put them at ease and you can ask them the following:

"How long have you lived here?" The better the neighborhood, the less turnover there's likely to be. Besides the person you're speaking to, try to find out if the majority of residents have been there a long time.

"Do you know anyone who is moving out?" Neighbors often hear about properties coming onto the market long before local real estate agents. Any inside info could give you a leg up.

"What do you like most and least about the neighborhood?" The most revealing insights always reside at the extremes, especially when it comes to negatives. Try to also get them talking about any controversial changes that are in the works, such as developments of rezoning plans.

CHAPTER CHEAT SHEET

Gut Check

What is your instinct telling you? Does moving make sense for you now? Should you rent or should you own? (Follow your heart.)

Reality Check

Did I just tell you to follow your heart? Well, not so fast. Remember, austerity is the new bling. You want everyone to think you are doing well, but there are times when you are not doing well, and that is okay. Make the move that works for you, when it works for you, because it works for you, not because it works for someone else.

Your Balancing Act

Function—Will the move meet your needs, now and in the future? Cost—Can you afford the move you are planning? Delight—Will it make you happy?

Key points to remember

- Renting is not a dirty word. Don't rush to own a home just because you think you're supposed to.

- If you are selling a home, remember, the value of your home isn't what you want it to be, but what the market will support.

- If you are ready to own, consider all the options within existing and new homes.

- Real estate is local; don't worry about the national picture; look at what is happening in your town or the city where you are planning to move.

- Consider where you will be in five to seven years, in terms of your job, your family, and your social life. Ask yourself, How do your current plans to move work with your long-term goals?

Chapter 3

Setting Your Budget

id you ever dream of acing your math final in high school? Did you imagine what it would feel like, but couldn't quite get there? Now is your time, and this chapter is your guide. Instead of an A+ at the top of the page, your reward is thousands of dollars, if not tens of thousands, in savings. Acing this test is easy if you know the questions to ask and are honest about your financial realities. This is particularly true for homeowners, for whom the stakes are highest, but if you are a renter, you'll also need to take a sharp pencil and candid eye to your personal budget.

More than ever, deciding where to live requires that you understand financing on two levels: first and foremost, your personal finances, and second, the new rules of home financing. Although lax lending practices are often blamed for the millions of foreclosures and underwater mortgages that continue to be a drag on the housing market, the fact of the matter is that a lack of personal responsibility on the part of homeowners has been a major factor. It's up to government to rein in the mortgage industry, but it's up to you to take responsibility for your financial situation. Even in today's buttoned-up lending climate, it's possible to end up with more home than you can afford.

Honesty is absolutely crucial when it comes to getting on the path to responsible home financing. The moment you start veering into speculative waters—for example, basing crucial financial decisions on the salary you hope to earn someday, rather than the one you currently take home—you run the risk of biting off more than you can chew. But with total candor and a bit of acumen, there's actually a very clear method to shopping around for a mortgage today, and following it could save you tens of thousands of dollars in the long run.

Take the example of a $200,000 loan secured at a thirty-year fixed rate. If you're able to pay just half a percentage point less on that mortgage—say 4.5 percent instead of 5 percent—your monthly payments will differ by only about $60 ($1,015 versus $1,075) but you'll end up paying somewhere on the order of $22,000 less over the life of the loan. Not bad for a few hours' worth of homework.

That's why this chapter is so important. I will present the information in the clearest possible manner so that the amount of extra legwork you put in really will be measured in hours, not days or weeks. The point is to demystify the process so that what in the past looked like a bunch of numbers on a spreadsheet will now be part of your formula for long-term happiness. Returning to the above example, it's about seeing how that mere half percentage point less on your mortgage rate can mean tens of thousands of dollars in savings, which with the right investment strategy could mean another $100,000 or more to live off during retirement—provided you're willing and able to take a long view of your financial picture and see the crucial role real estate plays in it.

Understanding Your Numbers

TALLYING YOUR COST OF LIVING

Pop quiz: How much of your current monthly income goes toward your home? What if you add in commuting costs? What did you spend last year on maintenance, gas, and upkeep for your car? How does the location of your new home reduce or increase how much you drive every day and each year? These questions are crucial to determining how much house you can afford. Don't worry if you don't know the answers to these questions off the top of your head. This section will walk you through the process of considering your budget for buying a home, or for renters the monthly rent, but also the costs of living in a home, in particular the expense of getting to and from the places that meet your daily needs.

To arrive at your actual number, you need to get a complete picture of your household budget. When deciding where to live, it is easy to focus only on the purchase price or monthly rent. This becomes the magic number around which all decisions are based. The old rule of thumb was that your housing costs should be approximately one third of your monthly after-tax income. Unfortunately, this formula ignores many of the other variables that go into owning and living in a home. A good number of people today are living "house poor." They're often in a home that, technically speaking, they may be able to afford, but all the extra expenses have them stretched way too thin—starting with the huge chunk of their disposable income that's consumed at the gas pump.

WORDS OF WISDOM

"The decision to refinance from our 30-year fixed rate mortgage to a 20-year fixed rate mortgage created a win-win situation for us. Our long-term interest payments will be significantly reduced without increasing our monthly out-of-pocket expense and our home will be paid off before we retire." Christine L., Hatfield, PA

"We had very little fixed income, plus some pretty hefty school loans, so we never would've qualified for a conventional mortgage. But we happened to know the son of the woman selling the home we wanted, so she agreed to seller financing—a one-year loan at a 6.5 percent interest rate, with the possibility of a six-month extension at an 11 percent interest rate. We ended up needing the six-month extension to finalize a 30-year fixed mortgage with a local credit union, but the seller chose not to raise the interest rate. There's something to be said for preserving the good karma of community!" Jessica D., Windham County, VT

Honestly Assess Your Personal Finances Before making a move, you'll need to get a full understanding of where you stand financially. You need to establish a clear understanding of your cash flow: what's coming in and what's going out. Not to state the obvious, but if the amount you spend each month is greater than the amount you bring home, you're living beyond your means. You probably have a rough sense of your budget in your head. But I strongly urge you to take advantage of one of the free personal finance calculators that are available at websites like Mint.com or SuzeOrman.com.

As you take a sharp pencil to your budget, be brutally honest. Account only for your actual income, not what you expect to earn someday. Look back over the last six months of expenses to understand which are fixed (student loans, car payments, insurance premiums, telephone, and so on) and which are variable (such as food, entertainment, and personal expenses). Consider setting up an Excel spreadsheet or Google Doc, like the example below, to calculate your weekly, monthly, and annual expenses.

Mapping Out Your Budget

Weekly Expenses	Monthly Expenses	Annual Expenses
Gas/Transportation	Mortgage/Rent	Life insurance
Groceries	Utilities/Phone/Cable	Health/Dental
Coffee/Lunch/Snacks	Health club dues	School tuition
Entertainment	Property taxes	Charity
Pharmacy	Car loan	Gifts
Child care	Homeowners insurance	Savings

Now, ask yourself, do you have an emergency fund set aside? Financial experts recommend at least a six-month cushion, and some advise having up to eight months' worth of accessible savings in the event that you lose your job or have an unforeseen emergency. If you don't have this cushion, you'll need to cut back on the variable expenses and build it up before you think about taking on a mortgage. And don't forget about saving for retirement, ideally putting 15 percent of your income into an IRA or 401K account. A little sacrifice now will likely have huge dividends down the road. Moving into a home you can't afford to own or to rent can diminish your comfort later in life.

These are challenging goals, and I realize they can feel overwhelming. If you find yourself drowning in data, meet with a financial adviser to understand your long-term financial outlook. This service doesn't always come cheap, which can make it seem counterproductive if the whole point is to spend less. But the simple act of meeting with a financial expert can help you focus on goals.

Calculate Your Transportation + Housing Traditionally the formula for determining your housing budget was to set it at roughly 30 percent or less of your household's monthly budget. With this formula, the location of the house in proximity to getting daily needs met rarely plays into the budget conversation. As a result, even before the price of gasoline surged past the $4 per gallon mark, some households spent a third of their total income getting around, without even realizing it. If you live far from work or school, transportation costs can actually exceed mortgage payments. This is a result of the so-called drive-till-you-qualify phenomenon, whereby people moved farther and farther away to find the cheapest possible home, not realizing that the ensuing transportation costs would quickly erase the savings.

A more realistic formula is to add housing plus transportation and aim to have this combined expense less than 45 percent of your household's monthly budget. This allows flexibility. The less you commute, the more you can afford to pay for housing.

The website commutesolutions.com, run by the Santa Cruz County Regional Transportation Commission, includes a True Cost of Driving calculator that adds up direct and indirect expenses, from gas to maintenance to auto insurance to taxes that go toward road construction. Even without allowing for tolls or an older vehicle, a person who commutes sixty miles five days a week can end up paying close to $20,000 annually.

Housing + Transportation Index

The Center for Neighborhood Technology and its collaborative partner, the Center for Transit Oriented Development, as a project of the Brookings Institution's Urban Markets Initiative, have developed an essential online tool called the Affordability Index (htaindex.cnt .org/). The interactive online tool lets you determine the H+T index for 161,000 neighborhoods across 337 metro areas. That covers about 80 percent of the U.S. population. For example, neighborhoods like Mt. Washington in downtown Pittsburgh fare especially well. The H+T costs for this compact, walkable community average 39 percent of residents' income, compared with 53 percent for the overall region, many parts of which are sprawling and car dependent. As you consider places to live, promise me you'll use this tool to better understand and compare the transportation costs. You don't want to buy a great home and then find out later that you are spending much more than you expected on transportation.

Account for Hidden Operating Costs I'll talk about maintaining your home in Chapters 16 and 17, but for now, the important message is this: *Do not move into a new home—whether you're renting or buying—without an understanding of how much it costs to operate the house on a monthly basis.* What are the monthly costs to air-condition in the summer and heat in the winter? Is there a yard to water? Is there a pool to maintain? Energy expenses can sneak up on you and throw even the best-planned budget out the window. A friend of mine learned this lesson the hard way when she moved from an apartment with a $75 utility bill into a house. She assumed that the monthly utilities would be higher, but wasn't prepared when a bill for $700 arrived in the mail. Luckily she was renting and moved out after a year, but if she had purchased the home, it would be a very different story.

If you're buying a home, ask (or get your real estate agent to ask) the seller for the last year's worth of utility bills to get an understanding of what you'll have to budget for. Renters should do the same of their landlord. And if you're building new, look for a builder who follows guidelines for energy efficiency set out by the Environmental Protection Agency (through its Energy Star program) or the U.S. Green Building Council (through its LEED—Leadership in Energy and Environmental Design—program).

Determine Your Debt-to-Income Ratio Once you have a firm handle on your personal budget, you'll be able to determine your debt-to-income ratio. This metric was all but lost during the housing boom, when people who didn't even have the prospect of a job, let alone a steady paycheck, were able to purchase homes worth several hundred thousand dollars. Fortunately, the debt-to-income ratio is back. Any reputable mortgage lender will be sure to ask about it, so you'll save yourself time and trouble by crunching the numbers.

As the name implies, debt-to-income ratio is a measure of how much debt you're carrying relative to the size of your household income. There are two basic calculations that you need to consider. The first takes into account only the debt incurred from your prospective mortgage, property tax, and insurance, also known as PITI, which stands for monthly **P**rincipal, **I**nterest, **T**axes, and **I**nsurance. Ideally, your PITI will not exceed 25 percent of your gross monthly income, that is, your income before taxes. The second calculation combines

Sample Debt-to-Income Ratio

Your gross monthly income	$4,000	
Your gross monthly income × .25	$1,000	Max monthly PITI
Your gross monthly income × .36	$1,440	Max monthly total debt

your PITI plus any other debt you're carrying, such as from your credit card, car loan, or student loan. (Refer to the expense chart on page 50.) Ideally, your debt will be no more than 36 percent of your gross monthly income.

These two targets are often referred to as the 25/36 rule. That's setting a pretty conservative benchmark, especially if you live in a region with high real estate prices and a high cost of living. In those cases, it might be okay to tweak the numbers a bit, perhaps to 28/40. But this should be a measure of last resort rather than your rule of thumb, since the debt-to-income ratio doesn't consider many of your other expenses, including transportation. Remember that your housing + transportation costs should not exceed 45 percent of your income.

Check Your Credit Score Your credit score is what creditors use to determine whether or not to lend you money. If you're looking to buy a home, your score could make or break the deal. Scores affect renters too, since landlords often run a credit check before signing a lease.

Credit-reporting bureaus collect your credit information. The three big ones in the U.S. are Equifax, Experian, and TransUnion. They keep track of everything from credit accounts (say for credit, gas, and store cards), your payment history (including its length and any late payments), court judgments, disputed information, and even your employment history. Based on all of this data, they arrive at a final credit score between 300 and 850, the higher the better.

A high credit score, say 750 or above, means you'll have a much better shot at getting a loan. What's more, your lender will reward you with a better interest rate, so your monthly payments will be lower. Consider the chart below, from MyFICO.com, for a thirty-year fixed mortgage on a $300,000 loan:

How Your Credit Score Affects Your Monthly Payment

Credit Score	Interest Rate	Monthly Payment
760–850	3.625%	$1,368
700–759	3.847%	$1,406

Credit Score	Interest Rate	Monthly Payment
680–699	4.024%	$1,436
660–679	4.238%	$1,474
640–659	4.668%	$1,550
620–639	5.214%	$1,650

You can get a free copy of your credit history from any of the three credit-reporting bureaus. Unfortunately, the agencies don't provide your credit score, which is what you really want to know if you're shopping for a loan. For that, you'll need to go to AnnualCreditReport .com, where you can pay a small fee (about $10) to get a copy of your reports, as well as a copy of your credit score. Stay away from supposedly free online credit reporting services, which are often full of scam offers that will cost you.

A low credit score can't be fixed overnight, but there are ways to repair bad credit. First, make sure there aren't any mistakes or errors on your reports. Next, start making all of your payments on time, and try to pay off as much debt as possible. Don't just transfer debt from one card to another, since this will only add to your debt in the long run. Finally, stop applying for new credit cards, since this will result in more credit inquiries into your account, each of which will ding your score.

Budgeting for Homeownership

THE COSTS OF HOMEOWNERSHIP

The debt-to-income ratio is the best place to start thinking about home financing, because it gives you a nice ballpark sense of how much house you can afford per month. But this isn't the end of the calculations. You need to look beyond the purchase price to all the other expenses that a home entails. Let's break them down into three categories: buying your home, owning your home, and living in your home.

THE COSTS OF BUYING A HOME

Here are the main expenses you'll incur before you set foot in your new home.

The down payment This could well be the biggest check you ever write. Although zero-down mortgages proliferated during the housing boom, many lenders now require a 20 percent down payment. Even if your pristine credit history qualifies you for less, you should still try to hit the 20 percent mark. Why? For starters, it proves that you're financially ready to buy a home. Also, the less you borrow, the smaller your monthly payments will be, and the less interest you'll pay over time. Finally, 20 percent down means you won't have to pay private mortgage insurance, which might save you a couple thousand dollars a year, depending on the size of the mortgage.

Admittedly, a 20 percent down payment is a big chunk of change that may take many years to save. This isn't necessarily a bad thing, because you'll be that much more committed to finding the right home when the time comes. But if you want to move more quickly, there are smart and not-so-smart ways to add to your savings. The best source of assistance is a gift or low-interest loan from your folks or other loved one. Roughly one third of all first-time home buyers go this route, assuming it won't push them into financial hardship or force them to dip into their retirement savings. Do be careful about taking too large a gift from relatives, especially your parents. Not only does this open you up to awkward relations and recriminations ("I see you have enough money to go on vacation, but needed money from us for a down payment . . . ") but it also makes it easier for you to purchase more house than you can actually afford.

If you have other assets, such as stocks or bonds, you might also think about cashing them in, even though you'll have to pay taxes. But do not under any circumstances take money out of your retirement savings for your down payment. Although first-time home buyers can withdraw up to $10,000 without paying an early-withdrawal penalty, the compounded loss in savings over time is too great. You're better off delaying homeownership or buying a less expensive house. Remember, you can take out a loan for a home or for college, but you can't take out a loan for retirement. If you can't afford a solid down payment on a home, you probably can't afford to buy the home.

Closing costs These miscellaneous fees differ from state to state, but they usually add up to between 2 and 5 percent of the purchase price of the home. Do the math, and that might mean $10,000 on top of the down payment for a $200,000 home. The good news is that some of the costs, including many mortgage-related fees, will be rolled into your loan, so you'll be able to pay them over time. But you'll still have to pay the first month's payment, transfer and property taxes, and homeowner's insurance.

Home inspection This might cost anywhere from $200 to $600 or more, but it's some of the best money you'll spend. Look for a professional who has been certified by the American Society of Home Inspectors or the National Association of Home Inspectors. They'll spot obvious problems, like a leaky roof or mold, plus less conspicuous ones, for example a hidden in-ground oil tank, which can lead to major problems if it springs a leak.

Legal fees You'll need to pay an attorney to handle a variety of tasks, such as reviewing the sales contract, checking for compliance, doing a title search, and representing you at the closing. Depending on the complexity of the deal, the total fee could run anywhere from several hundred dollars to several thousand. Some real estate attorneys

Do you have a long-term, short-term, or no-term plan?

In 2005 savings rates of Americans dropped to -0.2 percent, meaning that not only were we saving nothing, but we were spending more than we were earning. Not since the Great Depression have we seen numbers so low. Luckily, savings rates are coming up, nearing almost 4 percent. What is your savings plan? Keeping your long-term goals in mind while planning your move will pay dividends many times over in your later years.

charge by the hour, others by a flat fee. Make sure to get the agreement in writing, including when the lawyer will be paid.

THE COST OF OWNING A HOME

Here are the main ongoing expenses you'll pay after you move in:

PITI As discussed earlier, this includes your monthly mortgage Payments and Interest, as well as your property Taxes and homeowner's Insurance. The exact costs will depend on the value and location of your home.

Maintenance and repairs As a rule of thumb, you should expect to spend 1 percent of the purchase price of the home on its care and maintenance each year. So if the home is worth $200,000, you're looking at an annual maintenance bill of $2,000. Some of these measures are routine, for example tending to the lawn and periodically repainting the exterior, whereas some are unexpected, say fixing the roof after a tree lands on it during a violent storm. Even if you have insurance, at the very least, you will have a deductible. In the worst case, the fine print of your policy might mean you don't have the coverage you think you have. These unexpected costs are usually high, driving up the annual average.

Utilities That includes things like heating fuel, electricity, water, sewage, telephone, cable and/or Internet service, and trash pickup (assuming it's not part of your property taxes). The average American household spends about $2,200 on energy costs alone.

Homeowners association fees and assessments These apply if you live in a condo, co-op, town-house development, or gated community, and cover things like taxes, maintenance, landscaping, and staff salaries.

Remodeling costs The majority of these costs are borne during the first year or so of moving in. Obviously, they will vary greatly between a fixer-upper and a home that's in good, move-in condition. Structural repairs, where you're knocking down walls, pouring foundations, and installing new electrical and plumbing systems, will cost tens of thousands of dollars and usually require a professional. Cosmetic repairs, such as painting walls and laying new flooring, can be completed for a thousand dollars or less, especially if you do some or all of the work yourself. For more renovating advice, check out Chapters 18 and 19.

THE COSTS OF SELLING YOUR HOME

As I discussed in Chapter 2, your ability to sell your existing home is a key in deciding whether to move or stay. Be realistic about the actual value of your home. It's not your desired value or the price you paid that counts, but rather the price that meets the market. Let's assume you are able to make the sale. This will affect your financial portfolio in several ways. If you are not planning to purchase again, first, you need to take into account the capital gains tax that applies on profits above $250,000 for individuals and $500,000 for married couples. For example, if, as a couple, you bought a home for $250,000 and sold it for $600,000, you'd most likely have to pay a 15 percent tax on $100,000. Given how home values have tanked in recent years, most people will be lucky to have to worry about the tax. But as the market improves, capital gains will come back into play. Remember that you can deduct closing and selling costs, including some home repairs, from any capital gain. Following are additional selling costs to keep in mind.

Real estate agent commission This is typically around 6 percent, though it's worth seeing if it's possible to negotiate a lower rate. Even a 0.5 percent drop would result in $2,000 savings if the home sold for $400,000.

Closing costs These are often divided between the seller and buyer, though in a down market it's not unusual for buyers to ask sellers to foot the entire bill, which typically amounts to 2 to 4 percent of the selling price.

Moving costs It depends how much you own and how far you're moving. A typical renter might pay a few hundred dollars for a "man with a van" on Craigslist, whereas homeowners moving across the

Your Home Is Not an ATM

Real estate is a long-term investment, not a get-rich-quick scheme. Too many people lost sight of this fact during the recent housing boom and treated their homes like a liquid asset whose equity could be tapped into at any time. Just look at the spike in the early to mid-2000s in home equity lines of credit (HELOCs), which basically turn a home into an ATM by lending money based on the speculative increase in property value. In California alone, approximately 1.5 million HELOCs were issued in 2004 and 2005, which was more than the total number of homes sold in that time frame.

This attitude isn't nearly as pervasive in a down housing market, but I would still caution you not to think of your home as a liquid asset. Instead, think of your home as a savings account that will grow over time, rather than a stock or bond investment that can be cashed in virtually overnight.

country may need to fork over several thousand bucks to a moving company. (They might charge 50 cents per pound, with the contents of a typical three-bedroom house weighing upward of 10,000 pounds.) You can also hire a moving container (PODS is one of the best-known companies), which you load up yourself and then let them transport. This can cut costs and also lets you move on your own timetable, but don't underestimate how long the packing process can take.

SHIFTING FROM RENTING TO OWNING

In Chapter 2, I talked through the decision process behind renting versus buying. If you've decided to take the plunge into homeownership, you're on the brink of a hugely exciting journey, though you're also probably about to make the single biggest investment of your lifetime. Make sure to take into account all of your costs, and be careful not to assume a one-to-one relationship between your current rent and your monthly mortgage. Homeownership comes with PITI, but keep in mind that you will also want a little extra for the maintenance and upkeep that your landlord currently covers. Fortunately, some of these extra costs will be offset by the tax advantages that come with being a homeowner, namely the mortgage interest that you're allowed to deduct. That's particularly helpful during the early years of the loan, when most of your payment will be put toward interest.

Selecting the Right Mortgage

MORTGAGE BASICS

Mortgages make the housing market go around. The lending industry got a bad rap during the housing crash, when irresponsible practices led to the subprime mortgage crisis (more on that in a moment). But recent events don't change the fact that mortgages make owning a home possible for many Americans.

In the simplest terms, a mortgage is a loan given to you by a bank or other lender to purchase a property, with the property itself serving as collateral. If you stop making payments on the loan, the lender can step in and take back possession of your property. Of course, lenders need to make money on the deal, given the risk they're taking on. To do so, they rely on interest rates, which is the amount charged by a lender, calculated as a percentage of the total loan amount. Home mortgage interest rates dipped below 5 percent in the early 2000s, down from around 15 percent in the 1980s, and they remain at near record lows today. Economic turmoil leads to market volatility, however, which is why some experts predict that rates could start to creep back up.

Lenders also make money by charging "points" on a mortgage. The term is short for the percentage points of the loan amount that a lender may charge to issue a loan. This is a onetime fee that you pay when you take out the loan. A single point is equal to 1 percent of the principal on the loan. For example, one point on a $200,000 loan equals $2,000, and two points equals $4,000. Points provide a big chunk of change up front for lenders, but they can also work in your favor. That's because loans offered with points typically come with a lower interest rate, which will save you money over the long haul if you plan to stay in your home for a while.

What's the difference between prequalified, preapproved, and approved?

The terms preapproved and prequalified refer to processes by which a bank or lender tells you what size mortgage you can expect to take out. Preapproval is much more rigorous than prequalification. Prequalification typically involves a few back-of-the-envelope calculations based on your income and debts. It's a quick and free way to figure out what ballpark you're in with home prices. To be preapproved, on the other hand, you'll need to provide extensive paperwork, including pay stubs, tax returns, and bank records. You'll also have to pay a small fee, since the lender will run a credit check. It's a lot of work, but the letter of commitment you receive from the lender saying they'll lend you X amount will carry real weight with potential sellers. Prequalification and preapproval for your loan allow you to shop for a home and even make an offer. Full approval comes later after you have made your offer and your lender fully processes all of your paperwork. In some cases, if questions arise in the process, final approval is not given until just before closing.

Interest Rates

This chart shows how monthly payments go up with interest rates, using the example of a thirty-year, $100,000 fixed rate mortgage. Over the life of the loan, there's a difference of roughly $118,000 between the lowest and highest interest rates. Although current rates are at a record low, the actual rate you'll be offered depends on your credit score: The better the score, the lower the rate, which can translate into huge savings.

Interest Rate	Monthly Payment
4.0%	$477
4.5%	$507
5.0%	$537

Interest Rate	Monthly Payment
5.5%	$568
6.0%	$600
6.5%	$632
7.0%	$665
7.5%	$699
8.0%	$734
8.5%	$769
9.0%	$805

FIXED AND ADJUSTABLE RATE MORTGAGES

Understanding how interest rates and points work is easy enough. Where the mortgage games get tricky is when you start comparing the various loans offered. The following section covers the two basic types: fixed rate mortgages and adjustable rate mortgages (ARMs).

Fixed Rate Mortgage

How does it work? The interest rate on a fixed mortgage stays the same for the life of the loan. So if you lock in at a low 4.0 percent, that will be your rate until the loan is paid off, no matter how volatile the market becomes.

Pros: Predictability and stability, especially if you plan to be in your home for the long haul. Knowing exactly what your payments will be each month will help you manage the less predictable components of your household budget, such as unforeseen doctor's visits or the ever-changing costs of extracurricular school activities.

Cons: You pay a premium for peace of mind in the form of a higher starting interest rate, relative to what you'd likely pay for an adjustable rate mortgage.

Things to consider: If you opt for a fixed rate mortgage, you then have to decide on the length of the loan. Here are the options:

- **Thirty-year fixed rate mortgage** The most common and often the most prudent choice. Even if you don't plan to be in your home for that long, a thirty-year loan hits the sweet spot between attractive interest rates and manageable monthly payments.

- **Fifteen-year fixed rate mortgage** If you are closer to retirement age, this mortgage makes sense. Shortening your loan term could enable you to pay off your mortgage while you're still working. Your monthly payments will be higher, but that increase will be partially offset by a lower interest rate, typically half a percentage point less than what you'd get on a thirty-year loan. And there's no better way to secure your retirement dreams than by eliminating the significant monthly expense of a home mortgage. Even if you end up moving before paying off the entire loan, using a fifteen-year plan will allow you to accumulate greater equity in your home that you will be able to transfer to your next residence.

- **Forty-year fixed rate mortgage** Less common these days, but if you are able to find one, the qualification requirements are typically less than with a thirty-year fixed rate loan. The other upside is relatively low monthly payments. But you'll probably have to settle for an even higher interest rate, so the difference may not be so great. Plus, forty years is a very long time to be in debt, and the chances are you'll be carrying a mortgage into your retirement, unless you sell before then.

There is a middle road to consider when deciding between fixed rate mortgages—that is, locking into a sensible thirty-year loan, but then making higher-than-required monthly payments to your loan principal. This reduces the accrual of interest, which in turn lowers your total payments. If you find yourself struggling to make the higher monthly payments, you can always go back to paying the required amount.

Adjustable Rate Mortgage

How does it work? The interest rate on adjustable rate mortgages (ARMs) goes up and down during the life of the loan. These loans come with low initial rates. These rates remain fixed for an agreed-upon term, which could be anywhere from a few months to several years. After that, the rates fluctuate, depending on the market at each adjustment period.

Pros: Lower interest rates can result in much-reduced monthly payments, especially on "jumbo loans," which are above $417,000 in most regions, though they can top $600,000 in high-cost mar-

> **" ARMs give the illusion that you can afford more than your finances actually allow. "**

kets. To give you an example, let's say you're shopping for a $500,000 loan. If you choose a thirty-year fixed rate mortgage, you might end up with a 4.5 percent interest rate that results in monthly payments of about $2,500. But if you go with an ARM, the initial interest rate could be around 3 percent, resulting in monthly payments of roughly $2,100. The allure of ARMs is in that extra $400 each month.

Cons: Uncertainty over which way your interest rate will move when the starter rate comes to an end. Conceivably, it could move even lower. But with rates at historic lows, there's a good chance it will go up. Using the above example, the rate could increase 2 percent annually, in which case you'd be paying upward of $3,300 per month in a couple years' time. This is called "payment shock," and it's to blame for a good many of the 15 million foreclosures that happened during the housing crash.

Things to consider: I'm biased against ARMs. ARMs give the illusion that you can afford more than your finances actually allow. Although some people make the argument that ARMs make sense if you are planning to move in a couple of years, I would counter that if you know you are staying somewhere for only a couple of years, renting might be better. In today's economy, there is no guarantee that you'll be able to sell your home on demand or that your home will be worth more when you sell than it was when you made the purchase. This could leave you paying higher rates with no way out.

If you are seriously considering an ARM, ask yourself these questions:

- **Can I really afford to buy this home at this time?**

Beware of shortcuts when it comes to lending and homeownership. Safe lending practices are recommended not to crush your dreams, but to protect you from getting into financial trouble. If you can't afford a fixed rate mortgage, take very serious stock in your financial realities before opting for an ARM. It is substantially preferable to rent for a few more years or look at more affordable housing options rather than to find yourself underwater in a home you cannot afford.

- **How high will my mortgage payments potentially get?**

Ask your lender to give you a worst-case scenario so that you know exactly how high your mortgage payments could go. Remember that rates are at record lows, so there's a good chance they'll start to rise again before your fifteen- or thirty-year mortgage is up. There's no such thing as a sure job promotion, especially in a struggling market, so don't count on rising income to cover these increases. Inheritance or a gift is another story, but take a sharp pencil to how the infusion of cash will be taxed, and always remember, until money is in the bank and all taxes have been paid, it is not your money.

- **Will I be taking on other big debts in the near future?**

Whether it's college tuition or a new car loan, new debts can pile up quickly, and need to be taken into account when you consider an ARM worst-case scenario.

Tips for selecting an adjustable rate mortgage I seriously caution you against signing up for an ARM, but if you are absolutely set on the idea of it, here's what to look for to get the best possible loan.

- **Reasonable adjustment period.** ARMs are referred to by their adjustment period, or the time between interest rate changes. For example, a three-year ARM adjusts every three years, whereas a one-year ARM adjusts annually. Stay away from loans that adjust monthly.

- **Low, but realistic, initial interest rate.** It should be significantly less than the rate on a fixed rate mortgage, say around 3 percent on a $200,000 loan, to offset the risk of a later increase. But teaser rates that sound too good to be true usually are. Indeed, lenders often include "discount fees" in return for the supposedly bargain rate.

- **A stable index.** Lenders base ARM interest rates on an outside index, such as the Cost of Funds Index or the London Interbank Offered Rate, commonly referred to by the acronym LIBOR. These slow-changing indices are better than fast-changing, volatile ones.

- **Interest-rate caps.** These limit the amount your interest rate, and in turn monthly payments, can increase. There are two types. Periodic caps control how much your rate changes at each adjustment period; 2 percent is recommended for a one-year ARM. Life-of-the-loan caps control how much rates increase over time; 6 percent is recommended.

ALTERNATIVE TYPES OF LOANS

Fixed rate mortgages and ARMs make up the majority of mortgages, but there are other types to choose from if the traditional route is not an option.

FHA Loan

How does it work? These fixed rate loans are backed by the U.S. Federal Housing Administration, or FHA. Once a small fraction of the mortgages handed out each year, FHA-insured loans accounted for nearly a third of all home loans by 2010.

Pros: The big appeal of FHA loans is that borrowers can make down payments as low as 3.5 percent. Compared with a conventional loan, that might be a difference of tens of thousands of dollars, which could potentially get you into your new home years faster. Then there's the fact that the minimum credit score for an FHA-insured loan is down around 500, compared with the 600 and up that's required with conventional, bank-backed mortgages.

Cons: FHA-insured loans include a loan origination fee, plus a higher-than-average annual insurance premium that you'll have to pay until your equity in the home reaches 22 percent. If you're purchasing a condo, additional rules apply to reduce the FHA's risk. For example, no more than 15 percent of condo owners can be behind on their dues.

Also, although Uncle Sam's backing gives FHA-insured loans a lot of legitimacy, we must not forget that many of the subprime loans that precipitated the financial crisis were owned by Fannie Mae and Freddie Mac, two mortgage enterprises sponsored by the federal government. FHA-insured loans ideally won't prove so toxic, but they do raise some alarms, starting with the low down payment, which makes it easy to live beyond your means.

VA and USDA Rural Housing Direct Loans

How do they work? Zero-down mortgages are a thing of the past, except for these two limited-eligibility options. Veterans Administration loans are for veterans who have served the required active duty and have a minimum credit score of 620. Although the loans can be 100 percent financed, you need to pay a hefty finance fee of 2.15 percent. Rural Housing Direct Loans from the U.S. Department of Agriculture don't come with fees, but they're available only to low-income households. Once again, be very cautious when looking at any loan other than a fixed rate mortgage. Although they will offer a potential solution to those with limited financial means, they also will leave you with much greater potential to get in trouble and lose everything.

Seller Financing

How does it work? The seller basically functions as the bank, financing some percentage (or even all) of the purchase price for the buyer. The loans are typically short term, say between one and three years, after which the buyer will take out a new loan with a traditional lender.

The Pros and Cons of Mortgage Interest Tax Deduction

One of the biggest incentives for buying a home is the generous tax break it brings you, starting with the deduction homeowners can take for interest paid on a mortgage of up to $1 million. This is especially beneficial during the early years of your mortgage, when most of your monthly payment goes toward paying down the interest.

This tax deduction has been a boom for homeowners since it was embedded into the tax code decades ago as a way to spur real estate markets. But it has plenty of critics, including those in Washington, D.C., who argue that nixing the deduction could save the government upward of $100 billion per year. They also argue that the deduction ends up being more generous for high-income earners with more expensive homes. That's true, since homeowners in the top-earning 35 percent tax bracket get $35 of savings for every $100 paid in mortgage interest, whereas homeowners in the low-earning 15 percent tax bracket get only $15 for every $100 interest paid.

Both sides make valid points, but given the tenuous state of the housing industry, I don't think now is the time to eliminate any home-buying incentives, let alone one that's so deeply ingrained in our formula for homeownership. I also know that the deduction entices a lot of first-time homeowners, who are critical to turning the market around. But even if the mortgage deduction goes away, there are plenty of other tax-deductive expenses for homeowners, including property taxes, points paid on a mortgage, and home office expenses if you use part of your home solely as a home-based business.

Pros: Seller financing can be a win-win. Sellers can move a home that's maybe been stuck on the market for a long time. Buyers benefit from less strict qualifying requirements, including lofty credit scores and down payments.

AUTOMATIC PREPAYMENT PENALTIES

You can save thousands of dollars by paying off your loan before its term is up. Of course, that means lenders lose, which is why many boom-time loans came with steep penalties if you tried to pay them off during their initial years. These penalties were often hidden in the fine print, a common tactic with subprime loans. Since the crash, the government has cracked down on these penalties, especially for prime mortgages, so a lender who tries to impose them may not be playing by the rules. Take care to verify any restrictions or penalties before sending in extra payments. Also, note that you can have a prepayment penalty clause written into your loan in exchange for a lower interest rate.

Cons: Though it sounds fairly straightforward, seller financing is actually quite complicated. Both the seller and the buyer will need an attorney, and possibly a real estate agent too, to draw up the contract, promissory note, and other paperwork.

Things to think about: If you think seller financing might be an option (say the home has been on the market for a long time and you know the owner is motivated to sell), ask the listing agent to broach the possibility on your behalf.

Although it may seem like the seller is doing you a favor, you should still negotiate the best possible terms, including a competitive interest rate, low initial payments, and the right to extend the loan at a reasonable rate if market conditions preclude you from refinancing at the agreed-upon later date.

Reverse Mortgages

These loans are a way for older homeowners to live off their home. Here's how they work: If you're over the age of sixty-two and you own your house outright, or the mortgage is mostly paid off, you can cash in some of the equity in the form of a lump sum or regular payouts.

The amount you receive will depend on your age, the value of your home, and the interest rate. The older you are, the more you will get. The loan comes due only upon death or when you sell the house.

Pros: They let you stay in your home by drawing on your home's equity. Most are backed by the FHA, which ensures that if you decide to sell, you won't owe more than the value of the home.

Cons: Steep up-front fees amounting to 10 percent of the loan. Plus you still have to pay interest on the loan, which can quickly compound, so the loan might end up sustaining you only for about ten years, when you still have decades left to live. That's why they're a particularly bad deal for younger retirees. Also, lenders can foreclose if you fail to maintain your house, pay property taxes, or pay homeowner insurance premiums.

Other things to consider: Reverse mortgages should be thought of as a measure of last resort if you are well into your retirement years and have no other alternatives for income. If possible, selling your home and downsizing is almost always a better way to go. You can also explore less costly loan options, such as a low-cost home-improvement loan or state property-tax postponement programs.

Then and Now—What the Crash Means for You

Plenty has been written about the mortgage meltdown, but the crisis can be boiled down to a handful of factors and oversights. Here's a "that was then, this is now" look at the mortgage market to help you navigate today's much more regulated market.

UNDERSTANDING THE MARKET MELTDOWN

Market Fluctuations

Then: Home prices were surging. Between 2000 and 2006, home values more than doubled in the twenty metropolitan areas measured by the Case-Shiller Home Price Indices. In that time, the average annual gain of 12 percent made real estate a better investment than the stock market, which averaged 10 percent annual returns.

Now: After a precipitous fall, prices are now flat at best. Between 2007 and 2011, home values plunged more than a third. Some markets are starting to stabilize, but it will be many years before we'll see double-digit annual increases.

The Takeaway: When you factor in the boom and bust of the last decade, you're left with a gain of roughly 3 percent, which is in line with the long-term average. So that's what you should reasonably expect when you take a long view of your real estate investment.

Up and Down Credit

Then: Credit scores were practically irrelevant. A subprime borrower is one whose credit score is 600 or lower (on the FICO scale of 350 to 850). At the height of the boom, borrowers with scores as low as 400 were able to get mortgages. They had to pay higher interest rates, which was part of the appeal of predatory lending, but that they were able to close on the transactions at all is inconceivable today.

Now: Pristine credit is preferred, and a respectable score is absolutely required. To get the best rate and terms, you now need a credit score of 760 to 780, and it's not unheard of for lenders to demand 800. Even FHA-insured loans require scores of around 650.

The Takeaway: If your credit score has taken a hit during the bad economy, you'll need to repair it. Unfortunately, this can't be done overnight. Instead, it will probably take a year or two of effort to pull your score up. That includes making payments on time, paying bills in full when possible, and limiting your lines of credit.

> **Fast Fact** Talk about a credit swap. In 2006, 9 percent of home loans went to people with credit scores below 600. By 2010, that figure was down to just half a percent. That's why it's so important to know your score and to make the necessary repairs to get it above 700.

Away with Zero-Down Payments

Then: Zero-percent down payments were common on mortgages.

Now: A 5 percent down payment is the bare minimum, and many lenders want to see 10 or even 20 percent down. Not only that, but they also want to see up to six months' worth of cash reserves. On a $200,000 loan, that might mean another $10,000 cash in hand.

The Takeaway: To buy a home today with a conventional loan, you need to have significant skin in the game, as Warren Buffett likes to say. In other words, lenders of these mortgages want to see sizable cash investment to know that you're invested.

Lax Lenders

Then: Borrowers were often taken at their word when it came to their financials. The term *robo-signing* says it all. That's where bank and mortgage employees signed documents they hadn't read or used fake signatures to give loan applications the okay. Even when the documents were reviewed, they often relied on stated incomes, hence the proliferation of part-time workers who supposedly took home six-figure salaries.

Now: Your financials will be thoroughly vetted and verified. That means a long checklist of documents, including current W-2 forms, a month's worth of pay stubs, two or three years' worth of federal tax filings, recent bank statements, and more.

The Takeaway: There's no way around this verification process, so you should get your paperwork together before you start shopping around for a loan.

Revolving Owners

Then: Home flipping flourished. The practice of buying homes, making minor improvements, and selling them at a huge profit was so popular during the boom that it even had its own show—*Flip This House* on the A&E network. The series was canceled after five seasons in 2009, which is maybe a year longer than anyone in their right mind was still flipping.

Now: Homeowners are in it for the long haul, even when they don't necessarily want to be. In 2011, fewer than 5 million homes were sold, down from a peak of 7 million in 2005, and roughly 20 percent of homeowners with a mortgage owed more on the loan than their home was worth.

The Takeaway: Even if you hope to move again in a few years, be prepared for a worst-case scenario in which you're forced to stay in the home longer.

DISTRESSED PROPERTIES

The 15 million or so foreclosure notices that have been issued since 2008 are a major drag on real estate prices. If you're in the market for a new home, however, you might be able to land a deal on one of these distressed properties. Indeed, more than half of all buyers entering today's market at least consider either a foreclosure or a short sale. Although some of these bargain hunters will land their dream home for a fraction of its market value, others will end up with a home that turns into a major money pit. Here's what you need to know to improve your chances of winning in the game of distressed properties.

Foreclosure

What is it? When a mortgage lender takes possession of a property and sells it in an attempt to satisfy the debt. The process begins after a homeowner defaults on his or her mortgage and is deemed incapable of making payments. In some cases, foreclosures come onto the market through the bank (these are referred to as bank owned or real estate owned), in which case you'll probably have a chance to do an inspection. Others are sold through third-party auction companies, in which case you might need to close on the property "as is," often within twenty-four to forty-eight hours. That's a risky proposition, so you should definitely make sure you're dealing with reputable auction companies by looking them up through the Better Business Bureau (bbb.org) and the National Auctioneers Association (auctioneers.org). It's also a good idea to attend a few auctions to get a feel for the process before making any actual bids.

> **Fast Fact** According to the 2011 *National Association of Realtors Profile of Home Buyers and Sellers Survey,* "more than half of buyers considered purchasing a foreclosure but didn't buy one for a variety of reasons: 29 percent couldn't find the right house; 15 percent each reported poor condition and a difficult process."

Pros: The best bargains are on foreclosures, and as more come onto the market, the opportunities are only going to get better.

Cons: You forfeit most of the protections afforded during a normal home purchase. That often includes the option of performing an inspection, since most transactions are "as is." And properties are often in bad shape after months or even years of neglect. The other big problem with foreclosures is that they take a long time, especially in states where former owners are allowed to buy back their property, usually within a year of foreclosure. If that happens, you'd get your money back, but it's a long time to be in limbo on the deal.

Smart strategies: Work with a real estate agent who specializes in distressed properties. The National Association of Realtors awards a SFR (short for Short Sales and Foreclosure Resource) certification to Realtors who receive advanced training in distressed properties. Some 210,000 Realtors have so far earned the SFR certification.

Take note of the community surrounding the house. Many newer tract developments are filled with homes in foreclosure and short sales. Watch for neighborhoods in a downward spiral. Vacant homes invite squatters, college student renters, and a myriad of other potential problems. The odds are stacked against many of these neighborhoods coming back. A cheap house in the wrong place will give you headaches.

Short Sale

What is it? An attempt by the lender to avoid foreclosure after a borrower defaults on his or her mortgage payments. Rather than foreclosing on the property, the lender agrees to accept the proceeds from the sale of the property as fully satisfying any outstanding debt on the mortgage, even if the amount of the debt is greater than the sale proceeds.

Pros: These homes tend to be in better shape than foreclosures because the owners are still living there and want to get the best possible price.

Cons: Lenders take a long time to review offers, often four to six months. And the seller could end up rejecting the deal at the last minute if the lender inserts unfavorable language into the deal, perhaps saying that the seller may still be on the hook for some or all of the outstanding loan.

Smart strategies: As with a foreclosure, work with a real estate agent who specializes in distressed properties. Find out whether the seller has already notified the bank about the sale, because this will streamline the process.

CHAPTER CHEAT SHEET

Gut Check

Is your current budget realistic? What changes do you need to make to be more financially sustainable?

Reality Check

Are you being honest with yourself about your financial realities? What is your realistic budget?

Your Balancing Act

Function—What type of financing works best with your life phase and financial realities? *Cost*—Can you afford to purchase and still have a six-month emergency fund to cover job loss, illness, and other unforeseen cuts to your income? *Delight*—Would you be happier living below your means and saving more or living within your means and having a nicer home?

Key points to remember

- When shopping for a mortgage, look for the lowest possible inter-est rate, since even half a percentage point will save you tens of thousands of dollars over the life of the mortgage.

- There are great deals to be had on distressed properties, whether a short sale or foreclosure, but you should be prepared for extra legwork and some element of risk. Using a real estate agent with special training in this area will improve your chances of success.

- The cost of buying a home is one thing, but to understand true affordability you must also calculate the costs of owning a home and living in a home, including transportation costs. Housing and transportation should never exceed 45 percent of your household's total monthly budget.

- Even during a hot housing market, it's best to think of real estate as a long-term savings plan rather than a hot stock that can lead to a sudden windfall.

- A 20 percent down payment is always best, but you should strive for at least 10 percent, or else hold off on buying a home.

- Check your credit. If your credit score is below 700, you should spend the next six months to one year getting it back above that mark before you start looking to buy a home.

Chapter 4

Understanding Your Preferences

o you take cream and sugar with your coffee? Prefer Coke or Pepsi? Are you a Republican, Democrat, or Independent? Some of these preferences run deep (fans of Rush Limbaugh and Bill Maher can attest to this), whereas others are more flexible. (I prefer raw sugar in my coffee, but live on the edge with Splenda every now and again.)

Whatever the intensity, preferences are either learned or innate. If you grew up drinking Coke, Pepsi probably tastes like syrup, and vice versa. There's no genetic predisposition for soft drinks, no genome in our DNA that makes us Pepsi or Coke drinkers. Rather, the taste for one or the other is nurtured over time. Other preferences are there from the beginning, such as a person's natural tendency to enjoy certain types of music or have a favorite color. Anyone who grew up with siblings understands the extent to which two people raised in a similar environment can have very different appreciations.

The nature-versus-nurture debate has been roiling for centuries, of course, with no clear victor in sight. I'm not about to wade into the contest. But I do want to get you thinking about the ways in which personal preferences shape your notion of home, and also how external forces can affect that perception.

Companies are well aware of the power preferences have over decision making, and they'll often spend millions of dollars trying to win your business. These efforts have evolved into a true science, with major retailers hiring mathematicians to track consumer spending patterns and develop algorithms aimed at predicting future purchases. Target (the retail store) has become so sophisticated in its "predictive analytics" that it can deduce from basic spending habits if a customer is pregnant and have coupons for cribs, diapers, and other baby paraphernalia in her mailbox months before she'll need them. "We knew that if we could identify them in their second trimester, there's a good chance we could capture them for years," a senior Target statistician told *The New York Times* in a 2012 article headlined "How Companies Learn Your Secrets." "As soon as we get them buying diapers from us, they're going to start buying everything else too."

So why let the corporations have all the fun? You can try it too. By understanding how your mind works while making decisions and determining preferences, you'll be able to make more informed choices in all areas of your life. This is especially true when it comes to finding a home, given the complex web of preferences that go into the decision. That's the goal of this chapter. And the good news is that you don't have to be a math whiz to reach it.

The Science of Preferences

Humans are sentient beings. We think, therefore we are. Given that power of perception, it's easy to believe that your decisions are always your own, especially if you're among the more sure-minded bipeds walking the Earth. But in truth, many decisions aren't the result of personal preference, at least not directly. A variety of outside factors come into play, including the number of options and the order in which these options are presented. It's crucial to keep this in mind when you're looking for a home. To help navigate the decision-making process, let's take a closer look at the science of preferences.

EMOTIONAL VERSUS LOGICAL DECISIONS

Are you an impulsive person, or do you carefully weigh all the pros and cons before making a final decision? The one approach is emotional, the other logic based. Which is best? Stereotypes dismiss people who make emotional decisions as impulsive, whereas those who are logical are generally considered more prudent.

Don't rush to judgment! Exercising too much logic, at the expense of emotional insight, often leads people to make the wrong decision. Consider the so-called poster test, conducted by University of Virginia psychologist Timothy Wilson. In the study, two groups of female students were asked to choose their favorite poster from five options: a Monet landscape, a Van Gogh still life, and three humorous cat posters. The first group of students simply had to rate each poster on a scale from 1 to 9. The second group had to explain why they liked or disliked each of the five posters. Simply asking the students to think about and explain their preferences dramatically changed the results of their selections. Whereas 95 percent of the "nonthinkers" chose either the Monet or the Van Gogh, the "thinkers" were evenly split between the fine art and the cat posters. The reason, according to Wilson, is that even though most of the thinkers reacted positively to the fine art, they had trouble processing and explaining their thoughts, so much so that they ended up forming negative impressions. Upon reflection it seemed odd to them that a haystack would be attractive. Cats, on the other hand, were easier to understand, so the overall impression was more positive.

An even more interesting finding came during the follow-up interviews conducted several weeks later. Whereas none of the students who chose the fine art regretted their decision, 75 percent of the cat choosers wished they had made a different decision.

THINKING ABOUT HOMES

Picking posters for a dorm room wall is one thing. But what about real estate? It turns out the same phenomenon applies, with logic getting in the way of preference. Imagine two homes. The first is a nice three-bedroom apartment in the middle of the city about ten minutes from work. The other is a handsome five-bedroom house in the suburbs with a forty-five-minute commute to work. When faced with this type of choice, studies have found that most people will think through the trade-offs and give disproportionate weight to the importance of more living space. They imagine holiday times, with visiting relatives gathered around the dining room table and sleeping in spare bedrooms. Or birthday parties, with a gaggle of screaming toddlers tearing through the expansive backyard. The more they think about it, the more they believe the bigger house is right for them.

What they don't take into consideration is the ninety minutes they'll spend in a car *every day of the workweek,* and the huge toll this will take on their mind and body, to say nothing of their household budget. Study after study shows that commuting is one of the least pleasurable activities in life, and yet, given the choice, most people will suffer through it daily to get extra space they'll use, at best, a few days out of the year.

> **It's the physical characteristics of a home that are simplest to quantify, but it's your daily experiences that matter most.**

Crazy, huh? Yes, but also incredibly common. I meet many people who have made themselves miserable by not considering the factors that have the greatest effect on their emotional well-being. In the poster experiment, funny cat images were easier to quantify, but ultimately less gratifying. In real estate, it's the physical characteristics of a home that are simplest to quantify (like price per square foot), but it's your daily experiences that matter most.

Bottom Line: Follow your instinct and don't overthink your decisions. Remember that it's next to impossible to put a quantifiable value on an experience, like time spent in a car or the ability to walk to a park or get a cup of coffee. On the other hand, the extra bedroom or additional square footage can be quantified. So always ask yourself, Do I want to live in this home because the overall experience feels right or because it looks good on paper? As you assess your preferences, consider both the quantifiable and the experiential.

ARE YOUR PREFERENCES YOUR OWN?

Emotions have a huge influence on preferences. So does the number of options and the order in which they're presented. Too many options, and it's easy to become overwhelmed and either not choose anything or choose quickly and incorrectly. If you've ever been to a shopping mall food court or by-the-pound deli buffet, with a zillion offerings ranging from Chinese dumplings to chicken-fried steak, you know what I'm talking about.

Having an option in the mix that's clearly the wrong fit can also wreak havoc on the decision-making process by changing your view of the other choices. Dan Ariely, a professor of psychology and behavioral economics at Duke University, has written extensively about this phenomenon, and concludes that we're not in control of our decisions nearly as much as we think are.

Consider the following experiment, in which Ariely gave a group of students the following three subscription options to *The Economist* magazine:

Online only: $59

Print only: $125

Print/online together: $125

The print-only offer is clearly a lousy deal. Not surprisingly, none of the students chose it, with the majority selecting the combo package (84 percent) and the rest opting for online only (16 percent). Ariely then removed the print-only option and asked another set of students to choose between the two remaining subscriptions. This time, the results flipped, with 68 percent choosing the online-only option and 32 percent opting for the combo. What happened? Essentially, the presence of a bad option in the first scenario changed the way the students looked at the other two. More of them paid for the combo, even though they were probably cash strapped and do most of their reading online, because they felt they were getting a deal. The study shows that we don't know our preferences that well, and as a result we are susceptible to external forces, including falling for the default option. We defer to the better deal as it appears in relation to others, rather than how it might fit our lives.

Now let's look at this principle in the context of real estate. Imagine you're considering the following three homes:

Option A Ten-minute commute to work, kids can safely walk to school, home meets most of your needs, price easily fits your budget.

Option B Long commute, kids take the bus to school, large house more than meets your needs, price exceeds your budget.

Option C Long commute, kids take the bus to school, large house more than meets your needs, price just fits the high end of your budget.

You'll probably eliminate Option B right off the bat, since it doesn't have any real upside. But if you're like most people, you won't forget about it completely. Instead, as you weigh the remaining options, you'll find yourself considering Option C in the context of Option B, even though B was never viable. As you do, Option C will look better and better. After all, you get the huge house at a price you can afford, even if it is a bit of a stretch financially. In the process, you'll forget all about the grinding commute, which, as we learned earlier, is going to really diminish your overall satisfaction.

Now pretend you were presented only with Options A and C. You would consider the merits of the two options only in context of each other. Which sounds better: more house than you need, for more than you want to spend, far away from places that meet your daily needs OR a house that fits your life and budget and is also close to those places that meet your daily needs? All of a sudden, Option A looks like the much better deal.

This type of scenario plays out in many home searches, especially today, when foreclosures are often added into the mix. There's the million-dollar home that's now available for $500,000. Even though your budget might be only $350,000, you find yourself reworking the numbers and seeing how far you can make things stretch to make it work. The "great deal" has swayed you away from your realities.

Bottom Line: Don't let negative or unrealistic options distract you from your viable choices. Keep your priorities in mind as you search for a new place to live. If you find yourself seriously contemplating a home that doesn't fit your needs just because it is a good deal, take a long, hard look at your priorities and make sure you are really meeting your needs. Be hypercritical about why it seems like a good deal. Are you comparing it with homes that were never really an option or are you comparing it with other viable choices?

WORDS OF WISDOM

"I'm a stay-at-home mom, and even though we feel a bit squeezed in our home, we decided to stay where we are rather than try to buy a bigger house with a bigger mortgage. Our house is small, but it works for our family—the schools are great, close by, and our neighborhood is fantastic. The fact that I don't have to return to work to cover the expense of a mortgage and all the cost that goes with a bigger home makes it worth it." Carolyn B., Anchorage, AK

"We've learned that living close to the things we value most (work, school, friends, shopping, church, and so on) always trumps living in a 'charming' location in the boonies." Linda and Mike P., Surprise, AZ

"My husband and I both knew the location of our house would be wonderful for resale because of proximity to the downtown and the views, but the pleasure of living here comes from the sense of community, the walkability, and having a diverse neighborhood. Now that we are just coming out of the downturn, I am so glad we invested in what is considered a 'platinum' location." Carnie M., Salt Lake City, UT

TAKING STOCK OF HABITS AND CHALLENGING THE STATUS QUO

There's an old saying that habits are first cobwebs, then cables. Once we become set in our ways, it can be difficult to break out of the routine and chart a new path, even when doing so could have many upsides. That being said, there are moments in life when it's possible to take stock of our habits and determine which are working for us and which are better left behind. Moving to a different home is one of those moments.

As you begin the search for a new home, I'd encourage you to take stock of your daily routines, perhaps even keeping a journal so that you can jot down any major likes or dislikes. Take the same critical eye to the status quo. Let's go back to commuting: If you grew up with parents who commuted, you might take it as a given that you'll do the same. I get that, and I also understand that commuting makes it possible to live away from the hustle and bustle of the city. But I also know that the average American now spends more than $7,600 annually on transportation, more than they spend on food, according to a 2012 government study. That's in large part because the road infrastructure used by commuters is outdated, beyond capacity, and in poor repair. Bottom line: Commuting is getting harder and costlier, so you need to make sure it's worth it for you.

We require of our homes certain givens: a roof that doesn't leak, heat in the winter, running water, just to name a few. Over time these requirements have grown from providing shelter to those that increase comfort. The Pew Research Center conducted a study that challenges many assumed givens. They found that many Americans were coping with economic hardship by reassessing which home appliances were necessities and which they considered a luxury. Just 54 percent of respondents said they needed air-conditioning in 2009, down from 70 percent in 2006, and 66 percent said they needed a clothes dryer, down from 83 percent. I'm not saying you have to suffer through long, hot summers or line-dry all your clothes if you want to achieve financial freedom. But it's worth noting that the balance between luxury and necessity is in constant flux. You need to make decisions because they work for you.

Here are some questions that will help you identify negative habits or assumptions that your current home is fostering, and that your new home could help you break:

- What do you like most about your day?
- What do you wish you could change about your day?
- What do you like most about how you live?
- What do you wish you could change about where you live?

Bottom Line: Where and how you live now are not the only options. Use your next move to bring positive change to your life. Your current situation does not necessarily define where you will be happiest living after you move.

Housing Profile Variables

WHO'S YOUR HOUSE?

Your **housing profile** is the snapshot of your preferred house type, budget, and neighborhood. Housing profiles usually change over time, as people's salaries change, they enter into relationships, or they start a family. But you can also have several housing profiles at any one given time, depending on several external variables. Here are a few examples:

Housing Profiles Change by Price

Let's say you're in the market to buy. You have a stable job with a nice salary, and you've been preapproved by the bank for a $400,000 loan. You might base your housing profile on that number, even though the high monthly payments mean you won't have much of a safety net. What if instead you decided to look for a home that costs $275,000? It might have one less bedroom and less luxurious finishes, but the reduced payments would give you a bigger cushion and more capacity to save. You could even set aside $25,000 for renovations and still be ahead. Is an extra bedroom worth $100,000?

Now imagine a $200,000 home. What trade-offs would you consider to save a substantial sum of money? The point here is that it's

The Greatest Luxury in Life Is Financial Independence

If you can accept this one simple truth, your chances of achieving real wealth in life will go way up. You'll know that it's best to live not just within your means, but well beneath them in some areas. You won't have to buy a new car each year, not when your current one is running just fine. When it comes to your home, you won't feel the need to fill it with expensive status symbols. Fortunately, there's less pressure to chase bright shiny objects since the housing crash, which makes it easier to focus on what's truly important.

okay, and even somewhat trendsetting, to spend less than you can technically afford on a home. If your ideal home is not available in your price bracket in the location that you want, give this serious thought before paying top dollar for a home with too many compromises. Instead, consider looking for something below your means. You'll laugh all the way to the bank as you save every month.

Housing Profiles Change by Proximity

It's an age-old question of real estate: Is it better to live in the wrong house in the right neighborhood or the right house in the wrong neighborhood? This question goes back to the examples we looked at earlier in this chapter. As you get closer in proximity to the places where you meet your daily needs, how might your housing profile vary? Consider the trade-offs you would make if your commute was shorter and your home was within walking distance of restaurants and shopping. The house you select in a walkable community will look very different from one in an auto-dependent neighborhood. Keep the larger context in mind as you look for homes. Even for the same family, one size might not fit all.

Housing Profiles Change by City Type

Housing profiles will vary greatly from one city to the next. Imagine a typical family of four. In downtown Miami, they might be able to find an apartment in a high-rise building for a reasonable price. That's one housing profile. Now let's say a job transfer sends them to a car-dependent locale like suburban Atlanta. Their housing profile would reflect this, perhaps taking the form of a larger house with a garage. If instead the job transfer relocated them to Washington, D.C., where the transit system connects most places, they might be looking at a town house in a neighborhood near the urban core.

The same family with the same needs, yet their housing profile changes pretty dramatically as they change cities. If you're moving to a new city, or considering such a move, it's important to be flexible with your housing profile so that you don't end up jamming a square peg into a round hole, imposing your perceived housing profile onto a city that can't support it.

Finding Your Balancing Act

The chapters that follow in Part 2 of this book will explore in detail the many variables to consider as you look for your next home, including the big-picture scale of the region and city, the local scale of the neighborhood and street, right down to your ideal property type, layout, and materials of your home. Finding the right home requires balancing all of these elements. Here are three actions that will help in this balancing act:

DEFINE YOUR MUST-HAVES, WOULD-LIKES, AND DON'T-WANTS

You will be prompted throughout the chapters in Part 2 to think about the character of the place you want to live, your daily experience, and how you live in and use your home. As you move through the chapters, make lists of your Must-Haves, Would-Likes, and Don't-Wants. Do your best to keep the list fluid, yet streamlined.

Although some elements may feel absolute, finding the best home for you requires a lot of give and take. Don't overthink your list or discount options that are experiential rather than quantifiable. And, a point I will repeat many times over, if your ideal isn't available, look for ways to make what is available ideal.

REMEMBER, FAMILY MATTERS

Unless you're single, you'll have to balance the needs of multiple people in your search for a home. That's sure to complicate the process, especially if there are kids in the mix who have close friends in your current community. Committee decisions are tricky, and you don't want your ten-year-old ruling the conversation, but maintaining open lines of communication and getting buy-in from all members of the family, young and old alike, will make the process go more smoothly.

Be open and honest about your own needs and preferences. Holding back in an effort to spare someone else's feelings will only lead to trouble down the line. Making a move is a big project and, especially if you're buying, a long-term commitment. You want to make sure everyone is on the same page as much as possible.

REALITY CHECK: ARE YOU BEING HONEST WITH YOURSELF?

You're going to look at dozens of homes in your search for the perfect one. That's part of the fun, but you need to be careful about overexposure. Although you can't pretend that properties beyond your price range don't exist, you can keep them from coloring your reality. Budgets are easy to stretch, and if you're taking out a mortgage, the extra expense can seem inconsequential since it will be spread out over many years. Avoid this rationalization trap. You need to figure out how much you can spend in the context of your needs and desires—including vacations, retirement savings, and a rainy-day fund—and then stick to that number. People don't become "house poor" overnight. The process tends to happen slowly. After a few years of living beyond their means, they check their financial portfolio one day and realize their homes own them, not the other way around. Honesty now will bring prosperity later.

CHAPTER CHEAT SHEET

Gut Check

What is your ideal housing profile? Does your current housing profile work for your life? What changes would make it better?

Reality Check

Could your preferences be guided by external factors?

Your Balancing Act

As you start to define your housing profile, ask yourself these questions: *Function*—If you move closer to work or your kids' school, how would that change your requirements for your home? *Cost*—What is your budget range, and how does that change your housing profile? *Delight*—What are the variables that matter most in your housing profile?

Key points to remember

- As you assess your preferences, consider all factors, including quantifiable (square footage or number of bedrooms) and experiential (time spent commuting or kids walking to school). Don't underestimate the importance of the experiential factors.

- Don't let unrealistic options sway your preferences for your viable choices.

- Your habits aren't set in stone. If you don't like something about your lifestyle, use this move as a catalyst to make changes in your life.

Part 2: Searching

Chapter 5

Starting Your Search

iven the 130 million or so homes in the United States, choosing the right one for you is a bit like finding the proverbial needle in the haystack. The prospect gets easier if you're moving within the same city or town, but even then, you could be faced with hundreds of options.

Before the age of the Internet, touring open houses was the primary method of seeing available properties on the market. Real estate websites have changed that forever. This is good and bad. On the one hand, the Internet is empowering by allowing us to direct our own searches (saving a lot of legwork in the process). On the other hand, it floods us with unfiltered options to wade through on the path to finding a new place to live.

So where do you begin, and how can you channel these resources to work for you? By breaking the complex, overwhelming task of finding a home into small manageable tasks, you will be empowered to make the best decision possible. Let's get started!

> **Fast Fact** Today, 35 percent of people start their search online, and only 4 percent start with open houses. Over the course of their search nearly 90 percent of buyers searched for homes online, and just 45 percent attended an open house, according to a 2011 survey of home buyers conducted by the National Association of Realtors. We've seen a similar movement online for renters, who are abandoning brokers in favor of sites like Craigslist and Apartments.com.

Where, What, and How Much?

Every move starts with three basic questions: **Where** do you want to live? **What** do you want to live in? **How much** can you pay? When you begin your search online through real estate websites like Zillow or Trulia, you typically start by plugging some version of the following details into their search engine:

Where: City and/or Zip Code
What: Square Footage and/or Number of Bedrooms
How Much: Price Range

Let's call this the **limited search criteria,** the result of which is a laundry list of unfiltered options. Although it's a fine starting point, there's not much rhyme or reason to the results. In one typical scenario, searching for a three-plus-bedroom home for less than $350,000 in a New Jersey county with various bedroom communities of New York City, the search engine spit out more than 1,000 results. Yikes! You might as well be throwing darts at a map of the county.

So how do you refine the search? As I'll discuss throughout this part of the book, finding the best home in the best community means you need to give serious consideration to how you want to live. That means thinking through the total life experience that home will afford, from the time you wake up in the morning to the time you go to bed. The time getting to and from work, the amount of sunlight in your home, and the ways in which you like to spend your free time are just some of the points to consider.

To gather all the right data, you need to develop a set of **advanced search criteria** that goes beyond what you'll find on any real estate site. Though it starts with the same basic questions—where, what, and how much—the result will be a more measured and streamlined list of results. Here's how I define this advanced search criteria.

Where: Character of place and proximity to places that meet your daily needs

What: Type of home, livability, adaptability, flow, and function

How Much: Realistic range allowing for retirement savings and emergency fund

DEFINING AND REFINING YOUR HOUSING PROFILE(S)

In Chapter 4, I introduced you to the idea of your housing profile, the quick snapshot of your ideal neighborhood, house type, and budget (aka the where, what, and how much of your search). You might have several housing profiles, depending on your budget range, proximity to places that meet your daily needs, and the variety of building types in your city. Coming up with your housing profile and applying it to your search is a five-step process.

1. Assess: Consider how you currently live and how you want to live after your move.

2. Understand: Learn all the options, including characteristics/types of cities, neighborhoods, streets, yards, building types, and homes.

3. Articulate: Understand your priorities and define your housing profile(s).

4. Search: With an understanding of your preferences, priorities, and profiles, begin your search.

5. Review and Refine: Check back frequently with your preferences and options to make sure you're achieving the best balance between trade-offs.

Your search will be informed by both the available options and your understanding of your priorities. I'll help you define and refine your priorities so that you can identify your best housing profiles. As you read these chapters and start your search, keep these main points in mind:

- Keep your Must-Haves, Would-Likes, and Don't-Wants streamlined yet flexible
- Allow yourself to dream, but don't lose sight of your realities
- Find balance between the big picture with the small details
- If your ideal isn't available, look for ways to make the available ideal

GOOD AND BAD MODELS OF NARROWING YOUR OPTIONS

To define your housing profile, you need to first understand your entire range of options. Only then should you narrow your choices. In his classic career-planning guide *What Color Is Your Parachute?* Richard N. Bolles illustrates good and bad methods of narrowing choices for finding a profession. His method applies equally well to housing. Bolles uses two shapes to represent the two paths.

Your search will be informed by both the available options and your understanding of your priorities.

In the first, a triangle represents the wrong approach. This method starts with a wide range of options and then narrows them down by process of elimination. For example, if you don't like to work outdoors, jobs like forest ranger and construction worker are eliminated. This seems logical enough, but it doesn't allow you to fully explore all the possibilities. The better approach takes the shape of a diamond. You start by broadening your horizon to see all the possibilities, and only then do you start to narrow down the possibilities.

Methods of Narrowing Your Options

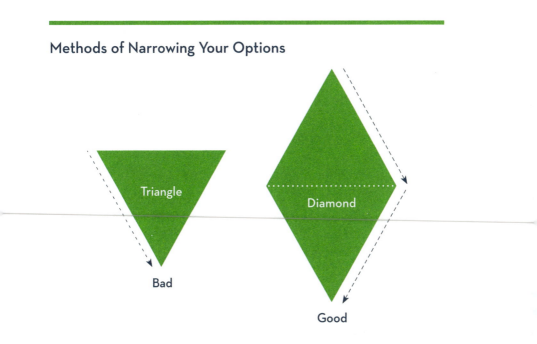

There are two main approaches to narrowing your choices. The first, represented by a triangle, illustrates starting with a list and eliminating options until you have made a decision. The second, the diamond, shows a preferable method. In this example, you first broaden your search before narrowing the options. This allows you to entertain, and often select, options that might otherwise have been passed over.

Most people take a triangular approach when searching for a home. For example, "knowing" they want a big freestanding house, they cast a wide net over only those types of property listings and narrow the search from there. What they (and you) should do instead is consider all types of homes—not just big houses, but smaller ones too, as well as town houses, lofts, and garden apartments—and then narrow the field. You may still end up in a freestanding house, but chances are it will be a better fit for your housing profile since you'll have considered it in the context of all the available options.

Conducting Your Advanced Search

Most real estate sites do in fact have some type of advanced search function allowing you to refine your search with various filters. They might be able to tell you if a particular home has a fireplace or swimming pool, but they won't indicate more experiential features such as the flow of the floor plan or the quality of natural light. You might be able to identify the closest schools, but not the distance from the house or whether the walk is safe for your kids.

Conducting your own advanced search is a back-and-forth process, combining online research with legwork in the field. I realize it takes a little more work, but if you know the questions to ask and the places to look, the process can be both fun and empowering, making the extra effort well worth it in the long run. The chapters in Part 2 of this book are dedicated to guiding your advanced search and to helping you define and find your "where, what, and how much." Before engaging with the details, let's take a moment to consider the overall arc of your search.

STEP ONE: FINDING YOUR "WHERE"

Where you start will vary, depending on one major question: Are you sticking with your current city or moving to a new one? If you're moving to a new city, your search will start with Chapters 6 and 7: "Selecting a Region" and "Finding Your City." If you're staying local, your search will start with Chapter 8, "Selecting Your Neighborhood," and continue into Chapter 9, "Streetscapes."

Selecting Your Region and City

Chapters 6 and 7 represent the 30,000-foot view. If you're relocating to a different part of the country, you need to take a big-picture look

> **Fast Fact** When searching for a home, buyers looked for twelve weeks on average and visited twelve homes, according to 2011 statistics compiled by the National Association of Realtors.

at such characteristics as climate and culture. You'll also want to pay close attention to the opportunities that matter most to you. If you're looking for work, the job market will be a top priority. If you're looking for love, a vibrant social scene will take precedence.

> **Conducting your own advanced search is a back-and-forth process, combining online resources with legwork in the field.**

Finding Your Neighborhood in a New City

If you are planning a move to a new city, you need to learn the character of the different parts of town and get a feel for your neighborhood options. Is there a right and wrong side of the tracks? Are some neighborhoods more walkable than others? Where are the best schools? Talking to locals, meeting with real estate agents, and doing online research will give you multiple points of view on these matters. Chapter 8 walks you through the process.

Finding Your Neighborhood in Your Current City

If you're staying local, you'll have an inside track on the neighborhood search. Still, try to see the options with fresh eyes. As I discussed in Chapter 4, moving to a new home is a perfect time to take stock of your habits and routines and eliminate those that aren't working for you. For starters, reassess your proximity preferences so that your next neighborhood has the amenities you need and desire. Target three or four neighborhood options that might be a good fit so that as you narrow your search to individual homes, you'll have more flexibility.

STEP TWO: DETERMINING YOUR "WHAT"

Once you figure out where you want to live, you can start to think about what you want to live in. There are multiple factors that go into this decision, beyond basic metrics like square footage. We'll go through them one by one in Chapters 10 through 14. Here are the main topics to consider:

Consider Different Building Types

You might be in the market for a single-family house, but it's important to consider the full range of available housing options covered in Chapter 10. You may be surprised to find that a new alternative is a better fit for your housing profile.

Learning to Read the Outside of a Home

Determining which type of home is right for you involves looking at lots of potential options, both in person and online. The process will go faster if you can read the outside of the home to know what it says about the inside of the home as well as the community at large. Although you don't want to judge a book by its cover, you also don't want to waste your time on homes that don't live well. For example, if a hulking three-car garage takes up the front of the house, chances are the floor plan doesn't flow well and the streets and sidewalks aren't kid friendly. I'll explain why in Chapter 11.

Assess How You Engage with the Outdoors

To determine the best type of property and yard for you, you need to understand how you like to use the outdoors. I meet many people who ended up with a huge yard only to realize they don't have much use for it and now have to pay (in time and money) to keep it up. As you decide on the best place to live, you need to determine whether you want to be actively engaged or passively engaged with the exterior. In Chapter 12, we'll explore this question in detail by learning the various ways in which people interact with outdoor spaces.

Touring Inside Your House

Not all square feet are created equal. In Chapters 13 and 14, I'll cover the design elements that make some homes live larger than others, maximizing their live-in value, as well as the red flags to avoid. For example, many new homes have too many hallways and corridors, which are counted in the overall square footage but serve only to confuse the floor plan. Or you'll find bedrooms with no logical spot for the bed because of the placement of the windows and doors. I'll also help you identify the elements that matter most to you in a home by getting you to focus on your lifestyle, both current and future.

STEP THREE: DON'T FORGET YOUR "HOW MUCH"

There are two parts to this equation: how much you can really afford and how much the home is really worth. Both figures are subject to irrational exuberance, to borrow a phrase. Many people spend more than they can afford, and many others think their homes are worth more than they are. Try not to get caught in this vicious cycle. As recent history reminds, the music always stops sooner or later.

What is your "How Much?"

In Chapter 3, I outlined the steps for coming up with a realistic number for how much you should be spending on your home. This number must stay at the top of your mind as you begin your search. Throughout the process, it will be easy to be tempted by properties that are beyond your price range. Remember, if you choose more house than you can easily afford, you may be saying no to other treats in your life, dinners out, vacations, and early retirement.

The New Home Value

What Matters	What Doesn't
Number of bedrooms	Square footage
Good price	Best possible deal ever
20 percent down payment	Zero-down payment
Proximity	Location
Quality of life	Keeping up with the Joneses
Eat-in kitchen	Formal dining room
Spacious shower	Whirlpool tub
Walk-in closets	Media room

WORDS OF WISDOM

"We grew up in suburbia and were looking for a house like we grew up in. We were so disappointed when we put in four offers on our 'dream houses' and were denied each time. We ended up renting an apartment in the city. It has been three years now and we don't ever plan on leaving. Being in walking distance from work and all our daily errands is priceless. In an apartment we have a yard, a pool, a hot tub, a gym, a spa, and no maintenance responsibilities for it—and the sense of community is terrific. Now we're so thankful for the way things turned out." Katie and Ruben G., Miami, FL

"In 1984 I interviewed for a job as an editorial writer at the *Providence Journal*, and on a walk through the city's downtown, whose beautiful string of old classical buildings curved gently toward the Providence River, I told myself that I really had to get the job because the city was so beautiful. I did and I never regretted it." David B., Providence, RI

Comparables

As you keep your number in mind, remember that there's often a big difference between what a house is listed at and what it actually sells for. Many home sellers have an overly optimistic idea about what their house is worth, especially if they've invested a lot of TLC in it. That's why it's important to base your search for a home on the sale prices of homes that are comparable to the type of home you're interested in, known in real estate lingo as "comps." If you're working with a real estate agent, one of their jobs will be to pull together a comps list for you at the beginning of your search.

You can also pull comps on your own by using the Multiple Listings Service (MLS), a database of real estate listings that can be accessed through the website mls.com. Always look for comps for homes that sold in the last six months in the same general vicinity (within six blocks is the rule of thumb) and with similar features, including number of bedrooms and bathrooms, lot size, and overall condition.

Case-Shiller Index

Developed by the economists Karl Case and Robert Shiller, the Case-Shiller index is the most often cited indicator of real estate prices in the country. It tracks the changes in the value of residential real estate both nationally (released four times a year) as well as in twenty metropolitan regions (released monthly), from Los Angeles to Denver to Atlanta to New York. Especially if you're considering a move to one of these areas, it's worth looking at the action of the index in recent months and years.

Though the Case-Shiller index goes back only a couple of decades, Shiller was able to plot the real estate data going all the way back to 1890 in the second edition of his book *Irrational Exuberance.* His findings showed that, with the exception of a period from the late 1990s to the market crash in 2007, home prices on average increase less than 3 percent each year.

Calculating Compound Interest

To calculate the 3 percent interest, either use the formula below, or go online to any compound interest calculator and use 3 percent as the interest.

One calculator is interestcalc.org/.

$M = P (1 + i)^n$

M is the final amount, including the principal.

P is the principal amount.

i is the rate of interest per year.

n is the number of years invested.

The boom-bust of the last decade has thrown real estate prices out of whack. So how do you know how much a home built before 1995 is really worth today? If you can establish its value in 1995, either by asking a real estate agent or tracking its public sales records, you can get an accurate sense of its current value by calculating its compound interest at a rate of 3 percent. If the home is priced way above this figure, think twice about pursuing it.

One more reminder about your number: If you're moving into a hot market, don't base your budget on projections about how much the home is going to be worth down the line. Sure, some markets will start to see double-digit increases in property values again, but the real estate cycle is never ending, so in the long run, 3 percent annual appreciation will always be the best number to bank on.

CHAPTER CHEAT SHEET

Gut Check

What is the where, what, and how-much of where you currently live? What changes would you like to make?

Reality Check

Are your aspirations for a home realistic? Are you starting your search grounded in your realities?

Balancing Act

Function—Are you considering all of the options before narrowing the list? *Cost*—Are you looking in the right price range at homes that are realistically priced? *Delight*—Where do you see yourself being the happiest?

Key points to remember

- Every housing search starts with three basic criteria: where, what, and how much. The more detail you put into answering these questions, the better a fit your new home will be in the long run.

- When searching, assess your needs and your available options. If the ideal isn't available, look for ways to make the available ideal.

- Be realistic about pricing, both for a home you are planning to sell and anything you are considering purchasing.

Chapter 6

Selecting a Region

Which would you prefer, flip-flops in January or a wooly parka? Do you like four seasons with beautiful fall colors, deserts with cacti, mountains with evergreens, or palm trees on the beach? At the start of your search, you might know exactly where you want to live. You may choose to live where you grew up, staying close to an established community of family and friends. Perhaps you work in a specialized job that narrows your choices to a small group of cities. Or you may end up in a city for any number of reasons and just know it is the only one.

But for some of us, myself included, selecting a region and city is not a clear-cut decision. The New Economy has created a new mobility. The golden handcuffs of corporate jobs with big bucks, and even bigger bonuses, have been released. Although for many this has been a very difficult time, for others it has been liberating, creating the opportunity to follow their dreams and build a new life in a new place.

If you are one of the millions considering a move to a new state or region of the country, you might be weighing several options. These next two chapters will outline characteristics of different regions as well as everything you need to consider when looking for a city. You don't need me to tell you that it's cold in the North and warm in the South. But taking the nationwide view will get you thinking about the fundamental ways life experiences differ from one part of the country to the next. (And, for the record, I did recently hear about a woman who moved to Fargo, North Dakota, without anticipating the harshest, most bone-chilling winter of her life; suffice it to say she doesn't live there anymore.)

To organize the information, I started with the U.S. Census Bureau's four main regions: the Northeast, Midwest, South, and West. To provide more specific context, each region is divided into two or more subregions, which vary slightly from the Census Bureau. As Cynthia Enloe and Joni Seager write in their wonderful book *The Real State of America Atlas,* "In the U.S., as elsewhere, it matters where you live. Healthcare is not the same in Massachusetts and Texas. The prevalence of guns in everyday life may seem a nationwide phenomenon to an outside observer, but in fact Americans' relationship to guns differ markedly if they live in Arizona rather than New York." Drawing from their book and other sources like it, I give you this quick snapshot of the country as a whole.

Region: Northeast

SUBREGION: NEW ENGLAND

Consisting of Maine, New Hampshire, Vermont, Massachusetts, Rhode Island, and Connecticut.

Geography: Ruggedness marked by mountain peaks and jagged coastlines, giving way to rolling hills and valleys. Much is undeveloped, preserving the region's natural beauty.

Climate: Four seasons, to varying degrees of intensity. Long, dark, cold winters in the far north. Warm, humid summers to the south. Splendid autumn throughout because of foliage. Increased risk of flooding as a result of recent supestorms.

Character: New Englanders are known for hospitality and reserve— that is, they're warm once you get to know them. In studies of geography-based personality traits, they're especially open to new experiences, with higher-than-average levels of creativity.

U.S. Regions

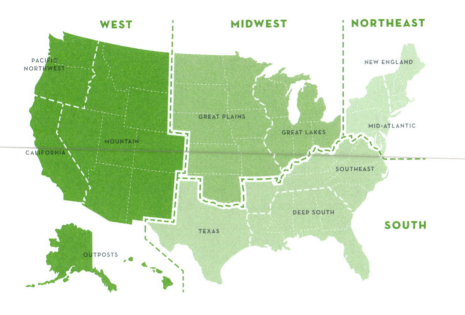

Economy: Regional unemployment on par with national average; Rhode Island has high rate of 11 percent. Boston is a hub of biotech industries and educational resources.

Housing Market: Dominated by the Boston metro area, this region is largely made up of smaller markets with fewer than 10,000 home transactions per year. Average prices have stabilized since the housing crisis, with markets in Maine and New Hampshire typically faring better than Connecticut and Vermont.

Fast Fact Before the Affordable Care Act, just 5 percent of Massachusetts residents didn't have health insurance, the lowest rate nationwide. Texas has the highest rate at 26 percent.

Politics: Mostly blue, with a pocket of red in central Maine. Vermont, New Hampshire, Connecticut, and Massachusetts have all legalized gay marriage.

Religion: Largely Catholic and Protestant. Massachusetts, Vermont, and Connecticut have a relatively large proportion of Jewish people. In general, fewer people say religion is important in their daily life than in other parts of the country.

SUBREGION: MID-ATLANTIC

Consisting of New York, Pennsylvania, New Jersey, Delaware, Maryland, and Washington, D.C.

Geography: Bridge between the North and South combines highly developed, densely populated metropolitan areas with wide swaths of wilderness, farmland, and beaches.

Climate: Four seasons like New England, with less bite in the winter and hotter, more humid summers.

Character: Rich cultural diversity owing to role as original gateway to immigration. Home to many ethnic groups, both English and non-English speaking.

Economy: Unemployment rates at or below national average. New York City strong in finance and business, with the most headquarters of Fortune 500 firms in the country, plus arts and culture. Politics dominate the D.C. area.

Housing Market: The New York, Philadelphia, and Washington, D.C., metro areas make up half of all home transaction activity in this subregion, with seventy-some smaller markets making up the

> **Fast Fact** New Jersey has the densest system of highways and railroads in the country, and also one of the busiest airports, making it one of the easiest states to travel to and through, traffic permitting, of course.

rest. Of those top three markets, Washington, D.C., has seen the best home price stabilization, with average prices continuing to rise.

Politics: Solidly Democratic.

Religion: Predominantly Catholic and Protestant, but with a strong Jewish and Muslim presence in New York and New Jersey.

Region: South

SUBREGION: SOUTHEAST

Consisting of Virginia, West Virginia, Kentucky, North Carolina, South Carolina, Tennessee, and Arkansas.

Geography: Rich coastline giving way to coastal plain and mountainous terrain of the Blue Ridge and Appalachian ranges.

Climate: Mostly temperate conditions, with warm, pleasant summers in some parts, humid and hot in others, and mild winters. Cooler temperatures prevail at higher elevations. Hurricanes a minor threat in the Carolinas.

Character: Primarily outgoing, conscientious, and agreeable.

Economy: Unemployment mostly on par with national average. Hopeful growth in tech and financial sector, especially in Charlotte, North Carolina, and northern Virginia.

Housing Market: Nashville and Charlotte are the largest markets in this subregion, although both make up less than 10 percent of total market activity. Smaller markets, such as Clarksville, Tennessee-Kentucky, are seeing some of the strongest rebounds since the recovery.

> **Fast Fact** West Virginia has the nation's highest rate of homeownership, at 79 percent.

Politics: Region is evenly split between red and blue states. Liberal areas clustered around major cities, following national pattern.

Religion: Largely Southern Baptist, with many residents saying religion is a big part of their daily life.

SUBREGION: DEEP SOUTH

Consisting of Louisiana, Mississippi, Alabama, Georgia, and Florida.

Geography: Subtropical conditions create a landscape of bayous and swamplands and unique flora, including magnolia trees and Spanish moss. Coastline is a major draw.

Climate: Very hot and humid, especially during the summer, when temperatures are routinely above 90°F. Upside is a pleasant off-season, except for the threat of hurricanes.

Character: High rates of agreeableness and extroversion. Strong Latino influence, especially in Florida, which also has a high number of retirees.

Economy: Unemployment rates higher than the national average in many parts. Tourism a big sector. Florida also sustained by arts and entertainment.

Housing Market: Miami and Atlanta make up nearly one third of all housing transaction activity in this region by themselves. Eight of the top ten metro areas are in Florida. Florida alone accounts for more than 60 percent of transactions. Average home prices continue to rise in this subregion, and the Orlando and Cape Coral markets in particular are seeing impressive gains. Meanwhile, markets in Alabama and Georgia tend to have less positive, or even negative, price trends.

> **Fast Fact** The nearly 22 percent of Mississippi residents who live below the poverty line is the highest nationwide.

Politics: Historically conservative. Florida is the exception, with many northern transplants importing liberal values.

Religion: A big part of daily life for many people, most of whom are Southern Baptist. Florida and Georgia have more than fifty megachurches each, the highest number nationwide.

SUBREGION: TEXAS

Geography: Ranked second in size and population, Texas has many topographies, from gently rolling hills to thick forests to desert valleys.

Climate: Variable conditions owing to size, but hot summers and mild winters are the norm. Threat of intense tornadoes and hurricanes.

Character: Expansive, independent spirit pervades much of state. Strong influence from immigrant population, namely arrivals from Mexico and Latin America.

Economy: Strong economy. The energy sector is a dominant force, with many corporations huddled in Houston. Technology is also strong.

Housing Market: Dallas and Houston account for half of all housing transactions by themselves, and if you add in San Antonio and Austin, you have nearly 70 percent. Of those markets, Austin average home prices are doing the best. Statewide, average prices are rising.

Politics: Mostly conservative.

Religion: Catholic to the south, thanks in part to immigrant population, and Southern Baptist to the north. High distribution (fifty or more) of megachurches.

> **Fast Fact** Texas is tough on crime, boasting one of the nation's highest prison rates and the highest number of executions (463 between 1976 and 2010).

Region: Midwest

SUBREGION: GREAT LAKES

Consisting of Wisconsin, Michigan, Illinois, Indiana, and Ohio.

Geography: Primarily flat topography giving way to rolling hills, forests, and the coasts of the Great Lakes; inland parts permeated by tens of thousands of smaller lakes.

Climate: Seasonal, with potential for bitterly cold winters and warm, humid summers, depending on proximity to water.

Character: Agreeable, outgoing, and fairly conscientious.

Economy: Many factories have been shuttered in this former hotbed of manufacturing, resulting in some of the highest unemployment rates in the country.

Housing Market: Chicago is the largest market in this region, constituting 15 percent of home transaction activity on its own. Average home prices in the subregion are fairly stable. Evansville, Indiana, and Lansing, Michigan, are some of the better performers among the larger markets. Meanwhile, Cleveland; Fort Wayne, Indiana; Dayton, Ohio; Flint, Michigan; and Chicago are still struggling.

Politics: Region as whole votes Democratic, but many states are decided by a narrow margin, suggesting an even balance of liberals and conservatives.

Religion: Range of faiths, including Catholic and several denominations of the Protestant faith. Michigan is home to one of the largest Muslim populations in the United States.

> **Fast Fact** Made in the USA! Wisconsin and Indiana have the largest percentage of populations employed (nonfarm) in manufacturing at just over 15 percent.

SUBREGION: GREAT PLAINS

Consisting of North Dakota, South Dakota, Minnesota, Nebraska, Kansas, Iowa, Missouri, and Oklahoma.

Geography: Huge swath of flat land between the Mississippi River and Rocky Mountains, largely made up of prairies, bluffs, and plateaus.

Climate: Four-season climate marked by very hot summers and very cold winters. Tornado Alley runs a straight path through the region.

Character: In geography-based personality traits, this region stands out for its extroversion. People tend to be agreeable and outgoing, and are referred to by some as "salt of the earth."

Economy: North Dakota, South Dakota, and Nebraska have the lowest unemployment rates in the country, down around 4 percent, largely because of a booming energy sector.

Housing Market: St. Louis and Kansas City make up a quarter of all activity in this subregion. Oklahoma City is the third-largest market but has seen better price rebounds.

Politics: Many of the states vote Republican as a whole, with pockets of Democrats.

Religion: A diverse mix of faiths, including Catholic, Lutheran, Methodist, and Southern Baptist.

> **Fast Fact** Approximately 12 percent of adults in this region hunt, compared with a national average of 5 percent, which dips as low as 2 percent on the coasts.

SUBREGION: MOUNTAIN

Consisting of Montana, Idaho, Wyoming, Nevada, Utah, Colorado, Arizona, and New Mexico.

Geography: The Rocky Mountain system forms a spine through the region, defining the terrain with soaring peaks and receding foothills.

Climate: Variable, depending on proximity to Rockies and the Pacific Ocean. Arizona, Nevada, New Mexico, and Utah are known for hot, arid conditions. Elevated parts of Idaho, Montana, and Wyoming experience harsh winters. Colorado has a mix of climates. Depending on location, many homes in this region will need to be designed to accommodate heavy snow loads.

Character: A spirit of conscientiousness and inwardness pervades. The exception is Utah, which scores high for extroversion in geography-based personality.

Economy: Unemployment is relatively low throughout the region, and job growth is expected to be strong in coming years, thanks to natural resources and mining sectors.

Housing Market: Phoenix, Las Vegas, and Denver are by far the largest markets in this region, making up half of housing transaction activity. In addition to being the largest metro area in terms of activity, Phoenix is also enjoying a long-awaited rebound in home prices.

Politics: Mixed, with Arizona, Idaho, Montana, Wyoming, and Utah skewing Republican, and Nevada, Colorado, and New Mexico skewing Democratic.

Religion: Largely Catholic, but with a strong Mormon presence in Utah and parts of Idaho and Arizona.

> **Fast Fact** Wyoming residents drive more than any other people, thanks to the state's sparse population, wide-open spaces, and major interstate highway system. The state has the single highest vehicle miles of travel per state per capita, at 17,735.

> **Fast Fact** Washington and Oregon have some of the lowest percentages of obese or overweight adults—50 to 59 percent, compared with 65 percent or more in states like Mississippi and Alabama.

Region: West

SUBREGION: PACIFIC NORTHWEST

Consisting of Oregon and Washington.

Geography: Natural beauty abounds, including lush forests, majestic mountains, and a pristine, rugged coastline, especially through Oregon.

Climate: Mostly mild, though inland parts experience colder temperatures. Damp, rainy weather affects much of the region year-round.

Character: Liberal attitude and openness to new experiences defines this corner of the country.

Economy: Unemployment rates on par with the national average. Job growth in natural resources as well as leisure and hospitality could have a stimulating effect.

Housing Market: Seattle and Portland are by far the largest markets in this two-state subregion, but a standout performer is the

Healthy Town

Some communities are built to be healthier than others. The fact that just 15 percent of kids today walk or bike to school, down from about 50 percent in 1970, is one factor in this. Some states, like California, have provided funding specifically for the creation of crosswalks, sidewalks, and bike lanes in and around schools; they are doing the most to combat the problem.

Kennewick-Pasco-Richland metro area, also called the Tri-Cities, which has a healthy housing market thanks to a strong local economy and high quality of life.

Politics: Both states are blue. But they turn red the farther you travel from the coast.

Religion: Mostly Catholic and Protestant. But compared with the rest of the country, fewer people say religion is a big part of their daily life.

SUBREGION: CALIFORNIA

Geography: The country's third-largest state behind Alaska and Texas has the largest population. Take your pick of topography, from coastal to desert, flat to mountainous.

Climate: Conditions vary from north to south and with the topography. Outside of the extremes, much of the state has a mild, Mediterranean climate. Buildings must be engineered to withstand earthquakes and seismic activity. Recent fires have ravaged parts of Southern California, creating new requirements for noncombustible materials on all homes.

Character: Primarily laid-back and open to experience.

Economy: California has been hit hard by the recession, with higher-than-average unemployment and foreclosure rates, but it remains the country's largest economy, and the world's eighth-largest, equal to Brazil's.

Housing Market: The greater Los Angeles area makes up a quarter of the state's housing activity, and with an average price over $440,000 is one of the pricier areas in the nation. But both in the Los Angeles

> **Fast Fact** A total of 54 percent of the workers in California's Silicon Valley are Asian or Asian American, compared with the national average of 16 percent.

> **Fast Fact** At the peak of the housing boom in 2005, just four states—California, Florida, Georgia, and North Carolina—accounted for nearly a third of all new housing permits, and job growth rates there were 50 percent above the national average, according to Harvard's Joint Center for Housing Studies. But since construction started slowing down in 2008, job growth rates in these states have been among the most sluggish.

metro area and statewide, housing recovery has been fairly weak. The diverse and beleaguered housing markets across the state have some more waiting to do before they are likely to see anything close to robust price appreciation again.

Politics: Predominantly Democratic, but the state gets more red the farther inland you go.

Religion: Primarily Catholic/Protestant with moderate levels of devotion, though the state does have more than fifty megachurches.

WORDS OF WISDOM

"We each made a list of what we wanted in a city and then we compared lists. Thankfully they were very close. Then we drove to visit each. Although we thought seriously about moving closer to our families, in the end we determined that on a daily basis we wanted to be where we fit best. We ended up moving to Portland, OR, and it was a great decision, worth the time invested." Kathryn V., Portland, OR

"We came to realize that when you're in a competitive field like academia, you have to relocate for the right position even if it means moving far beyond your home city or state." Kara B., Pittsburgh, PA

SUBREGION: OUTPOSTS

Consisting of Alaska and Hawaii.

Geography: Alaska is the largest state with the longest coastline. Hawaii is among the smallest, and the only one made up of an archipelago.

Climate: Arctic and harsh throughout much of Alaska, warm and tropical in Hawaii. Both states are in the Pacific Ocean's "ring of fire," an area with a high frequency of earthquakes and volcanic eruptions.

Character: A rugged, frontier spirit is embraced by many Alaskans, whereas the Hawaiian culture is warm and hospitable.

Economy: Unemployment rates are lower than the national average in both states, on the strength of natural resources and mining sectors.

Housing Market: Although part of the same subregion, these two states couldn't be more different in terms of housing. Alaska is the largest state in the union by land area but sees less housing transaction activity than Hawaii, one of the smallest states. Honolulu and Anchorage account for the bulk of activity, totaling more than 60 percent of all the subregion's housing activity combined. Average prices for the subregion overall are flat.

Politics: Alaska is bright red, Hawaii bright blue.

Religion: Hawaii is largely Catholic and Protestant, whereas Alaska has religion in virtually every stripe, from Seventh-Day Adventist to United Church of Christ.

> **Fast Fact** More than 50 percent of Alaskans live in a household with a gun, and fewer than 20 percent of Hawaiians do.

CHAPTER CHEAT SHEET

Gut Check

What region best fits your lifestyle and needs?

Reality Check

Are you able to find work in your ideal region?

Your Balancing Act

Function—What region logistically works best for your family, allowing you to participate in the activities you enjoy? *Cost*—What is the cost of living in the region you are considering? *Delight*—Is it important for you to live near family and friends, or could you be happy moving to another part of the country and starting a whole new social circle?

Key point to remember

• Regions vary not just by climate and geographical features, but also by cultures and character. Finding the right fit might mean returning to what you know or exploring a new place. Keep an open mind.

Chapter 7

Finding Your City

f you believe everything you read, you might pick up and move to Louisville, Colorado, which the editors of *Money* magazine recently called the best place to live in America. *Men's Health,* on the other hand, would send you packing to Madison, Wisconsin, that is, if you're a single lad on the prowl, given the city's high number of eligible bachelorettes. Looking for the inside track on investments? *Real Estate Trends* pegged Akron, Ohio, as the top U.S. market for buying and investing. If you've got a school-age brood, Falmouth, Maine, was the place to be, said GreatSchools.org, and retirees should look no farther than Winchester, Virginia, named the most affordable place to live out your years by AARP.

Although it's fun to pass time online and in magazines clicking and flipping through any number of themed "Top Ten Cities for *Insert Topic Here,*" it's not the best way to find your new home. That's because these "Best Of" lists are consistently inconsistent. For one thing, they aren't always guided by the most rigorous or transparent methodology. For another, real estate markets are changing all the time, so the hot city one year could turn cold the next. But the biggest downside to these lists is that no matter how thorough and current their selection process, they'll never be able to speak to your individual needs.

Every city has its own unique personality. I don't mean the personalities of the people who live there—although this is one element that contributes to the overall personality of a place—but rather the personality of the city itself. This is informed by many elements, such as

> **Fast Fact** The average American moves once every seven years. Nationwide, that translates into 40 million people relocating each year. And out of these, 15 million people move a distance of fifty miles or greater.

its larger regional context, its natural features, climate, size, population, local history, industry, economy, transportation infrastructure, built environment, civic institutions, and even sports teams.

If you take away only one thing from this book, make it this: Where you choose to live has an immeasurable effect on your total well-being. It affects what job you hold, the people you see, the activities you engage in, and even what kind of children you raise (assuming kids are in the cards). That's true whether you're looking across the entire country, narrowing your list to a few cities within a given region, or finalizing your plans to a specific place. What city has the right personality for you? Let's find out.

Who's Your City?

Who is your city? In his book of that title, the American urban studies theorist Richard Florida examines our biggest life decisions. Asked to name their biggest life decisions, he asserts, most people will say one of two things: career path or spouse. Both make sense. What we do for a living determines how we spend a good chunk of our time, not to mention our source of income. And the person we share our life with is central to our happiness.

Florida agrees that these are two very big decisions, but he goes on to argue that finding the right place to live is just as important, if not more so. "The place we choose to live affects every aspect of our being," he writes. "It can determine the income we earn, the people we meet, the friends we make, the partners we choose, and the options available to our children and families."

QUIZ: YOUR JUST RIGHT CITY

So what is the best city for you? Let's first examine where you currently live, consider the elements that matter most, and then start compiling your list of options.

Assess Your Current City

1. What characteristics do you love most about your city?

2. What would you change about your current city?

3. Is it easy to get around the city? How does this affect your days?

4. Do you connect with the people in your city? Is it easy to make meaningful friendships?

5. Are you suited for the job market in your city?

6. Can you afford the cost of living?

Imagine Your Ideal City

1. What size is your ideal city?

2. Is it urban, suburban, or rural?

3. What part of the country would you live in?

4. What types of people live in your ideal city?

5. What type of industry would you find in your ideal city?

6. What amenities and activities would you like in a city?

7. What is the weather like in your ideal city? Four seasons or hot year-round?

Compile a List of Potential Cities

1. Is there a city, or list of cities, that meet your ideal criteria?

2. Are you able to find work or make a living in this city?

3. If you can't find a city that meets all of your criteria, which ones meet some or most of your ideal elements?

Assess Your List of Potential Cities

1. What is the cost of living?
2. What is the traffic like in your potential city?
3. Are there good schools?
4. Are there civic and cultural amenities?
5. Are there parks or exercise trails?
6. Will you be able to find meaningful work?
7. What is the character of the place?
8. Will it be easy to meet people and establish friendships?

Keep these questions and your answers in mind as you read this chapter. Assessing your needs is a back-and-forth process. Return to this section frequently as you learn more about the characteristics of different cities.

Assessing Cities and Towns

Here are the main elements to consider when matching your wants and needs to the personality of a new city, or taking stock of your current city.

OVERALL CONNECTIVITY: TRANSIT, TRANSPORTATION, AND GETTING AROUND

How you get around a city will have a huge effect on your quality of life. This has to do with your means of travel—foot, car, bus, bike, mass transit, and so forth—but also the proximity between the places you visit regularly. In Chapters 8 and 9, we will look more closely at the proximity of activities in your neighborhood as well as the types and characteristics of different streets. For now, consider the overall connectivity of a city and start by asking yourself these questions:

• What are your options for getting to and from the places you need to get your daily needs met in this city?

• Is it easy to get from Point A to Point B?

> ## Making Your List of Cities
>
> Your list of potential cities will develop from any number of sources. You might consider places where you have friends and family; your list could also be informed by possible jobs, or you might be considering a place you have visited in your travels. You will find many websites that promise to help you find the perfect city. Some are better than others, but to date, none offer a comprehensive search tool that will offer perfectly calibrated results. All should be used only as a starting point to generate a list of cities that *might* fit your needs and desires. You still have to do the due diligence, visiting places in person, talking to the natives, comparing job/housing markets based on your specific requirements, and more.

- Is there a lot of traffic congestion?
- Are there walkable places in the city?
- Is there a transit system in place, and is using it a viable option?

Here are five aspects of getting around to consider when looking at a new city:

Walkability There's no better mode of transportation than your own two feet. First and foremost, it's free. It also promotes physical health (twenty minutes of sustained walking per day is needed to keep our bodies functioning properly) and mental health (no stress from traffic, honking horns, road rage, and so on). And it's good for the environment, curbing harmful greenhouse gas emissions and consumption of fossil fuels. Last but not least, walking encourages community, since it gets you out talking with others on the street. See "Walk Score," page 130, for advice on comparing walkability rates from one city to the next.

Biking Experts say biking is a reasonable option for trips three miles or less. To make biking a viable alternative, there need to be safe, dedicated lanes for biking as well as accessible bike racks at your destination. If you are an avid biker or interested in starting, most

Walk Score, walkscore.com

The surest way to measure a city's walkability is to get out and walk it. Walk Score is the next best thing, and it lets you assess more than 2,500 cities nationwide. Here's how it works: You plug a specific address, street name, or zip code into the search box and hit go. Walk Score spits out an overall score using a complex algorithm that crunches such factors as the presence of a town center, proportion of mixed-use buildings, population density, and pedestrian design. There's also a commuting function that calculates the time and expense needed to walk, ride, drive, and take mass transit to your place of work.

Here's a breakdown of the possible scores:

Walk Score	Description
90–100	Walker's Paradise —Daily errands do not require a car.
70–89	Very Walkable—Most errands can be accomplished on foot.
50–69	Somewhat Walkable—Some amenities within walking distance.
25–49	Car-Dependent—A few amenities within walking distance.
0–24	Car-Dependent—Almost all errands require a car.

cities have online resources and links to keep you up to date with local initiatives and local routes.

Personal Vehicles Unless you live in a major city, you probably will need a car to get to and from some if not all of your daily needs. Once upon a time, traveling by car was a real luxury. Today, it can be a burden, when the journey is spent parked in traffic rather than driving. When assessing a new city, look into average commute times, and get an understanding of realistically how long it will take you to get around, not just in terms of miles, but in terms of travel time. The

Fast Fact Transportation accounts for 27 percent of greenhouse gas emissions and 72 percent of petroleum use in the United States.

website WalkScore.com lets you search commute times by foot, bike, car, train, and other modes of transportation.

Mass Transit Ideally, you'll find a variety of options for getting around in town. Subway systems are efficient, though they're mostly limited to big cities. In smaller metros, light rail and bus rapid transit (BRT) systems are a quick way to get around, stopping every mile or so; systems with GPS-enabled time-to-arrival clocks make waiting times more bearable. Traditional buses and streetcars stop more frequently, making them less efficient but better at spurring economic activity. For a transit system to be viable, users must be able to reach the transit stops by foot on at least one of their journeys, and preferably two. Park and rides, whereby you drive to a source of mass transit that takes you the rest of the way, are another viable option, provided you don't have to hop in another car to reach your final destination—an inefficiency that defeats the purpose with some systems.

Coming and Going from a City or Town We used to enter cities, and now we follow exit signs into them, a telling progression about the health of our urban planning practices. The three main ways to access a city are by highway, rail, and air. The best fit for you will depend on how often you need to come and go—Are you an air-miles platinum traveler, or are you lucky to leave once a year for a vacation? Or somewhere in between?—as well as where you typically go when you leave. Ask yourself these questions:

• Consider how and when you visit family. Do you plan on driving?

• If you are driving to visit family, what would be the maximum length you would drive?

• Do you travel for work?

• Does your work travel take you to major cities or to smaller cities?

• Do you need an airport hub, or are you fine with connecting flights?

ECONOMY AND INDUSTRY

Health of Local Industry The economic health of the area is especially important if you will be looking for a new job once you arrive. Although it is ideal to move to a city with a strong economy, that doesn't mean you shouldn't move to a place that is struggling. The key is making sure that you first have a stable means of employment. If you have a secure job already lined up, moving to a city with a struggling economy might help you get a better price on a new home.

Take the local economy into consideration when deciding between renting and owning. If the economy is particularly bad in a certain city, it might seem like a great time to find a deal on a home. But remember the warnings of buying a foreclosure from Chapter 3. If you are moving to a place that is doing really well, take care before jumping into a house too fast before understanding the overall stability of the place.

Even if you won't be working for one of the big area employers, the health of local industries directly affects the health of the entire local economy. To find the most recent economic and industry reports for potential cities, visit www.city-data.com. Ask these questions:

- Who are the largest employers in the area?
- How strong are the industries of the largest employers in the area? (Oil companies in Texas are a safe bet, whereas cities with economies tied to manufacturing might be less stable.)
- Have there been large layoffs in the area recently?
- Are new companies moving into the area?
- Is there positive or negative growth in the region?
- How do unemployment rates compare with the national average?

Cost of Living and Taxes Cost of living varies wildly from region to region, city to city, and even neighborhood to neighborhood. Indeed, affluent neighborhoods tend to be "high-consumption," with residents driving luxury cars, putting in swimming pools, and paying attention in general to status symbols. That can easily land a person on the "earn-to-spend treadmill," a phrase from the 1996 book *The Millionaire Next Door* that still resonates today. There are many cost-of-living calculators on the Internet, but the one I like best is by Salary.com. It tells you exactly how much you'd need to earn in your new city to maintain your current standard of living.

Beyond standard of living and the keeping up with the Joneses factor, perhaps the biggest determinant of cost of living is tax burden. I couldn't believe how big a tax break I received after moving from New York to Florida. Not surprisingly, New York has one of the highest tax burdens, along with New Jersey and Connecticut, whereas Florida is much farther down the list. Here's how the top and bottom ten compare, according to a 2011 study by the Tax Foundation.

Tax Rates Nationwide

Top Ten	Taxes paid as percent of income	Bottom Ten	Taxes paid as percent of income
New Jersey	12.2	New Mexico	8.4
New York	12.1	Louisiana	8.2
Connecticut	12.0	South Carolina	8.1
Wisconsin	11.0	New Hampshire	8.0
Rhode Island	10.7	Texas	7.9
California	10.6	Wyoming	7.8
Minnesota	10.3	Tennessee	7.6
Vermont	10.2	South Dakota	7.6
Maine	10.1	Nevada	7.5
Pennsylvania	10.1	Alaska	6.3

Source: Tax Foundation

Housing Market All real estate is local. Every city, and even every neighborhood within each city, has its own highs, lows, and economic indicators. You can track the recent fluctuations on real estate websites like Trulia or Zillow, but for the most in-depth reports, visit HousingIntelligence.com. Follow the link to Reports and you will be able to purchase a detailed forecast for most markets in the United States. These reports track unemployment, housing permits, housing sales, and household growth, among other factors, to offer a forecast of each market.

BASIC SERVICES

Schools Schools will no doubt be one of the primary factors in your city search if you have school-age kids. Colleges and universities aren't essential, since many kids go away for higher learning, but they can add greatly to a community's cultural richness. Great Schools (www.greatschools.org) is an independent organization that lets you assess schools in a potential community. Ask locals about the schools. The more specific you can get with the conversation, the better. For example, instead of asking if the schools are good, ask if they offer language immersion classes, or if the seats and desks are arranged in rows or circles—anything to make the conversation as detailed and meaningful as possible.

If you don't have kids, you should still look at the community's primary and secondary schools, since they're a good indicator of the strength of other local services, as well as a solid tax base. That being said, less-than-stellar schools shouldn't be a deal breaker for empty nesters or those without children, since there are plenty of great places to live (especially within the city limits) that aren't necessarily known for their great school systems.

Health Care If you're in your later years or plan to be in the community for a long while, health care services are especially important. States in the Northeast have the highest percentage of doctors per population, which is a big reason why cities such as New York, Boston, and Trenton attract retirees over the age of sixty-five, despite the often harsh winters.

Consumer Reports' website (consumerreports.org) has a state-by-state rating of hospitals, based on such factors as patient experience, percentage of surgical-site infections, and quality of information on medications. You have to subscribe to the website to access the ratings, but it might be worth the $7 monthly monthly or $30 annual fee, especially since you'll also get access to all the other product ratings and information.

Safety and Crime Basic services also encompass fire, safety, and crime protection. Research fire department response times—for the city, and for your neighborhood. As cities have grown and budgets have been stretched, fire and ambulance services have often been cut.

• Where is the nearest ambulance or fire station?

• What are average response times in your city or your neighborhood? One minute? Four minutes? Ten minutes?

In general, smaller cities have lower crime rates than larger ones, although a single crime in a small town can reverberate further and deeper than 100 in a large city. Keep in mind too that there can be big differences from one neighborhood to the next. Here are a couple of online resources that can help you assess crime in any city. Once you have narrowed down your search to a specific area, contact the local police departments to get a report from the last six months. This will give you a sharper snapshot of the area.

CrimeReports.com Type in any address or zip code and get a map locating and identifying the residences of all registered sex offenders in that area. Names, photos, and addresses are included.

Homefair.com Under "City Reports" you can type in your zip code and learn the city's total crime risk, personal crime risk (including crimes like robbery and assault), and property crime risk (including things like burglary and motor vehicle theft).

Religious Institutions It's a good idea to attend several houses of worship, be it a church, synagogue, temple, or mosque, to make sure the community is one that you can integrate into. Many people realize too late how important their faith is to them, and find themselves living in an area without the requisite religious institutions in which they can feel at home.

PHYSICAL WELLNESS

Personal Health and Life Expectancy Your personal health, as well as life expectancy, depends a lot on genes, diet, and exercise, but your zip code can also be a factor. Variables include region (consider the healthy lifestyles maintained in a place like Boulder, Colorado, versus the sedentary lifestyle you find in less active cities), air quality, and transportation options (are you sitting or walking?). Look at the overall healthiness of a place. The American Fitness Index ranks cities based on such factors as number of smokers, percentage of exercising residents, and rates of chronic health concerns like obesity, asthma, cardiovascular disease, and diabetes. Visit AmericanFitnessIndex .org to see cities by their overall rankings, as well as personal health and community health scores.

Local Food The local and organic food movements have picked up steam in recent years, but there's still a ways to go. The website LocalHarvest.org is a database that helps you locate the best organic and local foods in your area. Type in your zip code or address and search for local farmers' markets, farms, and co-ops.

Exercise and Bike Paths See if the city has any trails or paths for biking, jogging, walking, or horseback riding. These multiuse trails are often built on old railroad lines, so they are away from streets and traffic. Some cities have hundreds of miles of trails, which makes exercising easy and safe for all ages and abilities, from parents pushing strollers to youngsters on training wheels to competitive bikers to senior adults out for a daily two-mile walk. Look for some of these trails in your state or city at railstotrails.org.

THE INTANGIBLE, YET ESSENTIAL

Real estate prices, test scores, tax rates, and other hard data provide a useful snapshot of a place. But to paint a complete picture, you need to take into account several less tangible factors.

Aesthetics: Natural and Man-Made Beauty, as they say, is in the eye of the beholder. But when it really comes down to it, some places are objectively more beautiful than others. This matters more to some people than others, but it always matters. All cities have natural as well as man-made aesthetics. The natural aesthetics might include the color of the sky; indigenous plants and trees; the topography, from mountains to wide plains; and water elements such as lakes, rivers, or the ocean. Man-made aesthetics include gardens, trails, architecture, parks, roads, and so on.

Having lived in both South Bend, Indiana, and Miami, Florida, I understand firsthand the difference the color of the sky makes in the look and feel of a place. Even though I love the crystal-clear blue skies of Miami, I miss the fall colors in South Bend, where a lone bright red tree will stand out among its yellow and orange neighbors. Every place has something that makes it naturally beautiful and special. Look around and ask yourself which of these elements matter most to you.

When it comes to the man-made world, there are two distinct types of development: Somewhere, USA, and Anywhere, USA. Somewhere, USA, has an identity all its own, whether it be the main street of a small town like Greenville, South Carolina, or the hustle and bustle of Pike Place Market in Seattle, with fish flying over your head. Anywhere, USA, on the other hand, lacks individual identity. If you were to be blindfolded and dropped into the sprawl that rings most American cities, chances are you would be hard pressed to identify your location. What makes a Walmart in Tampa different from a Walmart in Omaha? Not too much.

Most cites will have a blend of areas that are Somewhere and Anywhere. As you look for a new city, whether it be urban, suburban, or rural, look for one that includes areas that make it feel like Somewhere to you.

Sense of Community We experience a connection to our community on two levels: the larger whole and the individuals with whom we engage on a day-to-day basis. Connection to the larger whole can be seen when a city's team wins the Super Bowl or World Series and strangers unite from all socioeconomic tiers to celebrate the same events. Your unique experience and the people with whom you engage on a daily basis also inform your personal sense of community. These might be connections from work, school, or church, or within your neighborhood.

When deciding where to live, make sure the city you're looking at meets your needs for connection and social interaction. Cites that have the best sense of community and pride in place typically have places where residents can physically gather. Although social media is great for keeping us all connected, nothing replaces actually getting together in person. You can get a pretty good picture of the character of a place by reading the local papers and watching the local news. But the best way to get a real sense of the place is to get out and talk to people.

Transient Versus Stable Population A final intangible relates to the issue of transience versus stability in the population. The great thing about moving to cities like New York or Miami is that it is easy to meet new people, mostly because the people you are meeting are most likely transplants as well. The downside of this is that although it is easy to make friends, it is harder to keep them, because the nature of these places is that people come and go. On the other hand, some cities like Boston or Philadelphia have more stable populations. It's nice that once you are settled, your social group will be more stable, but it can be a bit trickier to make friends in the beginning.

College towns and cities with military bases have more transient populations. This can make buying and selling a house easier because of a forced movement in the market. Smaller cities and towns often have more stable populations, which makes purchasing more of a commitment. This is not the most important factor when looking for a new city, but one that can help you find a city that reflects your own character. Ask yourself these questions:

• How long do you plan to stay in your new city?

• Do you know people there already?

• Do you respond best to stability or do you like the excitement of new people?

Types of Cities and Towns

Pop quiz: What city do you currently live in? This is a straightforward enough question, but how you answer it speaks volumes. Most people respond by rounding up to the largest or most recognizable city close by. I go to visit my parents in Palm Springs every year for Christmas, but they actually live in Indian Wells, California. My college roommate was from Detroit, but actually lived in Troy, Michigan. Then again, sometimes we are literally from where we say we are from. I grew up in Anchorage, Alaska, and had the postal code that said so. Although how you identify where you live will depend on whom you are talking to, it also speaks to your connection to your city and the elements that mean the most to you.

As you consider a move to a different city, keep in mind that what we loosely define as a *city* is very often a metropolitan area composed of many smaller municipalities and communities, each with a unique identity and character. You might find you identify with one of these communities much more than the others.

When you name the city you live in, what do you think of first? What defines your city for you? Do you think about traffic? Do you think about a sports team? Do you think about positive or negative elements? Or both? How you identify your city will help inform you about the elements you value most. Think about these questions as you read the rest of this chapter. As you do, take note of what jumps out as a priority for you, and use that list to help you select your new city.

WHAT IS A CITY?

City is a broad term that means many things to many people. Technically speaking, it's defined as an incorporated municipality, usually governed by a mayor and city council. But for the purposes of this book, I'll use the term a little more loosely to also describe large metropolitan areas that are made up of smaller cities, towns, and neighborhoods. As I mentioned earlier, cities have their own personalities. The same is true for the subsections that are part of it. So although New York City is very different from Dallas, the New York neighborhoods of Greenwich Village in Manhattan and Staten Island's St. George are also quite different.

SIZE AND POPULATION

I love that scene in *City Slickers,* the 1991 film starring Billy Crystal, where the best friend, played by Bruno Kirby, is pitching his idea of a dude ranch vacation. "The three of us, New Mexico . . . driving cattle," he says.

"What, like in a truck?" Crystal responds. It's a universal gag, since everyone gets the schism between the urban huckster and the rugged frontiersman.

These archetypes are deeply ingrained in our culture, and, as is often said of clichés, they wouldn't exist (or be so funny) if they weren't based on a certain amount of truth. Be that as it may, they're too simplistic when it comes to figuring out the best place to live.

You may consider yourself a city person, but that doesn't necessarily mean the largely iron-bound island of Manhattan is your only choice. Instead, you might have in mind a walkable city center in a boutique city like Denver or Austin. Here is a snapshot from urban to rural of different types of cities.

Large Metros These cities have huge population bases (800,000-plus in the individual city or 3 million or more in the metro area). Examples include New York, Los Angeles, Chicago, Houston, Philadelphia, Dallas, Atlanta, and Washington, D.C.

Although these cities all move at a fast pace, the overall lifestyle can feel different, depending on the transit options and density of mixed-use areas. For example, New York's superior subway and bus system means you can live easily without a car, whereas in Los Angeles you might spend half your life behind the wheel. Similarly, many neighborhoods in Washington, D.C., are eminently walkable, including Georgetown and Dupont Circle, whereas the sprawling, single-use, car-dependent neighborhoods of Atlanta now extend all the way into Tennessee.

As we will discuss in more detail in Chapter 8, you will also find neighborhoods with many varied characteristics in all cities, especially large ones. You might also find areas of large cities that feel more like small towns. Living in a large metro area does not necessarily mean the feeling of an urban city center.

Big Cities These cities typically have populations ranging from 300,000 to 800,000, with metro areas up to 3 million. Examples include Austin, Charlotte, Nashville, Denver, and Pittsburgh. They tend not to have quite the hustle-bustle or the industry and commerce of their large metro brethren, but thriving cultural scenes are common. These scenes often define the character of the city, at least for a time, as with country music in Nashville and the arts scene in Austin. The proximity to nature, at least compared with larger metro areas, engenders an outdoor spirit, especially in places like Portland and Denver. To call these hobbyist havens is a little minimizing (Austin has Whole Foods' headquarters, and Charlotte is a banking hub in the Southeast), but it's fair to say that people in these cities are defined as much by what they do after work as by their jobs.

Midsize Cities With populations between 150,000 and 300,000 and metro areas ranging up to several hundred thousand, these cities include Greensboro, Spokane, Des Moines, Salt Lake City, and Tallahassee. The downtown areas of these cities will often be bustling during the day, anchored by a smattering of skyscrapers, but can often have limited residential options in the urban centers. Whereas big cities are often full of transplants and transients, small cities tend to be home to people who are from the area. This can be nice if you want to settle in for the long haul.

Small Cities Small cities fall between 50,000 and 150,000, some with and others without metro regions. Examples include Savannah, Topeka, Ann Arbor, Santa Barbara, and Biloxi. All of the categories offer a wide range in economic and cultural opportunities, perhaps none more so than in this group. Although some cities of this size might offer limited cultural opportunities, many, such as Savannah and Santa Barbara, are rich in architectural character and history. They might have a few midrise buildings, but high-rises are rare. As with midsize cities, people are often from the area, offering a more stable population.

Petite Cities and Towns These are "Small Town America" at its best, with cities ranging in size from 10,000 to 50,000 that may or may not have a metro area. They are often rural in character but can also be individual municipalities connected to larger cities. Living in a town can afford a quiet and peaceful lifestyle away from the larger cities. The cost of living is typically much lower than in cities, making homeownership easier and your money go further. You might find shopping and cultural opportunities more limited, but so too will be the need to keep up with the Joneses. Economies vary greatly, depending on local industry and proximity to larger cities. Petite cities are becoming wonderful refuges for the new breed of the telecommuting workforce.

Villages and Hamlets Small villages and hamlets are rural in nature, often defined by an economy based on agriculture or tied to natural amenities like beaches or ski slopes. Populations might range from 500 to 10,000 and can offer an idyllic form of human settlement when not overrun by rural sprawl (more on this in Chapter 8). Although it is easy to romanticize living in a small village or hamlet, the challenge is making the quiet life work with your career. There are people who put up with an extreme commute, traveling three or more hours each day from their country home to their city office. If those hours are spent on a train or bus, you might be able to use them productively. But you need to think long and hard about the toll that commuting great distances by car can have on your mind and body before making the move. Far more preferable is a situation where you're self-employed or making only occasional visits into the city.

SPECIAL TYPES AND CHARACTERISTICS OF CITIES

Beyond their physical size, cities can also be defined by special characteristics that add value and enrich life. These places are often talked about as destination cities, and make frequent appearances in travel magazines. But why only visit a great place when you can live there all the time? Even if you don't engage daily with the available amenities, you will benefit from their influence on the culture. The downside to these special places is that their popularity means they often carry a high cost of living. But you can often offset that by downsizing—trading square footage for connection to a great place. Here are a few examples:

College Town This includes Durham, North Carolina; New Haven, Connecticut; and Austin, Texas. These places offer a high-energy, intellectual atmosphere, often with access to great libraries and lectures; rich cultural experiences, including theater, concerts, museums, and lectures; robust sporting and athletic events, especially if the college is on the National Collegiate Athletic Association (NCAA) circuit; and often thriving job markets tied to research, technology, or medicine. Bottom line: College towns are not just for college students. Indeed, they're often a popular destination for retirees and empty-nesters looking to downsize. Wikipedia has a complete list of college towns, in the United States and abroad, with links to detail pages on each city.

Resort Town Aspen, Colorado; Palm Springs, California; and Palm Beach, Florida, all qualify as resort towns. They're defined by their natural beauty and appeal to outdoor types. Building on that, these places typically offer many outdoor amenities, including skiing, golf, boating, and more, which attracts retirees. That cohort also likes the often-warmer climate and the excellent health care. The emphasis on health care, in turn, stokes the economy, creating jobs for younger people looking to work in medicine and related fields. Do keep in mind that resort towns will often have a "season." Whether it is snowbirds flocking to sunny Florida in the winter or city-goers escaping to beach homes in the summer months, choosing to live year-round in a resort town means you will have to deal with longer lines, extra traffic, and booked restaurants in the busy season. A search of the word *resort* on Wikipedia will offer links to popular resort towns by categories.

Historic Town This category includes Newport, Rhode Island; Charleston, South Carolina; and Savannah, Georgia. They offer rich heritage and history, often boasting a high level of architectural beauty and urbanism, even if the actual historic core is very small. There is always a strong sense of identity and appreciation of place in historic towns, because people seem acutely aware of the connection to the past. Like resort towns, they may have a higher volume of tourists during certain times of the year, although since tourism is typically the mainstay of the local economy, visiting guests are usually welcomed with open arms. Finding a historic town requires a little research. Searching the terms *historic town* and *old town* will produce links to historic towns nationwide.

Cultural Destination These take the form of cities large and small, from New York to San Francisco to Los Angeles to Asheville to New Orleans. Common denominators include a thriving arts scene, often underpinned by world-renowned museums and theaters in the big cities and niche festivals in the small cities. Great food is common in every cultural destination, and their citizens tend to boast strong civic and cultural character. Finding a city with a thriving cultural or arts scene is a Google search away. Search terms like *arts cities* and *cultural cities* will yield results of cities large and small nationwide. Follow the links and read the articles to find the latest news on established arts communities like Austin, Texas, or Portland, Oregon, or discover the newest up-and-coming arts scenes.

CATCHING CITIES ON THE RISE

Boom-and-Bust Towns The economic fortunes of a region are in constant flux. A century ago, the Rust Belt states of the northern United States were the so-called foundry of the nation and home to many of the most robust local economies. But toward the end of the twentieth century, many manufacturing jobs started migrating overseas and South, and the Sun Belt was born. Alas, many of these southern boom-towns became epicenters of the housing bubble. When the bubble burst in 2007, places like Las Vegas, Phoenix, and Fort Lauderdale were the hardest hit. Yet, although only a few years ago they were considered down for the count, all three are making surprising comebacks. At the same time, lo and behold, some northern locales assumed completely dead, such as Bent Harbor, Michigan, and Milwaukee, Wisconsin, are seeing a revival in manufacturing.

As a general rule, the more meteoric the rise of a city tied to a bubble economy, the harder its fall is likely to be when the bubble finally bursts. Think of gold rush–era communities, which thrived while the gold flowed but turned to ghost towns once the panning sieves and sifters

> **Fast Fact** More than 50 percent of the foreclosures since the housing bubble burst have occurred in five states—California, Nevada, Arizona, Florida, and Michigan—according to Hanley Wood Market Intelligence.

starting to come up empty. Of course, San Francisco was a product of the gold rush, so there are examples of cities that are able to adapt.

How can you predict the fortunes of a city? In the recent housing market, most of Florida was hit hard, as were huge swaths of the Southwest, namely Las Vegas and Phoenix. There will always be highs and lows in both the housing market and in the economy. If you are looking at a city that has suffered greatly in the bad economy, be careful when making a purchase even though there might be great "deals" on the market. Refer to the sections on foreclosures in Chapter 3.

If you are looking in a place that has a booming economy, don't make the assumption that it will always be great. Remember the simple law of gravity: What goes up must come down. Be careful not to overpay. Look at historic values and assume that housing prices should go up a little (3 percent annually is the rule of thumb), but if there is a spike, be *very* careful. Refer to the Rent Ratio section in Chapter 2, since you might be better off renting if things are too hot. You don't want to get caught upside down in a mortgage.

Commerce Connections A new trend in business today is in-sourcing, whereby companies in larger cities create back offices, or even sub out work to offices in smaller cities to reduce overhead without reducing services. Examples include law firms from San Francisco opening "back offices" in Pittsburgh, where the cost of living is lower. The same trend is seen in Omaha, Nebraska, which dominates the insurance industry. Employees trade partner-track jobs with high salaries for the luxury of controlling their own hours and having more time to enjoy family life and recreational activities. The result is an affordable place to live while being connected in commerce to the rest of the nation.

As you look for a new city, consider some of these midsize or boutique cities, such as Des Moines, Iowa; Milwaukee, Wisconsin; or Minneapolis, Minnesota, that link through commerce to larger metro areas in other parts of the country. Although you will earn less than in a major city, in return, the cost of living will be lower and you will have more time to enjoy your family life and recreational activities. Working with a career counselor or recruiter with experience in global relocations can help you find these types of jobs.

Megaregions A megaregion is a cluster of cities with a total population ranging from 7 to 60 million connected by shared resources and economic linkages. Connections might include intercity railways to facilitate the movement of goods and people as well as regional master planning and land initiatives that support strong patterns of growth.

The United States has about a dozen megaregions, starting with the biggest, Bos-Wash, which extends from Boston to Washington through New York. It's home to more than 50 million Americans and is second worldwide only to the Greater Tokyo megaregion. Other U.S. megaregions include Charlotte-to-Atlanta, Dallas-to-Austin, Chicago-to-Austin, and Southern California.

Understanding the rise and value of the megaregion is important because it expands our sense of the city as a singular entity. "Currently we are tied to a nineteenth-century approach, which isolates the big city unto itself, without taking advantage of the connections and opportunities it could enjoy simply by planning and linking to smaller nearby cities," explains Dr. Catherine Ross, director of Georgia Institute of Technology's Center for Quality Growth and Regional Development.

To truly work well, megaregions need to be supported by high-speed rail. It could turn Philadelphia into a true sibling of New York, likewise Dallas and Houston, Portland and Seattle, and many other potential pairings. But the United States is woefully behind in its high-speed rail investments compared with other nations, such as China, Japan, France, and Spain. That needs to change before megaregions can reach full fruition and power the economy for the next century.

If you are looking at a city that falls in a megaregion, consider the benefits of being linked to a larger whole. You may find better transit infrastructures and easier access to civic resources in your city and beyond, as well as a stronger economy supported by connected commerce between cities. Proceed slowly though, since you might also find some drawbacks in megaregions that lack viable mass transit systems. Linking only via highways and roads creates substantial congestion that makes the process of connecting between cities difficult and often miserable.

CHAPTER CHEAT SHEET

Gut Check

What is the right city for you? Where is your greatest opportunity? Where would you feel most at home?

Reality Check

What are your realities? What external factors are at play in your decision?

Your Balancing Act

How do the cities on your list balance your wants, needs, and realities? *Function*—Does a particular city work with your job? Does it work with your spouse's job? Do the schools and activities work for your kids? *Cost*—How does the cost of living in your current city compare with the cities you are considering? What are the associated trade-offs in terms of employment, housing, and lifestyle? *Delight*—Where would you have the most social opportunities? What activities are important to you?

Key points to remember

- Cities and towns come in all shapes and sizes, and every city has its own unique personality that is informed by many elements, such as its larger regional context, natural features, climate, size, population, local history, industry, economy, transportation infrastructure, built environment, civic institutions, and even sports teams.

- Metro areas are made up of both neighborhoods and smaller municipalities, each with its own identity and characteristics. You might find that your right city is actually a city within a city.

- How you get from Point A to Point B in a city is crucial. What are the transportation options? Are there viable alternatives to individual cars, such as walking, biking, or mass transit?

Chapter 8

Selecting Your Neighborhood

You've heard the expression "The whole is greater than the sum of its parts." When it comes to cities, the parts in the equation are the various neighborhoods that knit together to form a thriving metropolis—the sum. There will usually be distinct differences from one neighborhood to the next in terms of size, architecture, ethnicity, character, and more. But the identity of each neighborhood will retain its place in the larger context of its city.

Miami is a great example of this neighborhood variation. Depending on where you are in the busy metropolis, you'll experience a vastly different type of urbanism. There's the downtown neighborhood of Brickell, for example, with its gleaming residential towers, nexus of international banks, and high-end restaurants and shops. Due east is South Beach, which offers a similar opulence, though set against a backdrop of art deco architecture and teeming nightlife. Little Havana is the city's best-known ethnic enclave, with its concentration of Hispanics and virtually year-round festival atmosphere. Looking for a slower pace? Check out the streetcar suburb of Coral Gables in southwest Miami, a quiet, pedestrian-friendly community with well-to-do homes and main-street businesses. Farther out from the city center, Miami starts to break into suburbia, including Kendal, with its modest residences laid out primarily in suburban subdivisions, and Pinecrest, which offers a more intimate, villagelike experience for those able to afford the loftier real estate prices.

Proximity Priorities

Make a list of the places you go every day, once a week, once a month, and once a year. Think about how long it would ideally take you to get to each of these places. Using the list below, check your ideal travel time for each of the following activities:

	5 min. walk	5 min. drive	15 min. drive	30+ min. drive
After-School Activities				
Airport				
Bank				
Bar				
Coffee Shop				
Day Care				
Doctor's Office				
Drugstore				
Dry Cleaner				
Grocery Store				

I could go on and on (indeed, a typical neighborhood map of Miami will include upward of fifty locales), but you get the point. Any city, whether large or small, is going to offer more than one type of living experience. The exact mix of neighborhood types will differ from one place to the next, with some cities serving up more options than others. But whether there are just a few neighborhoods to choose from or a few dozen, the trick is to figure out which one is right for you. That's what this chapter is all about. If Chapters 6 and 7 took the view from 30,000 feet, a vantage point that allowed us to see and dissect the distribution of land and populations within a region and

	5 min. walk	5 min. drive	15 min. drive	30+ min. drive
Health Club				
Hospital				
Library				
Museums				
Natural Amenities				
Parks				
Post Office				
Restaurants				
Schools				
Shopping				
Transit Stop				
Work				
Other				

cities, this chapter is like coming in for a landing, looking in detail at what each neighborhood and community has to offer.

Your Neighborhood Preferences

With tens of thousands of properties on the market (hundreds of thousands in larger metros) it would be next to impossible to sort through all of your options without targeting a few areas. To narrow the scope, you first need to determine the elements of a neighborhood that matter most to you. These will be your neighborhood preferences.

QUIZ: YOUR JUST RIGHT NEIGHBORHOOD

Assess Your Current Neighborhood

1. What are the characteristics you like most about your current neighborhood?

2. What would you change about your current neighborhood?

3. Is it easy to get to and from the places that serve your daily needs where you live now?

4. Do you like the look and feel of your neighborhood?

5. Why are you considering a move out of this neighborhood?

Imagine Your Ideal Neighborhood

1. What neighborhoods have you visited or lived in that you love the most?

2. What characteristics of those places stand out the most?

3. What are your proximity priorities in your ideal neighborhood? (See chart, page 150.)

4. What can you walk to from your home in your ideal neighborhood?

5. What are the amenities in your ideal neighborhood?

6. What do the buildings look like in your ideal neighborhood?

7. In your ideal neighborhood, do you need to drive your car on the weekends?

Potential Neighborhoods and Characteristics

1. Are there any neighborhoods in your city that meet your ideal neighborhood profile?

2. What are the three most important characteristics of your ideal neighborhood?

3. Are there any neighborhoods in your city that meet your three most important characteristics?

4. Are there homes available in your price range that meet your housing needs in any of the neighborhoods you have listed?

Assessing Neighborhoods

The assessment process for neighborhood characteristics is similar to what we looked for in cities, just on a tighter scale. Like with cities, some of the elements will be more important to you than others. Focus in on the ones that matter most to you, but keep them all in mind. *This content is of utmost importance to any housing search.*

The Experience of Getting Around—Walkability, Traffic, and Transportation In Chapter 7, we looked at the menu of transportation options you might find in a city. Let's now consider the details of how you will get to and from the places you need to go every day. Not every neighborhood can offer the full gamut of transit options, but be cautious of having too many scenarios where the only way to get from Point A to Point B is to hop into a vehicle. Visit at rush hour to see if it is easy or hard to turn *in and out* of the neighborhood. See if the traffic is flowing or is clogged up. Look out for difficult left

Check Back and Keep Balanced

Once you have your list of potential neighborhoods narrowed down and are seriously looking at homes, come back to this section and double-check to see how your preferred neighborhoods stack up. It is easy to let your focus stray to the amenities inside a potential new home and forget your neighborhood preferences. In the end, housing amenities might win out, but finding the right place to live requires keeping everything in mind when you balance your final decisions.

turns or high volumes of traffic that create congestion. See if it is easy or hard to travel around inside the neighborhood. How does it feel to go for a walk around the block?

Once you have your neighborhoods narrowed down, ask these questions:

• What is the proximity to your work? How much time will you spend commuting each day? How will this affect others in your household?

• Are there things you can walk to in and around the neighborhood, or are you completely dependent on your car?

• Are there local transit options that would allow you to maximize the time you spend commuting?

Mix of Uses or Single Use Proximity, proximity, proximity! You might be seeing the catchphrase *live, work, learn, play* attached to a lot of new developments these days. This is because it is becoming widely recognized that the shorter the distance between you and the places you go every day, the higher your quality of life will be. Consider a mixed-use development or neighborhood in proximity to a mix of uses such as retail, restaurants, offices, libraries, banks, and post offices. If you are looking at a residential-only neighborhood, note your proximity to other amenities close by. Proceed cautiously when looking at residential neighborhoods that are completely isolated from business, schools, or stores. Although you might be getting a great "deal" on the property, the trade-off in terms of quality of life can sometimes be enormous.

Walkscore.com can help you start to narrow down the neighborhoods in a city that have a mix of uses, but the best way to really get a handle on this is to talk to a real estate agent to understand the different options.

Local Economy and Stable Home Values From neighborhood to neighborhood within a city, you'll find a wide range of home values and economies. Look for ones that are as stable as possible. You can get information from a local real estate agent.

Avoid neighborhoods with a high percentage of foreclosures or homes that are underwater. Although the deals might be great, you don't know who your neighbors will be over time. Crime is often much higher when neighboring homes are abandoned, even if those homes are worth hundreds of thousands of dollars.

School District and After-School Activities The neighborhood and school you select will determine not only the type of education your children receive, but also the experience they have engaging with other children and participating in activities. GreatSchools.org is an essential resource that offers reports on all schools nationwide, public and private. Supplement your online research by asking as many people as you can, to get a sense of the best schools.

When looking for a neighborhood, look closely at how your kids will get to and from school. Consider the following:

• Is it important for you to have your kids walk or bike to school?

• Are you interested in driving them every day and available to do so? Is there a bus?

• What type of after-school programs do your children participate in?

• Are you able to drive them to activities after school, or will they need to stay at school until you leave work?

Health Benefits of Walking to School Are Proven

In 1969, approximately half of all students walked or rode bikes to school, according to the Department of Transportation. Today, that figure is down below 15 percent, with more than half of all students arriving by private automobile and another 25 percent taking the bus. According to the Centers for Disease Control (CDC), between 1980 and 2010, the number of overweight children in the United States tripled from 5 percent to 15 percent. They cite a direct correlation between the reduction in walking or biking to school and the rise in weight. To combat this problem, the CDC has started a nationwide program to support and encourage the creation of safe routes to school for children. Visit www.walkbiketoschool.org for more information.

As you develop your list of schools, research to see what housing options are available within walking or biking distance of these schools. This single variable might greatly shift your housing profile. Consider what trade-offs you might happily make for your kids to be able to walk or bike to school.

And if you do plan on having your kids walk to school, double-check at pickup and drop-off time how safe the streets are for walking and biking. Remember, quiet roads with and without sidewalks can get busy before and after school.

Safety In Chapter 7 we looked at the big picture of crime. You can check online and scan police reports to get a general idea of crime stats, but when it comes to narrowing a neighborhood search, talking to locals is best. Stats tell you how often crimes occur, but people will tell you what it's like living in the place. Think about whether you or your spouse would feel comfortable walking alone at night, if you'd always feel a need to lock and double-lock your doors, and if you'd be okay with having your kids out of your sight for extended periods.

Architectural Character Architectural character will vary greatly, depending on the neighborhood type and architectural styles. Some aesthetics will feel better to you than others. This occurs for two reasons. One, we each have a natural preference for certain aesthetics. And two, some places simply have better designs. In Chapters 9 and 11 we will look in more detail at why some streets and buildings look and feel better than others. In the meantime, think about the following:

- What types of buildings do you want to look at? Tall urban buildings, town houses, small homes, large homes?
- What do you want these buildings or homes to look like?

Amenities—Sports Fields, Pool, Parks, Trails Connecting to the outdoors makes us healthier and happier. The easier it is to get out and enjoy the outdoors, the more likely you are to actually do so. Parks and nature trails are ideal for light-impact exercise. You might look also for places to play basketball or tennis. Great parks can be found in even the densest urban areas; take Central Park for example. Consider these questions:

- Are outdoor activities important to you? If so what type of activities?
- How often do you want to participate in these activities?
- How close do you want them to be to your home? Walk, short drive, longer drive?

Proximity to Cultural Experiences and Civic Institutions Although you may not engage with cultural and civic institutions on a daily basis, having them close by can increase the quality of life and might even raise your property value. Cultural experiences might include libraries, theaters, museums, or galleries. Not only is it personally enriching to live near cultural attractions, but you will typically find that they raise the caliber of restaurants and shopping nearby as well. Research online through chamber of commerce websites to see if there are local festivals, open gallery nights, or other cultural events.

Consider the following:

- How important is it to live near civic and cultural institutions like libraries, museums, theaters, and galleries?
- Is it important to you to live in a place that has local festivals, parades, and events?

Grocery Store Guide

Before you move into a new neighborhood, take a stroll through a couple of the nearest grocery stores. This will tell you a lot about the community. Grocery store chains stock different items in different areas of town depending on who lives there. Think about your own food-buying preferences. If the local grocery store can satisfy them, there's a good chance the neighborhood as a whole will be a good fit for your needs and desires. Interesting items to note:

Size of packaging Large bulk-size items will tell you that there are a lot of families, while smaller packaging could indicate more singles live in this area.

Location of organic foods If organic products are important to you, look to see if they are interspersed throughout the store within their respective product categories rather than clustered on a single shelf in a corner of the store.

Specialty items What specialty items are available? Do you want an olive bar and wide selection of imported cheeses?

Produce How fresh is the produce? Are there a good variety of colorful fresh fruits and vegetables, or are they bruised and wilted?

Natural Features Beyond the ecological benefits of streams, ponds, marshes, hills, and the like, natural features contribute greatly to a neighborhood's character and sense of permanence. They also increase property values significantly, as do human-helped natural features, such as parks, greens, and squares. Pay special attention to the presence of old-growth trees, which are a sure sign of a neighborhood's commitment to nature and recognition of its value. Conversely, don't fall for the trick developers often use of giving a community a nature-evoking name, even when the community is anything but—Fox Meadows, for example, with neither foxes nor meadows in sight, or Saddle Ridge, where horses haven't roamed in decades. Consider these questions:

• What natural features and amenities matter most to you?

- Do you wish to engage with the outdoors—hike, canoe, run, and so on?
- Do you prefer views of the outdoors—lakes, rivers, water features, mountains, and others?

Sustainability This starts with natural features, but then goes further by addressing such issues as wetlands preservation, soil maintenance during development, and water conservation. These can be difficult for the average citizen to measure, but there are some telltale signs of a neighborhood's commitment to sustainability. One sign concerns the way yards are landscaped. If the community has guidelines for xeriscaping, the practice of using less-thirsty plant species to landscape a home, there's a good chance water conservation is going on at the municipal level. Another positive sign is the presence of community gardens, which indicate a grassroots commitment to land and soil management.

To find areas locally that support sustainable initiatives for the natural environment and xeriscaping for water conservation, Google these terms and the name of your city. You should be able to find articles about local developments and links to local professionals.

Character of the Place The character of a neighborhood is defined not only by the physical elements and available services noted above, but also by the personality of the people who live in a neighborhood. Here are three factors to consider:

Pace Are you looking for the hustle and bustle of a city center, the peaceful quiet of a rural route, or somewhere in between? Note the speed of the checkout line in the grocery store or the tellers at the bank. This will be a good indication of the neighborhood pace. Look for one that matches your temperament.

Amount of civic involvement Effective leadership is key. Is there a cohesive community that gets out to support local initiatives? Pride of place will bring people out, even when they are busy. You will find that property values are typically higher in places where people participate in their communities. That being said, your level of involvement will depend on both your desire to participate and the ease with which you can engage. If you want to get involved, look for places that are open to new members participating. It is awful to arrive ready to jump in, only to find that newbies aren't welcome.

> **The highest property values are found in neighborhoods with a diversity of housing and building types catering to multiple needs as well as a diversity of incomes.**

The neighbors Will there be a yearly block party or do people keep to themselves? Watch out for the Joneses, America's most famous neighbors. Keeping up with them can be hard. If you have kids, look for neighbors who have kids of similar age so playdates can be easily facilitated. The best way to scope out the people living in a potential neighborhood is to visit in the evenings and on weekends. If people are out and about, start conversations. If no one is out, this may be an indication that you will have little engagement with your neighbors once you arrive.

Diversity Diversity takes many forms, such as age, income, profession, life stage, culture, and language. The highest property values are found in neighborhoods with a diversity of housing and building types catering to multiple needs as well as a diversity of incomes, which allow residents to upsize and downsize without moving away. Neighborhoods that allow granny flats are a perfect example of diversity enriching a community. The rental units in these homes can give up-and-coming professionals or college students an affordable place to live in a great community while helping the homeowner offset their mortgage. These same granny flats can provide homes for an elderly parent, allowing them the freedom of living in a real house rather than a "home." Don't discount diversity out of hand. You might find that it raises your property value and enriches your life.

Fast Fact Many metropolitan areas are made up of several small cities and even counties that look and feel like neighborhoods. Depending on where you are within the "city," you might actually be in a different city or town. For example, Coral Gables in Miami is its own city, with mayor and city council, yet is completely surrounded by the city of Miami. It is difficult to tell where one stops and the other starts. A search of Miami real estate might eliminate viable options in Coral Gables unless you spend the time to make sure they are included. As you search, open your criteria to include the metro area. This can be difficult on some real estate sites, but with a little extra effort, it might lead to a great house in a great neighborhood.

How to Research a Neighborhood

Finding the right neighborhood for you requires research. If you are completely new to an area, ask questions. If you don't know anyone, calling a couple of real estate agents can give you a jump start. Have an idea of your neighborhood preferences when you call, and ask for areas that meet those needs. Here are the online resources and in-person tips to help you research potential neighborhoods.

RESEARCHING NEIGHBORHOODS ONLINE

Nothing beats pounding the pavement to learn about a neighborhood, but the following websites can provide a useful overview and help you narrow your search.

Google The best place to start is a search with the name of your city and the word *neighborhood*. Although there is no national database of neighborhoods, many major cities have their own sites highlighting their local neighborhoods. Additionally, Google Maps and Google Earth give you a bird's-eye view of potential neighborhoods, and Google Street View lets you explore many 'hoods, and even exact addresses, through 360-degree street-level imagery.

Wikipedia This online encyclopedia often provides excellent snap-shots of cities and neighborhoods that are typically written by consensus by people who live there. The entries usually have lots of links to additional sources of information, such as municipal websites. Start by searching for the name of your city with the word *neighborhoods.* Not all cities will have a neighborhoods page, but many do, and that is a great place to start. Wikipedia can help you assemble a list of neighborhoods as well as research ones you know about.

WalkScore.com The best online resource for assessing the walkabil-ity and potential commutes to and from different neighborhoods is WalkScore.com. You can search by city, zip code, or specific address to see whether a neighborhood is walkable or not, and check the dis-tance to amenities of any area. WalkScore.com can help you assemble a list of walkable neighborhoods in a city as well as research ones you know about.

City-Data.com A wealth of information about cities and neighbor-hoods nationwide. Includes links to schools, median housing prices and incomes, maps, and general data. You will need to have your neighborhoods list already started to get the most out of this site.

Neighborhood Scout An excellent clearinghouse of information on neighborhoods nationwide, covering schools, crime, real estate prices, and more. As with City-Data, it is best to have your neighbor-hoods list started already to get the most out of this site.

Trulia, Zillow, and RealtyTrac These three sites are great for getting a sense of the real estate prices in a given neighborhood, as well as the foreclosure activity. Triangulating the data from all three sites should get you an accurate picture. Some of these resources, like Trulia, have incorporated a street-view option so that you can take a street-level view of homes listed on their site.

Realtor.org The official website of the National Association of Realtors contains rich industry data as well as extensive advice for home buyers and sellers.

RESEARCHING NEIGHBORHOODS IN PERSON

Although using online resources can be a huge help, there is no substitute for pounding the pavement. Here are a few tips to assist in your search:

Assess the Commute: Before buying a home, drive your possible commute at rush hour to see if it is something you can handle. It is one thing to use an online calculator to tell you how long the drive will be; it is another to sit in traffic and experience it yourself.

Walk and Talk: Walk potential neighborhoods to get a feeling for the character of the place. Visit during the evenings and weekends to see who is out. Bring your dog, if you have one. They can be a great conversation starter and a gauge of whether the neighborhood is pet friendly.

Check the Reputation: Like cities, neighborhoods have personalities—not just the personalities of the people who live there, but also the character of the place and feeling you get from being there. Although two neighborhoods might look similar from the outside, upon further study you will start to see differences emerge. Sometimes reputations are well earned, such as a local school that dominates in sports, or great shopping. Other times reputations are more general and reflect the character of a place—perhaps it is bohemian, or conservative. You might learn that some areas are known for families, whereas others are known for turnover. Take all recommendations with a grain of salt. After all, your information is only as good as the source, and sometimes your source might be prejudiced. Nonetheless, gauging the neighborhood reputation can give you a good grounding into whether it might be the right fit for you.

Be Thorough: Talk to as many people as possible; real estate agents, of course, but also friends, coworkers, family members, hotel staff, and even strangers.

Visit Late at Night: A place might feel great during the day, but when the sun sets, it could be a different story. Is it well lighted? Are lights on in the buildings? Do you feel safe?

Observe the Level of Cleanliness: The level of cleanliness can indicate the personalities of your potential neighbors. Look at how well manicured the lawns are or whether any personal belongings are visible from the street. Some people like everything to be in order, whereas others don't like the pressure of keeping everything tip-top all of the time. Look for the level of cleanliness that fits your personality, and you will find it easier to connect to your new community.

Understanding the Rules and Requirements of a Neighborhood

As you narrow down your search for different neighborhoods, you will want to gauge the rules and requirements that come with each one.

Codes, Covenants, and Restrictions (CC&Rs) Some neighborhoods have CC&Rs in place to regulate various aspects of the community. Some of these rules might relate to maintenance and upkeep, such as the requirement that everyone shovel snow or keep leaves raked in a timely fashion. Some CC&Rs regulate the colors you can paint your house or whether you can install a basketball hoop outside. Watch out for requirements for parking boats and RVs, if you have either of these, as well as guest parking or on-street parking.

An increasingly common type of CC&R sets age limits of fifty-five and older. Municipalities often favor these because they contribute to the tax base without adding children into the school systems. If you are considering moving into an age-restricted community, consider first whether you might have an adult child or even minor grandchildren who might need to live with you in the future. Although they are allowed to visit for extended stays, you could run into trouble if they are full-time residents.

Your real estate agent can give you a general idea of requirements, but if you are seriously considering a home in a community with a homeowners association, you will want to get a copy of their codes and requirements before purchasing. Some people love the idea because they keep everything regulated and standard, but others find certain regulations cumbersome. You will need to gauge the situation for yourself to find the right balance.

Homeowners Associations (HOAs) Homeowners associations determine and set the CC&Rs of a community. The level of activity will vary, depending on the neighborhood. Sometimes they are hard to engage with and influence. In other places, you will be elected president if you don't turn up at the meetings. Don't underestimate HOAs. They can fine you for not adhering to the rules and may even have the ability to foreclose on your home if you fall behind in dues.

Check Zoning and Local Codes If you are planning to build new, add on to a house, or build a backyard cottage, you will need to check local zoning and building codes to understand your parameters. If you are building a backyard cottage, look out for minimum square footages or restrictions on adding a second habitable structure to your property. In some places, codes are in the process of changing to allow these small cottages, called "accessory dwelling units." If they are not allowed, ask around to see if this might change in the future.

> **If you know the types of neighborhoods that will best meet your preferences, you will be able to narrow your list faster and find the one that is the best fit for you and your family.**

Types of Neighborhoods

As you begin to articulate your neighborhood preferences and start to compile your list of potential neighborhoods, it is helpful to have an understanding of the different types of neighborhoods you will most likely encounter. If you know the types of neighborhoods that will best meet your preferences, you will be able to narrow your list faster and find the one that is the best fit for you and your family.

Neighborhoods break down the volume and mass of the city to a human scale. This is true whether you live in a metropolis of 5 million or a township of 50,000. Time was, neighborhoods were divided into three neat categories: urban, suburban, and rural. Nowadays there's far more nuance as suburban development has blurred the boundaries between city and country. Following is a rundown of the most common types of neighborhoods found in cities across the United States. Not every city will have all of the types, but many have most of them. Following are common types of neighborhoods you might find in your city.

TYPE: Urban

Subtype: Urban Core

What is it? Think downtown New York, Chicago, Philadelphia, or any major metro area where a mix of tall and short buildings accommodate commercial and residential uses. Regionwide transportation systems will likely have a hub in or near the city center, and pedestrian traffic will be high, especially during the workweek.

Pros: Urban living at its best. A mix of uses allows you to walk to most if not all of the places you need to go every day. In some cases, you won't even need to own a car. Typically excellent mass transit. Proximity to city attractions, including nightlife, museums, and restaurants.

Cons: Can be more expensive than suburban alternatives. Crime in some areas of some cities can be higher. You will probably have to live with less space. Some parts of major cities are not set up well for residents, with limited numbers of grocery stores, schools, and services for those who remain after the business day ends.

How to Find: Follow the tall buildings! Some cities will have several urban areas to choose from. Advanced searches on real estate websites such as HotPads.com will be able to guide you to the urban core areas in a city by allowing you to specify high-rise buildings in your search criteria.

Subtype: Urban Periphery

What is it? These neighborhoods are still part of the urban spectrum and are typically adjacent to downtown, with low-rise buildings mainly serving residential use, though with sufficient commercial use mixed in. Examples include Georgetown in Washington, D.C., Lincoln Park in Chicago, and Boston's Beacon Hill.

Pros: Walkable, convenient, and trendy, featuring upscale condos, renovated town houses, farmers' markets, and high-end restaurants.

Cons: The style doesn't come cheap. Indeed, real estate prices will likely be the highest around, whether you're looking to rent or own.

How to Find: Not every city will have an urban periphery; some will go straight from downtown to streetcar suburbs. To determine if a city has these types of neighborhoods, ask a real estate agent if there are any neighborhoods with three- to five-story buildings, typically town houses and small apartment buildings just outside of downtown.

TYPE: Prewar Suburb

Subtype: Streetcar Suburb

What is it? As the name implies, these neighborhoods developed around a streetcar line that may or may not still be in use. Coral Gables in Miami and Myers Park in Charlotte are two examples. Others include Pittsburgh's Squirrel Hill, New York's Forest Hills, and Cleveland's Shaker Heights.

Pros: These enclaves are still part of a cohesive community plan, even in cases where the streetcars stopped running long ago. They tend to be pedestrian friendly, with ample, tree-lined sidewalks, since residents usually had to walk to the streetcar stop. They will often have corner stores and local shops, as well as churches and other civic institutions integrated into the community.

Cons: Like the neighborhoods in the urban periphery, these neighborhoods tend to be among the most expensive in a city.

How to Find: An online search of the name of your city with the words *streetcar suburb* should yield the location of these neighborhoods in any given city. Because of their beloved character, there are often extensive websites with images and details of these first-ring suburbs adjacent to most American cities.

Subtype: Bungalow Neighborhood

What is it? A type of neighborhood that spread throughout the country in the first few decades of the twentieth century, from Santa Barbara, California, to historic Boylan Heights in Raleigh, North Carolina. The Craftsman-style architecture, inspired by brothers Charles Sumner Greene and Henry Mather Greene, features small homes with low-pitched gable roofs, expansive porches, stone chimneys, and foundation walls. Often filled with Sears & Roebuck and other mail order homes from the early twentieth century.

Pros: Some of the closest neighborhoods to the city center. Compact with a strong feeling of identity. You know right away when you've entered and left a true bungalow neighborhood. Garages were to the back of the homes, either alley-fed or accessed by a side driveway. Streetscapes with sidewalks, on-street parking, and street trees make them ideal for pedestrians and bikes. Typically they connect to small retail areas.

Cons: The bathrooms, kitchens, and closets in the 1920s were very different from what we have come to enjoy today. If the home has not been renovated, you might need to budget for a fairly large renovation.

How to Find: Bungalow neighborhoods are typically adjacent to the streetcar suburbs. Your real estate agent can point you in the right direction. If you are searching online, a search of the word *bungalow* with the city name will usually give you the location of a few individual homes. You can use this information to learn more about the areas where they are located to see if they are in bungalow neighborhoods.

TYPE: Transitional

Subtype: Postwar Cottage Community

What is it? After World War II, the GI Bill provided loans for vets returning from war efforts. As a result, new neighborhoods quickly sprang up nationwide filled with modest little cottages. These homes created the iconic image of the house in the suburbs with the white picket fence.

Pros: Relatively close to the city center and near a mixture of daily uses, including shops and schools. Often considered "cute" houses. Garages were to the side of the house or in the back.

Cons: Homes tend to be small and might need significant updating.

How to Find: Like urban periphery neighborhoods, these are not found in all cities. Ask your real estate agent if your city has neighborhoods of postwar cottages.

Subtype: Ranch House Subdivision

What is it? Another product of the great suburban expansion that took place in the middle of the twentieth century, when millions of low-slung houses were mass-produced quickly.

Pros: Neighborhoods are typically close to downtown and urban amenities. Some of the homes have a certain nostalgic quality, leading to recent efforts by some preservationists to protect ranch houses under the National Register of Historic Places. They often include large basements, depending on their location in the country.

Cons: Rambling floor plans, low ceilings, and dark interiors can give ranch houses a cavelike quality. Lots are often oversized, resulting in large yards to maintain.

How to Find: Typically within a few miles of downtown and urban areas, these neighborhoods are often tucked in behind the earliest strip malls. An online real estate search within a twenty-mile range from downtown for the zip code should pull up local options for ranch homes.

> **Fast Fact** The country's 130 million dwellings are divided into three areas by government data. Roughly 38 million are in central cities, 65 million are in the suburbs, and 27 million are beyond the limits of a metropolitan area.

The History of the Gated Community

Gated communities have become a symbol of recent suburban development, but their origins predate the late twentieth century by a long shot. In fact, their roots reach all the way back to the Roman Empire, when soldiers who completed their military service were offered tracts of land in England. As you might imagine, the locals were none too happy about this, so the Romans built walls to protect their communities from angry mobs. Later, after the fall of the Roman Empire, communities in the Middle Ages commonly built walled fortresses surrounded by moats to keep out warring factions and protect their resources.

Fast-forward half a millennium or so, and it's estimated that more than 4 million homes in the United States are in gated communities. Although the gates aren't there to protect against roving marauders, they do provide a sense of security. (I say *sense* because let's face it, if someone wants to hop over the four-foot-wall, they can do so.)

Gated communities are also thought to be safer places for kids to play outside because traffic is limited. Although that may be true, I caution you to think hard about living in a gated community, since the cons are at least as significant as the pros. For example, these communities are typically completely detached and isolated from your daily needs (unless you are a golf or tennis pro). They also often have the strictest codes, covenants, and restrictions (see earlier references to these), and the architecture tends to be homogenous.

TYPE: Postwar Suburb

Subtype: Early Ring Suburbs

What is it? Postwar suburbs were conceived as master-planned communities based on mass-produced, cookie-cutter homes. Levittown, New York, developed in 1948, is the preeminent example, though it had many imitators, all built on the same single-use, low-density model. Split-level homes were common. Housing types are often fully separated from commercial buildings.

Pros: Homes in these neighborhoods are among the most affordable, and there's been some effort to introduce mixed-use back into these neighborhoods. Commutes to the city center are usually reasonable, taking advantage of transit.

Cons: Considered "starter housing" by most. Typically, these are the places you live until you can afford to live somewhere else.

How to Find: If these types of developments are in your city, your real estate agent will be able to direct you to them.

Subtype: Outer Ring Suburbs

What is it? These second-generation postwar suburbs proliferated from the 1980s to the mid-2000s. Cars are required for most if not all trips outside the home.

Pros: Meets the needs of those looking to get away from the faster pace of a city. Many are protected by homeowners associations, which enforce standards and bylaws designed to maintain quality.

Cons: Totally car dependent, often many miles from all places that meet daily needs and amenities. Real estate prices have been especially hard hit by the housing crash.

How to Find: Follow the big-box retail stores, and these developments will be close by. Another sign of outer ring suburbs are new developments by volume home builders, often signified with banners and flags along the street frontage.

TYPE: Rural

Subtype: Rural Neighborhoods

What is it? Small hamlets and enclaves of development surrounded mostly by agricultural land. Often close to the town center. Might include a few mansions (once belonging to the town doctor or local factory owner, for instance). Surroundings give way to farmland with farmhouses, barns, and other agricultural buildings.

Pros: Often picturesque settings. Can afford a quiet lifestyle without noise and traffic. Home prices are typically extremely affordable. Often near local shops and restaurants.

Cons: Often, struggling economic conditions result in dilapidated properties nearby. Many times rural locations near a metro area or city are being overrun by rural sprawl, as noted below.

How to Find: Rural neighborhoods are found on the outskirts of larger metro areas, as well as in small rural towns. Head out of town on a county road or search online under the term *rural* with the name of your city.

Subtype: Rural Sprawl

What is it? Developments of suburban homes and subdivisions in rural areas on former natural or agricultural land. Typically between and among large tracts of land, some with old farmhouses and historic barns, other plots with trailer homes.

Pros: Homes are often affordable and are close to nature.

Cons: "There is no there there." Inserting suburban models of development with cul-de-sacs and rows of homes in rural farmland slowly destroys the very quiet and the wide views that homeowners first sought.

How to Find: Rural sprawl is easily found by driving around rural areas outside a city.

CHAPTER CHEAT SHEET

Gut Check

What type of neighborhood feels right for you? What lifestyle are you drawn to? Where do you see yourself living?

Reality Check

Does the character of the neighborhood and do the elements within it meet your needs? How do your answers to these questions differ or vary from your spouse's or children's preferences?

Your Balancing Act

Function—Which neighborhood works best in allowing you to get to and from those places where you need to go every day? Are there multiple ways to get around the neighborhood such as walking, biking, and mass transit, as well as driving? *Cost*—Where can you afford to live? *Delight*—What is the one element in a neighborhood that would make you happiest? What elements matter most to you in the neighborhood when you are home before and after work and on weekends?

Key points to remember

• Different cities serve up a different mix of neighborhoods, each delivering a unique living experience ranging from urban and suburban to rural.

• Thriving neighborhoods have a distinct identity and sense of community.

• Walkability, traffic, and transportation are key. The process of getting to and from and in and around your neighborhood will define your daily experience.

Chapter 9

Streetscapes

Think back to the street you grew up on. I'll bet you can picture it perfectly, down to the pattern of cracks in the pavement (which, if you were prone to superstition, you avoided on the walk to school or the bus each day), the types of trees (or lack of trees), the way the leaves crunched distinctly underfoot each fall (or if you were like me, the way the snow crunched under my moon boots each winter), and the rows of homes on either side that housed your friends and neighbors. Whether you grew up on a cul-de-sac or a tree-lined boulevard, I bet you remember all the details.

Now think about the streets you have lived on in your adult life. Are they as clear in your mind? If you are like the average grown-up, the streetscape can easily slip to the periphery when deciding where to live, even though these details were once front and center as a child. This is because as adults we tend to experience streets primarily from behind the wheel of a car.

Through the buffering of your car, it is common to have some inkling whether a street is the right fit or not, even if you might not be able to put your finger on why. Yet all too often, as you cruise by, the design of the street is dismissed and all attention is turned to the potential house. As a result, many of us end up moving onto a street that's not quite right. This is a reminder that it is all too easy to question, and even disregard, our instincts when we don't understand what is informing them.

The goal of this chapter is to train you to read the design of a street, in an effort to help you avoid making these oversights. As I explain how to understand streets, your initial instincts will come rushing back, so you can start to identify the issues that matter most to you. There's an old truism of real estate that it's better to buy the worst house on the best block than the best house on the worst block. That tells me that there's a pretty good awareness of the importance of living on the right street. But as our homes and communities have shifted shape in recent decades, we've lost sight of the importance of a home's context. In the following pages, I'll reconnect those dots, laying out the different types of streets that are out there and then giving you the tools you need to pick out the winners and losers in any given neighborhood.

Your Ideal Street

Streets are easily overlooked when searching for a new home. Most people will skip from a search at the level of the neighborhood to go straight to the individual home. Yet, if you think about it, streets are the glue that holds everything together. Neither neighborhoods nor homes would function without streets. And as such, taking a moment to understand the street type and characteristics that best fit your life can streamline the process of determining the right neighborhood and home as well.

WORDS OF WISDOM

"Our neighborhood does not have sidewalks; as a result the families that live across the street from the school drive their kids to and from school every day because the drivers can be a bit crazy." Beth C., Norfolk, MA

"I choose to live in the city because when I'm not at work, I want to maximize my time with my family. I do not want to waste extra hours in the car, struggling through a commute to a larger house that I don't need and can't enjoy." Elizabeth and Eric S., Alexandria, VA

The content of this chapter may introduce a new way of looking at the streets you drive daily. After you complete this chapter, return and reevaluate these assessment questions. You might find that you want to revise some of your preferences.

QUIZ: YOUR JUST RIGHT STREET

Assess Your Current Street

1. Picture your current street.
2. Are there elements like street trees and on-street parking that slow down traffic?
3. Do you feel safe walking on your current street? Are there sidewalks?
4. What do you like most about your current street?
5. What do you like least about your current street?

Imagine Your Ideal Street

1. What streets have you lived on or visited that felt the best to you?
2. What does your ideal street look like?
3. What do the homes on your ideal street look like?
4. Where are the garages on your ideal street?
5. Are there children playing outside?

The Important Elements

1. Are there neighborhoods in your city that have streets that match the description of your ideal street?
2. If so, are there homes in these neighborhoods that match your price range and housing needs?
3. If your ideal street type isn't in your city, or the homes on it don't fit your needs, what elements can you find in the available streets with homes that do fit your needs?

Understanding Streets

CHARACTERISTICS OF GREAT STREETSCAPES

Streets create the framework for everything in the built environment. They're both the nervous system of a city, providing a means of travel between different places, and a skeletal system, providing the setting for the buildings. Contrary to what many believe, streets are not the exclusive domain of the automobile. They existed and thrived long before automobiles were even conceived, serving pedestrians, shops, cyclists, and buildings alike.

Great streets are destinations. Time and time again people will drive for miles to spend an afternoon walking down a great street. The character of the street defines how it feels and what you experience while you are on the street. Here are the four characteristics that make the experience of walking down some streets enjoyable.

A Feeling of Containment and Definition When you are on the street, are you in a place or traveling through a space? Feeling like you are somewhere is the first element of a successful streetscape. Do the buildings help to define an outdoor room, or are they set back behind parking lots? Even residential streets with single-family homes are most successful when they have a feeling of containment.

Eyes on the Street—Signs of Life In a phrase coined in 1961 by Jane Jacobs in her book *The Death and Life of Great American Cities,* "eyes on the street" refers to the natural protection that results when a neighborhood's residents are in constant visual contact with the street. This contact can happen passively through doors and windows that face the street, like a family periodically looking out their kitchen window to the sidewalk. Or it can be more direct, such as through a front porch where residents sit in the evenings, or the sidewalks that they walk along each day. Either way, the possibility for constant vigilance creates a sense of comfort and security that makes being outside feel safe. Even if no one is literally watching out the windows, knowing that they might be makes a street more desirable.

A Sequence of Places and Experiences As you travel through a great neighborhood, you will experience a sequence of places: a tree-lined avenue, a quiet street, a small pocket park. Some might be expected, like a central neighborhood square. Some will be a surprise, such as a view of a special building or a lake.

A Reason to Be There Other than being a conduit for travel by car, is there a reason to be on this street? Consider if there is something that you want to walk to and if you could make the walk if desired. Is it safe to take an evening stroll, take a child to a park, or go for an early-morning walk with a dog? Could your children play outside unattended? Are there sidewalks? If it is a main street, are there shops that you would actually shop in? The best streets have a reason to be. Ask yourself, does yours?

Short Drive, Long Wait

Americans now drive upward of 3 trillion miles every year. Much of that driving is for short trips, say to the supermarket or to drop the kids off at school. In fact, half of all trips are three miles or less, and 28 percent are one mile or less. The result is intense congestion in many cities and towns that could be eased if there were more options for walking, bicycling, and public transportation. In Boulder, Colorado, for example, two decades' worth of investment in sidewalks, bike paths, and pedestrian crossings has resulted in a 14 percent decline in the number of people who drive to work.

SEVEN STEPS TO FINDING YOUR RIGHT STREET

You might be saying to yourself, "This is all very interesting, but how can I apply this as I determine where to live?" Here are the seven questions that will help you identify the character of a street. As you narrow your search and begin to seriously look at homes in different neighborhoods, take a moment and ask yourself these questions.

How Fast Is Traffic? Nothing ruins a feeling for neighborhood faster than speeding traffic. Parents will keep the kids indoors, or at least sequestered in the backyard, and few people will walk for fun. And rightfully so, since excessive speed is a major safety hazard. Studies have shown that a pedestrian who is struck by a car traveling twenty miles an hour has a 95 percent chance of surviving, but if the car is going forty miles per hour, the survival rate drops to just 10 percent. That is a huge and terrifying decline.

The speed that traffic flows on a street is directly related to the width of the street and lines of sight available to the drivers. If streets are wider and houses are set far back from the street, a residential street performs more like a freeway. Even frequent monitoring and tickets from police won't slow drivers down.

Take note as you drive down a potential street to watch for the posted speed limits, and then see how fast you are driving. On many streets, even if you don't have a lead foot, you might struggle to keep under the limits. Here are some questions to consider:

• Would you feel safe having your kids play outside here?

• Would you feel safe having your teenage kids drive on this street?

• Would you feel safe walking here?

Garage-fronted street Pop quiz: Which street would you rather have your kids play on? Which feels safer? Streets faced with garage doors that do not have street trees and sidewalks encourage cars to drive faster.

Sidewalks: Is This Street Walkable? A safe sidewalk is one that allows a pedestrian to be protected from traffic. Typically this is done by setting the sidewalk back five or more feet from the street with a planting strip for street trees, and by allowing on-street parking. These two moves essentially insulate pedestrians from traffic. You might find as you drive through a neighborhood that some streets have sidewalks, whereas others don't. Having sidewalks on both sides of the street is ideal, but one is better than none!

While you look, ask yourself these questions:

- Would you feel comfortable having your kids walk to school on these streets?

- Would you let your teenagers ride their bikes to a friend's house on these streets?

- Would you enjoy a walk with a friend or a walk with your dog on these streets?

Sidewalks and tree-lined street Street trees not only slow down traffic by providing a barrier between pedestrians and vehicles, they also add value to the homes on the street.

Does the Street Form an Outdoor Room? Buildings and street trees act like walls of an outdoor room by providing a comfortable sense of enclosure. If houses and other street buildings are set too far back, the space will lose its feeling of intimacy. In compact city centers, apartment buildings and shops often sit right next to the sidewalk. In close-in neighborhoods, town houses and smaller apartment buildings might be set back ten or fifteen feet to create little areaways. In a typical suburb, freestanding houses can sit anywhere from ten to twenty-five feet from the sidewalk.

Commercial streets where the buildings are set back behind parking lots lack enclosure and limit walkability. Residential streets where houses are more than twenty-five feet from the sidewalk have a hard time keeping a feeling of containment. Historically, larger homes did have fairly large setbacks. But in these cases, trees with large cathedral-like canopies or gardens created a sense of enclosure.

Key Recommendation: When buildings are pushed back from the street to facilitate only the ease of the car, it is done at the expense of the person who owns that car—you. When touring a potential street, ask yourself these questions:

• Does this feel like an outdoor room?

• Are you comfortable standing here?

Garage Locations: Who Lives in the Home, People or Cars? It used to be that if a home had a garage at all, it took the form of a separate building tucked behind the main property. Postwar suburbanization and the rise of the automobile brought the garage front and center, starting with the split-level and ranch homes, where the garage for the first time was a dominant feature of the façade. Subsequent house styles, including the McMansion, were even more deferential to the garage. As a result, when you drive down the street in many U.S. neighborhoods, all you see is a line of garage doors on what are disaffectionately called "snout houses" (see page 185 for more details). Garage doors as a façade limit the number of eyes on a street and encourage speeding.

WARNING

BEWARE OF "GRATUITOUS SIDEWALKS"

To be usable, a sidewalk needs two characteristics: It must feel safe to walk on, and it must lead somewhere you actually want to go. If the journey feels dangerous or if you are walking just for the sake of walking, you'll be less likely to use a sidewalk.

Consider the garage location and ask yourself these questions:

• Are garage locations balanced with the house and street to support pedestrians and bikes?

• Can you see front entrances?

Are There Street Trees? Besides adding beauty to a neighborhood, trees create a barrier between the sidewalk and street that allows pedestrians to safely coexist with automobiles. Trees also enhance the feeling of containment that creates the outdoor-room effect, especially when their canopies knit together to form a charming allée. A sure sign of a thoughtfully planned community is when its mature trees have been planted the right distance apart so that their boughs just touch. Street trees also provide shade to help cool the neighborhood and reduce soil-eroding storm-water runoff (and basement or street flooding). Neighborhoods with a canopy of street trees will typically hold value better than neighborhoods without.

Street Trees Add Value to Your Home

A recent study by economists at the U.S. Forest Service in Portland, Oregon, determined that street trees can add close to $9,000 to the sale price of your home and reduced the time on market by 1.7 days. Additionally, you can benefit from your neighbors' trees. The study also found that homes without street trees but within 100 feet of homes with them had higher property values than homes in neighborhoods with no trees.

Are the Façades Simple? If the streetscape is interesting, every individual building doesn't need to be a work of art. In fact, cities and streets work best when the buildings are simple and work together to create a greater whole. Individual buildings combining to contribute to a larger context of place form the heart of every great street ever built.

As you look for a street, look for buildings that work together calmly to reinforce your experience of place.

Are There Audiovisual Elements to Consider? A great streetscape will have many layers, some of which we have talked about—buildings, trees, and sidewalks. Others are easy to overlook, especially during the day, but can make a big difference at night. Here is a list of sights and sounds to consider when looking for your right street:

- *Streetlights:* Streetlights have many pros and cons. Some people love them because they make the streets safer, but others dislike them because, depending on their location, they might light up your house at night.

- *Power Lines:* On a great street, power lines might go unnoticed because you have other things to look at, but on a bad street they might be front and center. Consider their placement if they are there. And if you live in a storm-prone part of the country, consider also that power lines above the ground might mean longer power outages after a big snow or strong winds.

- *General Noise:* Although you might be on the edge of your neighborhood on a quiet street, you could also find that you back up to a noisy street.

Take time to note if a potential street has lights and where they are to determine if they hit the right balance for you. Also, pay close attention to the noise level of both the street you are looking at and the adjoining areas. Just because you can't see a busy thoroughfare doesn't mean the light and noises can't reach you.

RED FLAGS

By keeping the elements of a streetscape in mind, you should be able to drive down any street and know pretty quickly whether it's a winner or a loser. But just in case, here are two red flags to watch out for. I'm not saying that you shouldn't live on a street with one or more of these problems under any circumstances. But there should be significant upsides to the home (a great bargain, proximity to your workplace, opportunity to create a granny flat, and so on) to balance out the potential negatives.

Snout House This type of architecture has become all too common on the streets of America. It includes any type of house with a front-facing garage that's so dominant that it takes over the entire façade (like a pig's snout, hence the name). Snout houses have actually been prohibited in some cities, including Portland, Oregon, because they make the streets look like the houses are for cars instead of people. A handful of street-facing garages on a block needn't be a deal breaker for you, but if every house is a snout house, I suggest you keep driving.

Wiggly-Worm Roads Gently curving streets are good for relaxing drivers' speeds and creating a sense of spatial definition within a neighborhood. Unfortunately, they've become so overused in many newer subdivisions that the entire street network consists of mindless bends and curves. If you've driven through one of these communities, you know how disorienting the experience can be. You might pull into the subdivision off the main thoroughfare heading north, but all of a sudden find yourself traveling east or west. There's absolutely zero concern for cardinal direction, a fact made worse if the homes in the community look similar. Sometimes not even a GPS device can get you to your destination. Living on a wiggly-worm road can be a real nightmare, especially if you are planning to have friends over to visit, since finding you can be a project.

Types of Streets

BUSY STREET, QUIET STREET, FAST STREET, SLOW STREET . . .

Think about your lifestyle, your work, your other time commitments, and what you like to do in your free time.

Before proceeding, it is important to note that the definitions below are the more technical meanings of typical street types. In recent years, the names of the different street types have been bandied about quite freely, with a small two-lane residential street carrying the bold name of *boulevard* or *avenue,* or, oddly enough, main streets emerging on the outskirts of town with nary a storefront in sight. Don't necessarily take the label on your local street to illustrate the real meaning of the type. And don't take too literally the definitions below. The important point of this section is for you to start to see that there are different street types, each with their own common features, so that you can determine your best fit.

TYPE: Primary Street

Subtype: Boulevard

What is it? A large multilane thoroughfare with traffic moving in both directions, often separated by a planted median, with side lanes separated by another median for slower moving traffic on each outer edge. They are common to major cities, with the example par excellence being the Grand Boulevards of Paris, from Montmartre to Madeleine. Most U.S. cities have a boulevard in some form. Streetcar suburbs are often connected to downtown areas by a large boulevard where the median was used for the streetcar.

Common features: Boulevards take on many types in the United States. The best examples have retail space at the street level and offices or apartment-style residences above. You will also find larger condo/apartment buildings on boulevards.

Pros: Living on a boulevard can afford total walkability and twenty-four-hour activity, which is great if you like being in the heart of the action.

Cons: The downside is constant traffic and steep real estate prices. Some boulevards have been overrun by strip development and parking lots that make them unfriendly to pedestrians.

Subtype: Avenue

What is it? Slightly smaller in size and scale to boulevards, often with a planted median. In traditional cities and towns, avenues usually connect individual neighborhood centers, and they often terminate on a civic building or space, such as a town hall or a public square. That makes living on an avenue highly social, though you can find sections that aren't in the immediate hustle and bustle.

Common features: Avenues have a mix of attached and detached housing. It is common in more urban areas to find apartments and midrise buildings. Typically this density drops as the avenue moves away from neighborhood centers. Town houses and apartment houses are common on avenues. In older, traditional neighborhoods, the largest and grandest single-family homes lined the avenues.

Pros: You can be closer to the action. Avenues often have the largest and most mature tree canopies in a neighborhood and often the highest property values.

Cons: Avenues have more traffic than neighborhood streets, which can make them less safe for kids to play outside. The picturesque setting comes at a price, and real estate can often be expensive.

Subtype: Main Street

What is it? Main streets are the primary retail corridors that form the heart of a town or neighborhood center. Often a boulevard or avenue will turn into a main street at the center of town. It's no accident that Main Street is among the most popular street names in the United States (just as its British equivalent, High Street, is in the United Kingdom).

Common features: Main streets are identifiable by rows of shops lining the street. Depending on the location, these shops might be local mom-and-pop stores or national chains, or a mix of the two. Above the shops are offices and residential condos and apartments.

Pros: You will be in the heart of the action. Walk out of your building and you can walk to restaurants, shops, and entertainment.

Cons: Housing options can be limited. Apartments can be small. You will most likely give up private outdoor space and the option to grill.

Subtype: Collector Roads and Arterials

What are they? Modern versions of boulevards and avenues, these large, busy thoroughfares are designed to collect traffic from smaller pods of development and connect other pods, both near and far. In addition to heavy congestion, collector roads are defined by a number of wide travel lanes and the absence of on-street parking. The wide distances and multiple turn lanes make it very difficult for pedestrians to cross intersections.

Common features: Mostly filled with strip malls and big-box development, set back from the street behind parking lots. Residences are typically set back behind buffers and berms accessed by secondary streets.

Notes: Although typically you won't find a residence on the collector or arterial, you most likely will have to engage with these types of streets in the process of getting to and from your home. Take care to note the amount of time you will need to spend on these road types and the ease with which you can move through them.

TYPE: Secondary Streets

Subtype: Neighborhood Street

What is it? Any part of the network of streets that branches off from the primary thoroughfares. Traditionally, neighborhoods contained a variety of neighborhood streets designed to handle different volumes of traffic. Those nearest to primary streets will be wide enough to accommodate two full travel lanes, and will contain more businesses than housing. Narrower slow-flow streets are for local traffic only, typically through more residential areas.

Common features: Single-family houses of all sizes and descriptions, some with granny flats where codes permit, as well as apartment houses and town homes.

Notes: Most residential development is found on neighborhood streets. Not all streets are created equal. As discussed in the sections above, the character of these streets can vary greatly. These could be quaint and picturesque tree-lined streets. In other cases, you might find garage-fronted motorways. Take time to look at the details noted in the beginning of this chapter so you can find the character of street that best matches your needs.

Subtype: Cul-de-sac

What is it? French for "bottom of the bag," *cul-de-sac* refers to a dead-end street with a crescent-shaped end. The large circle allows cars to easily turn around at the end of the street.

Common features: These streets have become common in subdivision developments in recent decades, where they are typically seen as the safest streets in a subdivision. They're made up almost exclusively of single-family houses, and the centers of some nicer cul-de-sacs are filled in and landscaped with a large tree to reduce the large amount of paving and soften the look and feel.

Notes: Cul-de-sacs can be seen as the solution to traffic problems because you might think that stopping connecting traffic will eliminate lots of traffic. In fact, the reverse happens. Cul-de-sacs create speeding traffic. This is because for every street they cut off, the traffic is rerouted somewhere else, adding more of a burden to the streets that do connect. (See more in Appendix 2, page 345.)

TYPE: Tertiary Streets

Subtype: Yield-Flow Street

What is it? Like slow-flow neighborhood streets but smaller still, often with a single lane designed to handle traffic movement in both directions. These streets are common in older, more established neighborhoods, where they provide access to low-density areas far removed from the city center.

Common features: Single-family houses with potential for granny flats.

Pros: Plenty of peace and quiet, plus room for large houses and yards.

Cons: You're unlikely to be within walking distance of stores, libraries, or post offices.

Subtype: Alley or Lane

What is it? Small tertiary corridors that run down the center of city blocks, providing access to garages.

Common features: Once found mainly in older neighborhoods established a century ago or more, alleys and lanes are reemerging in smart-growth communities where they help accommodate parking, trash maintenance, and utilities.

Notes: Although we don't typically think of homes being located in alleys, they can provide the setting for a pocket neighborhood or access to alley-fed garage apartments.

Your Ideal Street, Revisited

Keeping in mind the different characteristics and types of streets, take a moment to reassess your street preferences from the beginning of this chapter. Ask yourself these questions.

QUIZ: YOUR JUST RIGHT STREET—PART 2

1. *What street type best fits your needs?* Boulevard, avenue, neighborhood street, lane, etc.

2. *What do the buildings look like on your ideal street?* Apartments over retail, apartments only, large homes, small homes, etc.

3. *How fast does the traffic flow on your ideal street?* Slow? Fast? Is there traffic at all?

4. *What would it feel like to walk on your ideal street?* Country lane with no traffic? Urban street with sidewalk cafés? Neighborhood street with sidewalk and street trees?

5. *Which neighborhoods in your city have streets that meet your preferences?* Are there homes in these neighborhoods that meet your budget and housing needs?

6. *If not, are there areas in your city that meet some of your preferences with homes that meet your needs?*

CHAPTER CHEAT SHEET

Gut Check

Will you be better off on an active street within walking distance of restaurants and shops or a quiet one with more living space and land?

Reality Check

Does the street feel safe? Would you let your kids play outside?

Balancing Act

Function—Did you get lost driving through the neighborhood, or did the streets follow a logical order? *Cost*—Can you afford the homes on the street you are considering? *Delight*—Is the street designed in such a way that it encourages interaction between neighbors?

Key points to remember

• Streets have two very important roles. They are conduits for travel and the framework for buildings and places throughout a city.

• In a well-planned community, large and small thoroughfares combine to form an efficient network with multiple ways in and out.

• A successful streetscape provides the feeling of an outdoor room, such that when you walk out of a home onto one, you get the sense that you're entering a self-contained place. Streets that are designed around the automobile, with wide, fast travel lanes and front-loaded garages, are the least pedestrian friendly.

Chapter 10

Residential Building Types

When you think about the concept of home, what image comes to mind? Most people come up with a few basic types: the free-standing house, an apartment, a town house. Those dwelling types are certainly common, but there are many other ways to live—and I'm not talking about the yurts and igloos you see thumbing through the pages of *National Geographic*. In most towns and cities across America, there are a dozen or more types of housing, including some you've probably never even heard of, let alone considered in your search for a new home.

This chapter lays out ten of the most common dwellings, providing a quick overview, the main pros and cons, and a few key considerations. Keep an open mind as you take in all the various options, remembering that the nation's housing stock is in the midst of a major transformation at the moment. As a result, long-held truths about these various dwelling types are starting to shift course, if not change direction completely. For example, more and more people are renting houses in the suburbs and owning apartments in the city, turning old assumptions about urban renters and suburban owners on their head. And so-called granny flats, once outlawed in communities across America, are now considered one of the hottest trends in real estate. Read on for other surprises, as well as advice about the tried-and-true dwelling types.

Types of Dwellings

TYPE: High-Rise or Midrise Building

What is it? Tall multistory buildings found in city centers and urban areas, these buildings contain owner-occupied condo and cooperative apartments, as well as rental units. A midrise building is usually five to ten stories high. A high-rise is usually more than ten stories. The range in value and lifestyle is enormous, from luxury penthouses to inner-city projects. Buildings often include ground-floor retail businesses.

Pros: The urban locations and higher densities allow a walkable connection to restaurants, shopping, and offices. High-rises and midrises are great for people who like the security of a larger structure. If you travel a lot, you can lock your door and go without worrying about

---

Dwelling Types

There are roughly 130 million residential dwellings in the country, according to the latest American Housing Survey conducted by the U.S. Department of Housing and Urban Development. Here's how they break down by dwelling type.

82,472,000 detached units (freestanding single-family houses)

21,657,000 five-or-more units (high-rise condo, co-op, and rental apartments)

10,160,000 two- to four-unit dwellings (small apartment buildings)

8,769,000 manufactured units (modular and mobile homes)

7,053,000 attached (town houses and row houses)

your home. Some have a doorman or security on-site, and others are controlled with buzzers and intercoms. Higher-end buildings some-times offer additional amenities like swimming pools and rooftop terraces, and even coffee shops or a valet.

Cons: Noise can be an issue, depending on the thickness of the walls. If the building was constructed for rentals, you might find that you can hear every word your neighbor says, every TV show that they watch, and every noise they make in the . . . Well, you get the point. Don't leave it to the real estate professional or leasing agent to have the full story. Ask residents.

In addition to noise, larger buildings will also have more restrictions on what you can and can't do. For example, outdoor grilling is rarely allowed, even if you have a terrace. If you have a pet, check first to see if they are allowed or if there are size restrictions for animals.

Key Recommendation: Look at how the building meets the street. Well-designed buildings will define the street and make you feel safe while walking by. Always double-check with neighbors to see how much sound transmits between units, especially if you are planning to purchase.

TYPE: Town House

What is it? Single-family home attached on both sides to other homes. Built in long blocks, also called row houses, town houses are typically two to three stories tall. The first floor, or parlor floor, is often raised above the street enough to allow a basement level below to get some natural light. They are famous for large formal stoops, tall triple-hung windows, and bay windows. Town houses are typically in neighborhoods in the urban periphery and also off main streets or lining boulevards and avenues.

Pros: A town house is a great option for someone who wants to live in an urban area but does not want to live in an apartment building. You will most likely be able to walk to stores or restaurants, and there's the potential for having your own backyard. Town houses also provide a feeling of security for those who don't want the exposure of a single house. In older cities, town houses have some of the highest-valued residences. In new communities, they might be some of the most affordable.

Cons: As with apartments or condos, you will be sharing walls with neighbors. Even in older town houses with masonry walls between residences, sounds can travel. You might consider sacrificing a few inches of living space to build an extra layer of insulated wall on top of the existing walls. Another drawback is having windows on only two walls. This means that unless the design works to maximize light or you are on an end unit, it can get dark in the center of the house.

Key Recommendation: Look for buildings with simple forms that support the feeling of an outdoor room. Keep safety in mind, and think about how the building will feel when you're coming and going at night. Avoid places with hidden entrances. Watch out for town houses that step in and out toward the street between every unit. This is a common trick to add faux interest to a block of town houses or other group of buildings, but the arrhythmic arrangement takes away from the streetscape—and can be a safety hazard at night if the steps are too deep by creating shadows and hidden corners. Also steer clear of town houses that are floating in a sea of parking, also known as the town house without a town. See next page.

TYPE: Live-Work Building

What is it? An old type with a new twist, a live-work unit is the modern take on living above the store. It looks similar in size and form to a town house, with a shop on the ground floor and apartment on the upper floors. The shop can be attached to the apartment or be separate, allowing for two tenants. Live-works are a common building type in New Urbanist communities. They are found in and around main streets and throughout neighborhoods on the urban periphery.

Pros: Live-work units are great for small-business owners who can combine the mortgage of their home with that of their business.

A TOWN HOUSE WITHOUT THE TOWN, ESTATE MANSION WITHOUT THE ESTATE

The right building in the wrong place is the wrong building. A cottage in the middle of a bustling city wouldn't feel right, nor would a skyscraper in the middle of farmland. Although these examples are extreme, it's quite common to see a town house devoid of any actual town. Town houses are ideal in high-density communities, given their efficient footprints, and they're particularly suited to establishing borders of a park, town square, or other public space. But all too often, they're marooned in a random subdivision without a single amenity, let alone a full-service downtown. The result is a bedroom community where literally the only thing you want to do is sleep.

Another violation that has cropped up in recent decades is the estate mansion without the estate, which might also be described as a country house without the country. These homes are extreme versions of the McMansion, houses with 8,000 square feet of living space or more that have many accoutrements of luxury—the home theater, the infinity pool, the his-and-hers walk-in closets—but not the required grandeur of the surrounding estate. That disconnect makes the interior grandiosity seem way over the top and the exterior meagerness seem all the more deficient, as if whoever built the home blew all the budget on the home and forgot about the landscape, or forgot that the neighboring home is only ten feet away.

Take caution when you encounter either of these conditions, as they rarely deliver on the intended dream.

They also provide a great opportunity for someone wanting to live in an apartment in an urban area to rent out the shop space to offset the mortgage of the residence. Live-works can bring new businesses into a struggling main-street area, encouraging growth and economic development.

Cons: Combining residential and commercial uses into a single mortgage does not fit most lenders' formulas. Unless you have an open-minded or creative banker, it can be difficult to find financing.

If you can't get financing for a live-work unit because of the mix of commercial and residential space, consider building a temporary rental apartment on the first floor, which you can convert to retail space or offices later, if financing allows.

> ❝ If your find a building that you want to live in, ask around to the neighbors to get a sense of who lives there and when they might be moving out. ❞

TYPE: Loft

What is it? An urban building type known for its open and adaptable floor plan. The bathroom is often the only defined room. As manufacturing shifted to suburban locations and abroad, urban industrial buildings were left empty. Abandoned buildings were carved up into large lofts and sold or rented to artists and urban pioneers. Over time, these areas have gentrified, and now they have some of the highest property values anywhere. As such, the name has been slightly co-opted and is used fairly freely today in an attempt to add interest to a regular apartment.

Pros: True lofts have a lot of character. They are flexible and can accommodate many types of living, from the prototypical single urban dweller to young families. You can keep them rough with exposed brick and plumbing lines, or you can renovate and finish the space, even putting up temporary walls to create a bedroom or nursery. In some spaces, you might even discover large windows hidden behind walls or old hardwood floors from the factory days. Lofts are often in thriving walkable areas with restaurants and galleries.

Cons: Often fierce competition. Whereas these residences were once in unsafe and undesired areas, they're now in some of the trendiest and most expensive parts of town. That plus the fact that they're often quite large means they can be quite expensive to buy, heat, cool, and maintain. And if you prefer more formal living with separate spaces, a loft is not for you.

TYPE: Apartment House

What is it? Apartment houses are smaller apartment buildings that might include anywhere from four to eight units. At a glance, some of the smaller apartment houses look like large single-family homes. Commonly found on the boulevards and avenues of the early street-car suburbs, they're making a comeback in New Urban and infill projects, the term for new developments that fill in empty lots in older, often blighted neighborhoods.

Pros: Apartment houses provide the opportunity for people of varied incomes or family sizes to live in the same neighborhood. The frame-work of a traditional community allows this type to work seamlessly with single-family houses. You can usually walk to at least a corner store, pharmacy, or coffee shop.

Cons: Many of the apartment houses in older neighborhoods haven't been renovated. You might find that you are living without central air, a dishwasher, or other modern amenities.

Key Recommendation: Often the most desirable apartment houses in traditional walkable neighborhoods never make it to posted housing listings because they are transferred via word of mouth before a listing is necessary. If you find a building that you want to live in, ask around to the neighbors to get a sense of who lives there and when they might be moving out. A little legwork and a few lucky conversations can get you on the inside track.

TYPE: Apartment Complex

What is it? A large complex of apartment buildings typically arranged around parking lots and communal greens. Identifiable in many cases by wooden balconies and exterior staircases. Usually rentals.

Pros: It's often easy to find apartments in these types of properties. Most cities have a guidebook to apartments in local grocery stores or in listings online. Units typically include a washer and dryer. These apartments work well for roommates, as many of the buildings are designed with a bathroom attached to each bedroom. The developments may offer a pool, tennis court, or other amenities. Rents are usually affordable.

Cons: Often set in isolated auto-dependent locations far from all other uses. The buildings rarely form an outdoor room, making walking even within the complex difficult and unpleasant. Because they are usually built for rentals, thin walls between units may mean that noise is an issue.

TYPE: Duplex

What is it? A building that contains two residences, attached by a shared party wall. A duplex is a bridge between a single-family house and a town house and can be found in any number of architectural styles.

Pros: Affordable. Often in areas that are close to a downtown or neighborhood center.

Cons: Because of their affordable nature, duplexes can be a little run-down and seen as transitional housing.

Key Recommendation: Walk the area and get a feel for the neighbors, especially the ones with whom you'll be sharing a wall in the unit.

> **Fast Fact** Roughly one third of homeowners and one fifth of renters are doubling up to help make ends meet, according to a 2011 survey by Hanley Wood. That could mean an adult child moving back in with Mom and Dad (aka a "boomerang kid"), aging parents living with their grown children, or two or more friends sharing the same roof.

TYPE: Single-Family Home

What is it? This is the most common type of housing in the United States. Set on their own lots, typically in a suburban or rural setting, single-family homes range in size from a few-hundred-square-foot cottage to a 20,000-square-foot mansion. They are available in any number of architectural styles and materials.

Pros: For many, the single-family house is the housing type of choice. It provides privacy and a yard for gardening or for kids to play in. Depending on the location, you can get a lot more space for your money. They are often in large residential areas, which allows for a quieter setting. Single-family homes offer the potential for windows on all four walls, which makes a huge difference in bringing natural light into the home.

Cons: Taking care of a single-family home requires more time, money, and effort. You will have to keep up with maintenance of the yard and house. They are less secure than attached living, so single people and the elderly can sometimes feel uneasy. In many cases, single-family homes are in isolated, car-dependent areas.

TYPE: Accessory Dwelling Unit (ADU)—Granny Flat

What is it? A secondary residence in the backyard of a larger single-family home. An ADU, also known as a mother-in-law cottage or granny flat, can be a freestanding cottage or a finished apartment above a garage.

Pros: Ideal for elderly parents or a grown child, ADUs are an excellent option for addressing the needs of a multigenerational household. Loved ones can live close by without sharing the same roof. Or if you rent out the space, you can have added income to offset the mortgage. ADUs add to the character of a community by providing housing for students and young professionals—people who can be assets to a community but don't have large incomes.

Cons: In many cities and towns, building codes do not allow ADUs. They might be grandfathered into older communities but prohibited in newer ones. The good news is that nationwide, a major shift is taking place, and cities are awakening to the idea that these units provide real value to the community.

Policy Point: Legalize Mother-in-Law Apartments

Accessory dwelling units (ADUs) or granny flats are huge assets to a community. Once upon a time, they were standard fixtures in most neighborhoods, providing housing options for widowed or elderly parents, college students, or young professionals. Fear of overcrowding and concern that people would start building low-income rental units on their properties prompted some city officials in communities nationwide to prohibit ancillary dwellings of any kind in their zoning ordinances.

The rise in multigenerational housing has sparked interest in creating secondary living spaces either within the home or on the property. ADUs benefit communities in the form of expanded tax revenue and efficient land use. Many cities and municipalities are starting to make them legal again.

Check the neighborhoods in your city to see if and where ADUs are allowed. If your community bans in-law units, you might join forces with smart-growth advocates and green builders in your area to try to get the zoning laws revised. There are plenty of success stories out there, including the Santa Cruz Accessory Dwelling Unit Development Program, a California grassroots effort that managed a complete overhaul of the permit and approval process.

CHAPTER CHEAT SHEET

Gut Check

Does the type of dwelling you see yourself in match up with your ideal neighborhood, or do you need to consider other options?

Reality Check

Does your dream of living in a city apartment or suburban single-family house meet your needs and the needs of your family?

Balancing Act

Function—Which building type best fits the housing needs of your family? *Cost*—How do the available options balance with your financial realities? *Delight*—Which building type would make you happiest?

Key points to remember

- Freestanding single-family homes are just one of your many building-type options. Consider also apartments, town homes, live-works, and lofts, to name a few.

- In urban areas, how a building, whether residential or commercial, meets the street defines how it feels to walk in and around this neighborhood. If it defines the street with shops or other active uses, you will feel safe walking by. If the building is set back from the street or steps in and out, creating dark places where someone can hide, you will not feel safe walking by at night.

- Outdoor living and natural light are important in all building types. How they are achieved will be different, depending on the location of the residence, urban to suburban to rural.

Chapter 11

The View from Outside Your Home

Searching for a new home can be both overwhelming and exciting, especially when it comes to narrowing down the options. At best, the process can feel like a round of speed dating, with your real estate agent screening your potential suitors. At worst, you'll find yourself online for hours, scrolling through the real estate equivalents of Match.com. Luckily, unlike dating sites, homes usually look better in person than they do online!

First impressions happen fast, whether you're looking for love or a new home. Psychologists will tell you that a tenth of a second is all it takes for most of us to form an impression of a total stranger. We might not be quite so quick to evaluate physical structures, but initial opinions of homes tend to take shape pretty quickly. Indeed, veteran real estate agents can usually gauge a buyer's interest in a property before they've even reached the front door. There's really no getting around these split-second judgments, especially since a complex web of unconscious responses largely governs them. But at least where homes are concerned, you can arrive at a far more informed first impression by learning what common features unite the best residential architecture, whether it's a suburban cottage or a row house in the city.

If you read shelter magazines or watch HGTV, you've no doubt encountered the term *curb appeal*. Although there's nothing wrong with this expression per se, you could read one of those articles or watch one of those episodes on TV and believe that a fresh coat of paint and a few potted plants on the front porch are all that's needed to create an impressive exterior. In fact, the most appealing homes benefit from a series of simple yet often subtle elements that have nothing to do with decorative flourishes. In this chapter, I'll talk through these elements one by one, so that you'll know what to look for as your search for the right home moves off the street and onto the actual property. Just to be clear, the focus of this chapter is exterior design: the look and feel of the home. We will discuss understanding the condition of a home in detail in Chapter 16 and energy efficiency in Chapter 17.

Setting Your Vision

Determining which house has the best look and feel for you is a back-and-forth process. Start by imagining your ideal home, focusing on the elements that stand out in this vision. The questions that follow will help bring that image into focus. As you look at more homes, you might find your list of must-haves and don't-wants shifting somewhat. Revisit this section throughout the process and let your image evolve.

QUIZ: OUTSIDE YOUR JUST RIGHT HOME

What does your ideal house look like?

1. Do you prefer one story or two?
2. Where is the garage?
3. Where is the front door?
4. Is there a front porch?
5. What color is the house?
6. What material is it made out of?

7. Are there characteristics or architectural styles that you like more than others?

8. What do the windows look like?

9. What does the roofline look like?

Which exterior elements in your ideal home matter most to you?
Chances are, the picture-perfect house in your mind might not be available in the real world. The key to making available homes feel ideal is focusing your wish list on the elements that matter most to you.

For example, let's say you love the look and feel of a Craftsman bungalow, with its long, overhanging eaves and deep, shady front porch. If a bungalow isn't available in your area, consider homes with deep porches, even if they're from other architectural styles. Or perhaps you love the look of a modern home, with its clean lines and contemporary feel. If modern homes aren't available in your area, expand your search to homes that have that minimal ornament.

The key to making available homes feel ideal is focusing your wish list on the elements that matter most to you.

Are there deal-breaker elements?
One of the best ways to narrow the list of options is to eliminate homes that don't meet your needs. For the exterior of your home, make a distinction between elements you don't care for and those that are deal breakers. In my case, I dislike horizontal windows, but I could live with them. My deal breakers are a garage that takes up more than half the front of the house and double-height entries. Are there any elements that you would dislike greatly if they were on your house? Are there any elements you dislike that you can easily fix?

Remember, never say never. Keep this list flexible. You might find when balancing all of the variables of neighborhood, proximity, budget, and overall house layout and design that you will need to be flexible on certain points. Nonetheless, it's a good starting point to identify what you don't want so you can narrow your list faster.

VISUALIZE WITH IMAGES

As you narrow in on the look and feel of the exterior that best fits your vision, it can be helpful to collect images of homes and elements that you like. Here are a few resources, both online and off, to help you in this exercise.

Architecture Section of Your Local Bookstore: Flipping through books can offer great inspiration. You might find new ideas you didn't even know you were looking for.

Shelter Magazines: Magazines can provide great inspirations. They often cater to a certain type of architecture, from contemporary (*Dwell*) to traditional/transitional (*Better Homes and Gardens* and *This Old House*) to country (*Country Living*). It's nice to collect hard copies and create a clippings file, though most shelter magazines also have online counterparts with "inspiration" sections with images to help form your search.

James Hardie Visualizer: James Hardie, the manufacturer of fiber-cement board siding products, offers an in-depth online home exterior visualizer. Select your region, and then select from a range of different home designs. After that, you can change the color and type of siding, trim, and accent to adjust the look and feel of the house. This is a helpful tool to play with to help visualize different color and design options for the exterior of your house. The link is http://jameshardie2.swatchbox .com/ngcv/default.asp. Or simply Google "James Hardie Visualizer."

NOTES ON ARCHITECTURAL STYLES

Determining the architectural characteristics and details that you like is important in the process of finding a new place to live. But don't worry too much about the exact details of architectural styles.

Unless you are looking for a home in the historic district of an old town, the homes you are looking at will probably not fall into a defined style category.

Details That Matter

THE LANGUAGE OF ARCHITECTURE

In my first book, *Get Your House Right,* I explored the language of architecture in great detail. Like any language, architecture has a vocabulary and grammar all its own. Vocabulary defines the elements of a building—the windows, doors, eaves, roofs, and so forth. Grammar is the rules by which these elements are composed. When you look at a building and know that something feels wrong yet can't put your finger on exactly why, it's usually because there's something off with the grammar.

In its absolute simplest form, a building has two primary functions. The first is to stand up and be structurally sound. The second is to keep water out. Before the miracle of structural engineering and the invention of plastic as a building material, the design of a building itself had to perform these two tasks. Today, just about anything goes—design-wise, that is. If you can draw it, it can be built.

So shouldn't this be a good thing? On the one hand, yes. Many of the cool things we can build are fantastic: houses standing in the middle of waterfalls, buildings so tall they literally touch the clouds, and structures perched on the sides of mountains. The problem is that although some of the things we can design are in fact cool, a lot of what is being built today defies nature's logic.

By releasing us from the restraints of material limitations—columns were to support a beam, eaves were designed to keep water away from the building—we have forgotten the grammar. More often than not, buildings of all types, but especially newly constructed homes, are speaking gibberish. You don't have to have a degree in architecture to inherently understand that something is wrong when building elements serve no purpose. I can't sing in tune, but I know when someone else is out of tune. It is hardwired in every human being to understand nature's proportions.

So yes, although beauty is in the eye of the beholder, certain universal core principles make some buildings look, and live, better than others. Learning to recognize these good and bad design elements will help to inform your search, because you will start to see that the exterior design of a home reveals a lot about the design of the interior, the design of the community, and the overall experience of living in a place. You may not be able to avoid all the grammatical errors

> **Fast Fact** According to a survey of builders, designers, architects, and industry experts conducted by the National Association of Home Builders, a front porch is an outdoor feature most likely to be included in the average new home built in 2015.

in your available housing stock, but going in with eyes wide open will help you navigate to the ones that best fit your lifestyle and needs.

DESIGN ELEMENTS TO USE AND AVOID

Architectural designs vary greatly, depending on building type, climate, architectural style, and location—urban, suburban, or rural. Yet despite these many variations, the core principles central to proper grammar in the language of architectural design remain constant. Following are six elements to look for in a potential home, with tips about dos and don'ts.

Front Door The front entrance makes the biggest statement about your home. Although it may not be the primary entrance you use every day, it is the place where guests enter and leave, making it an important architectural feature. There are two common front-door conditions to avoid. The first is the hidden front door. This is common on homes where the garage dominates the front of the house. It can be unnerving to approach a home with a door hidden behind a corner or down a dark path. Even if you know you're in a safe neighborhood, you might worry a little when approaching at night.

The second condition to watch out for is the other extreme, the soaring double-height entrance. Rather than welcoming visitors, these rocket-ship entries look like they might take flight from the home. Typically, double-height entrances are on homes with numerous gables, window types, and gratuitous details. They're meant to call attention to the door. If this much effort is needed to focus attention on the door, it is usually an indication that the overall design of the house is chaotic, both inside and out. And it is a hint that you'll be faced with high utility bills down the road, as these areas are hard

> **Fast Fact** The percentage of U.S. homes with a three-car garage peaked at 20 percent in 2005 and was down to 17 percent in 2010, according to the U.S. Census Bureau. As recently as 1990, the figure was around 10 percent.

> ## The Greatest Value Is in What You Can Touch and Feel
>
> W hen was the last time you sat down to enjoy a cup of coffee on your fifth gable? I often toss this question out to the crowd when I'm speaking to homeowners. It's rhetorical, of course, but it often gets a few knowing nods from people who fell for the wrong kind of home their last time out. This was easy to do at the height of the McMansion era, when builders were engaged in a game of one-upmanship with one another, applying more and more detail and ornamentation to homes in an effort to stand out from the crowd.
>
> In that environment, it was easy for prospective home buyers to see that fifth gable as a measure of value. But once they moved in, they forgot about the gable and started noticing the exterior features with which they interacted every day, like the front porch where they might like to sit in the afternoon. As you assess homes, always place the greatest value on those features that you can interact with, rather than those there just to catch your eye.

to heat and cool. Keep the entrance modest, yet visible. Look for a front door that is clearly visible yet designed to the scale of a person. At the most practical level, ask yourself if the outside entrance could protect your waiting guests from rain.

Garage Location The location of the garage is key to the experience of living in any home. The garage's location speaks volumes about the overall design of the home and the surrounding neighborhood. In Chapter 9 we looked at snout houses and the effect garage-fronted homes have on the streetscape. Now let's look at the effect your garage has on your life. If you pull up to a house and its dominant feature is a double-wide garage door, you are clearly in for a car-dependent lifestyle. What's more, the floor plan of the house will have to make room for a multicar garage that's likely to impede its overall efficiency.

In an ideal design, the house itself will dominate the home's façade and the garage will feel like an added element. If the garage is facing the street, look for one that is pushed back behind the front face of the home. The ideal depth is eighteen feet or so from the façade so that it's shielded from view and cars parked in the driveway will be less conspicuous. But setting the garage back even three or five feet will make a difference.

The Sides A home has at least four sides and lives best when the architectural design includes windows and other design elements on all four of these sides. Not only will this make the house look better on the outside, but it will greatly increase the quality of life inside by providing more natural light and natural cross ventilation.

All too often with recent construction, only the front façade receives attention. Don't forget the sides: Use four-sided architecture. Look for windows on multiple walls. Even before you go inside a home, look at the sides of the house. If they are blank, take pause. A barren wall gives the house an unfinished feel, as if the builder ran out of money midway through the project. It also means the interior spaces on the opposite side of that wall will be devoid of natural light, making them dark and feel smaller. And since natural cross ventilation will be impossible, you'll have a heightened dependence on mechanical systems. On the other hand, if there are windows, look at how they are placed relative to neighboring houses. You don't want to look out of your living room into your neighbor's bathroom or vice versa.

> " A home has at least four sides and lives best when the architectural design includes windows and other design elements on all four of the sides. "

Windows Windows are a building's eyes to the world. They provide a visual connection to the outdoors as well as natural light and ventilation. The power of a window as a design tool is incredible. A small

Ask Yourself: Could It Work?

As you take in the exterior features of a potential home, ask yourself, Could that work? Even if the particular element will never be called into service, you want it to look like it would be able to function properly to contribute positively to the design of the home. What does this mean? Here's an example. Once upon a time, shutters served an actual purpose, providing security, privacy, sun screening, and protection from extreme weather. As a result, it was imperative that they actually cover the entire window. But these days, you can find purely decorative shutters that are too narrow to cover the window. This is the type of grammar violation that generates a nagging feeling in the back of your mind that there's something wrong with a house. As you look at a building, check to see if the elements at least look like they could work. Otherwise you are paying for elements that serve no purpose but will require maintenance and upkeep nonetheless.

number of well-placed and proportioned windows can transform a space, whereas a dozen awkward windows in the same home could result in dark and gloomy rooms. You can tell a lot about the quality of the interior natural light without even entering a home by taking note of the window placement.

Look for windows that have a vertical sense of proportion—typically two times as tall as they are wide. This enhances the look and feel of the house, the same way vertical lines in fashion help the human body appear tall and trim. Although there are exceptions to every rule, it's generally best to stay away from horizontal windows and houses with excessive numbers of arched windows.

Watch out for homes that compensate for blank side walls by covering the front wall with oversized windows, often arched or otherwise ornamented. At a glance, this gives the feeling of a house with a lot of light. And yes, at certain times of day, this is true. But in many cases, the homes get so much light that all homeowners can do at the peak of the afternoon is close the shades, turn on the lights, and crank up the AC. This is especially true when the large expanses of glass face south.

Roofline At its core, a roof is a source of shelter. Indeed, a roof over your head is the very definition of home. As with a clearly marked entrance, it's possible to go too far with a distinctive roof, which the gable-crazed rooflines that define McMansions make all too clear. It's fine to have a complex roofline. Indeed, many beautiful homes are a cascading arrangement of spaces, often with a single highest center, which creates a correspondingly complex roof system. But there's logic to the system that's lacking when gables and other roofline flourishes are applied gratuitously just to make the home look more interesting.

There are four unintended consequences of galloping gables on your roof. First, the harder a design tries to differentiate, the more alike everything tends to look. I discuss this more in "I'll See Your Six Gables and Raise You Three," in Appendix 3. Second, a crazy roofline is a red flag that the floor plan inside is a bit crazy as well. Third, the more ins, outs, ups, and downs, the more opportunity for a leak. And fourth, though these homes look large and spacious, often these extra roofs do not yield any extra living space—just extra attic space (and higher energy bills).

Keep the rooflines simple. Look for designs with clearly defined rooflines and simple proportions. Try to avoid a home with more than three gables facing the street or with roofs that overpower the home.

Material Selection Materials are literally the building blocks of structures. Brick and stone are both load-bearing materials, which means historically they supported their own weight, resulting in some very beautiful brick and stone houses. But over time, especially here in the United States, these once-structural elements became veneers, hanging from wood-frame homes—resulting in stone that is little more than wallpaper.

If you are looking at a house with a patchwork quilt of materials, proceed with care. This is usually a sign that the builder was trying to compensate for a bad design. Varied materials can add interest and texture, but unfortunately they are often applied haphazardly.

Changing materials is fine across the façade, but look for horizontal transitions rather than vertical strips of masonry running the full height of a home's façade and surrounded on both sides by siding. If the stone were actually load bearing, this would never stand up. Not every house needs a little of every material. If the design is good, it will stand on its own, without all the smoke and mirrors.

The Materials on the Outside of Your Home

EXTERIOR WALL MATERIALS

The materials that are used on the exterior of your home will define its look and feel and also determine its durability and weather resistance. In Chapters 16 and 17, I'll discuss in more detail the issue of maintenance and sustainability. Here, though, is a snapshot of what you need to know about the common materials in home exteriors today.

Vinyl The most affordable type of siding, and therefore the most common. It's often described as a no-maintenance material, though I take issue with that characterization because it applies only to the fairly short life of the product—say twenty to thirty years (less for inferior products). After that it requires a complete replacement. What's more, vinyl can also warp and discolor before the official end of its warranty, and it can feel flimsy. Despite those downsides, its low price makes it a necessary evil for homes that must stick within a certain budget.

Wood Wood can take the form of either clapboards or shingles. Both give a home a natural look. But depending on the climate and location, wood exteriors can require a lot of upkeep, typically repainting every five to ten years or so. Cedar shingles in the North work well and add value to the home, making them the exception to the rule. But if you are looking at a newer house in a hot, humid climate, real wood can be more liability than luxury.

The Benefits and Dangers of Material Ordinances

Everyone wants to live in a community that is thriving, looks great, and has a strong tax base. In a growing trend, especially in Texas, communities and municipalities are putting in place material ordinances in an effort to support these goals. It is not uncommon to find ordinances that require an arbitrary 80 percent masonry.

Although I'm all for keeping property values high and the tax base strong, these types of restrictions actually end up doing the opposite. Neighborhoods that allow a mix of durable materials are typically more desirable in the long run than communities with arbitrary percentage restrictions on specific materials, which end up feeling static. Take caution when moving to one of these areas or if your community is considering enacting such an ordinance. Look for codes that call out performance and durability standards rather than specify certain materials or percentages of materials.

Fiber-Cement Board Siding This man-made material is a great alternative to wood, offering the same look and feel with the durability of masonry. It's also termite- and rot-resistant, noncombustible, and rated to withstand hurricane-force winds. Clapboards come in two thicknesses: a more affordable option and a higher-end version. Paint on this factory-finished siding is typically guaranteed to last fifteen years.

Brick Another man-made material that's extremely durable and sound. As a load-bearing material, it was once used to build entire houses, and that's still the best look for brick. Avoid stage-set designs where brick is used as a veneer on the front only. This will look like you ran out of money. .

Stone Historically, this load-bearing quarried material was used to construct entire buildings. That can be cost-prohibitive today, so stone is commonly used only for the base of a building. That's okay, provided it's used on all four sides of the building in a true load-bearing manner. Stone applied piecemeal or in vertical strips takes away from the architectural credibility of the home. Fake stone that gives a hollow sound when knocked is even worse.

Stucco True stucco-on-concrete block is durable and attractive. Fake stucco hanging from wood-frame construction is a lawsuit waiting to happen, because it's often hiding water damage. Never buy a stucco house without having a deep-wall inspection. If you are looking at a foreclosure with stucco, take great care, unless you are able to have a thorough inspection done. Buying a stucco home sight unseen is an absolute no-no. The underlying water damage could include substantial structural compromises costing tens of thousands if not more.

PVC Trim and Accessories PVC (short for polyvinyl chloride) is an extremely durable plastic. Trim and accessories made with it can look natural, and are lighter and easier to work with than wood or fiber-cement and don't require special tools. Plus they are durable, long lasting, and rot-resistant.

OPENINGS
Windows Wood- and fiberglass-frame windows keep out the cold and rain better than units made out of vinyl, though they will need to be repainted periodically. PVC windows are a good alternative, because they have the look and feel of wood, are durable, and don't require painting. Double- or triple-glazed windows, which have a sealed space between two (or three) panes of glass, minimize heat loss, make a home more comfortable, and can reduce heating and air-conditioning bills by a third—saving hundreds of dollars a year. Low-E (low-emissivity) coatings are another efficiency feature to inquire about, since they lower utility bills by reflecting heat into the house in winter and blocking heat from the sun in summer. Look for simulated divided light (SDL) windows if possible. This is when there is a grille on the inside and outside face of the glass. Avoid grille-between-the-glass windows (GBG) because they look flimsy.

Doors Front doors are easy to replace, so a bad one shouldn't be a deal breaker. But look for doors that feel substantial. This includes the hardware. In terms of design, look for doors that are built tradition- ally with stiles, rails, and panels. Doors will feel unsubstantial if the panels are thinly pressed into the door and are smaller than the stiles and rails. Avoid etched glass and fake leaded glass in sidelights and transoms. Whereas genuine leaded-glass windows in old homes look beautiful, cheap imitations in new homes draw attention for all the wrong reasons. Better to keep it simple and substantial.

> **Carriage-style doors are nice, adding dimension to a very large and horizontal design element, thus relating the garage to a person, rather than the car.**

Garage Doors Finding great garage doors can be tough. Many models on the market today will be the bright white variety with thin pressed panels. These doors only exacerbate the situation when installed in a snout house. Carriage-style doors are nice, adding dimension to a very large and horizontal design element, thus relat- ing the garage to a person, rather than the car. You can find models that open up on tracks but are designed to look like they swing open. They can be expensive and are something that can be added at a later time.

ROOFING MATERIALS

Asphalt Shingles The most common roofing type found today. Not all shingles are created equal, however, so some will last longer. Laminated shingles (aka "architectural" or "dimensional" shingles) are layered, and their thickness and depth make them look more like slate or wood shakes. Three-tab asphalt shingles consist of a single layer. They're flatter and thinner than laminated shingles, offering less protection. An inferior roof shouldn't squelch the deal, but you can use it to negotiate the price down if a replacement will be needed soon.

Metal Durable and attractive, metal roofing comes in steel, aluminum, copper, and alloy strips, and in a variety of shapes and textures. But it's expensive, especially the copper, which over time develops a greenish patina that some people find attractive. A more affordable alternative to a standing seam metal roof is a 5 V-crimp roof. Historically used on utility buildings, this type of metal roof is becoming widely popular in residential construction. Advantages of metal include easy installation and ultralight weight, about half that of asphalt. It is also durable in hurricanes and doesn't burn in fires. Make sure you hire a contractor who is familiar with the material.

Slate, Shakes, and Tile These more specialized roofing materials tend to be attractive yet pricey. Slate and tile are both long lasting but extremely expensive to replace when the time comes. Slate is common on traditional architecture, such as Tudor houses with steep-gabled roofs or tile in Mediterranean-style architecture. If you're looking at a home covered with one of these materials, make sure you ask when the roof was last replaced. Shake roofs, like the kind you see on shingle-style homes, need to be replaced more frequently, about every ten years. The shingles are typically made of cedar, which weathers to a nice shade of silvery gray.

CHAPTER CHEAT SHEET

Gut Check

What stands out to you as the most important elements outside your house? Would you be proud to call this place home?

Reality Check

Does this house fit your lifestyle? Will you be able to maintain the outside of this home?

Balancing Act

Function—Does the location of the garage work to get groceries in and out of the house? Is there a good flow from inside to out? *Cost*—Can you afford to maintain the home? *Delight*—Do you like what it looks like?

Key points to remember

- When you look at a home from the street, the dominant feature should be a welcoming entrance of human scale, not an enormous garage door beckoning an automobile.

- Four-sided architecture, including windows on the sides and back of the house, is essential to function and form.

- Although it's important to identify with the home itself, you also want to have a strong connection with the surrounding block, neighborhood, and community as a whole.

Chapter 12

Your Yard, Lot, and Property

A house with a yard has been part and parcel of the American Dream for well over a century. As Kenneth Jackson writes in *Crabgrass Frontier: The Suburbanization of the United States*, "By 1870 separateness had become essential to the identity of the suburban house. The yard was expected to be large and private and designed for both active and passive recreation, in direct antithesis to the dense lifestyle from which many families had recently moved. The new ideal was no longer to be part of a close community, but to have a self-contained unit, a private wonderland walled off from the rest of the world." That identity was carried into and throughout the twentieth century, along with the devotion to a large, weed-free lawn, a cornerstone of the suburban idyll.

Although the house with a yard remains an ideal option for many, there are many alternatives that might meet your needs even better. For people choosing to live in or near the city center, with or without children in tow, being close to a park or expansive green space will be as important as the big yard was to their parents' generation. Elsewhere, there's a growing interest in xeriscaping, the technical term for landscaping and gardening in ways that reduce the need for water, for example through the use of drought-tolerant plants and gravel.

I'm definitely not anti-yard, and I don't want you to be either. Indeed, a lush green lawn truly will be the best fit for many millions of homeowners and renters alike. My position is that it shouldn't be the default setting that you blindly gravitate toward. In this chapter, I'll help you think about how you really intend to use your outdoor space so that you can define and find your own frontier.

Understanding How You Live Outdoors

The size and type of property that's the best fit for you will depend on two things: the type of activities you plan to enjoy outside your home and the amount of time and money you're able to commit to landscape care and maintenance.

Exposed backyard Design, not distance, creates privacy in a backyard. This house has a completely exposed backyard, despite being one of the most expensive homes in the development.

IDENTIFYING HOW YOU WANT TO USE THE SPACE

Here are the five main ways people engage with and use their land. Which fits you?

Passive Engagement Includes such outdoor living activities as relaxing, grilling, and eating. In urban settings, a small balcony or terrace is enough to accommodate these pastimes. In suburban and rural settings, a back deck, covered porch, or garden terrace will suffice. Quality of space is much more important than size. The best outdoor living areas for passive engagement are closely connected to the indoors with an easy flow in and out of the home, and with a sense of containment and privacy from neighbors.

Active Engagement This primarily applies to kids, who love to run, jump, scream, and yell. Specific activities will vary, depending on the age. If you have little kids, they might be happy to romp through a

Private backyard This house, by contrast, uses the design of the landscaping to create privacy for the residents, resulting in an outdoor place that will actually be used.

Design, not distance, creates a private yard

Large suburban lots often have less privacy than small urban lots where the neighbors' property defines your backyard. That's contrary to the original image of the suburban yard, the "self-contained unit, a private wonderland walled off from the rest of the world" about which Kenneth Jackson wrote.

What Happened? Poorly designed suburban developments sprang up in which yards became little more than exposed patches of grass devoid of shade trees and border plants because the yards were so large that landscaping was too expensive for the developer's budget. Often, there is a ten-by-ten-foot deck attached to the back of the house, with enough room for a grill. Unfortunately, this offers very little privacy. In an attempt to create privacy through distance, lots were pushed farther and farther apart. This is a case of treating the symptoms rather than the disease.

What Are Alternatives? Not all square feet are created equal, inside and outside the house. Smaller lots with well-defined yards can be more conducive to outdoor living, since they can create a sense of privacy and employ all corners of the property. Fences are another type of border, but they need to be tall enough, and on their own can't create privacy, since neighbors can look down from their upper floors. Look for natural barriers like hedges, pine trees, or willows. In the same way that floor plan efficiency is more important than raw square footage, how a yard is laid out tells you more than the acreage. I've been on quarter-acre properties that get far more use and deliver far more pleasure than properties with two acres or more.

sprinkler, dig in a sandbox, or play tag in the yard. If they are older, they might want a basketball hoop in the driveway. Ask yourself these questions:

- Do you see your family playing outdoor lawn games like badminton or bocce ball?

> **Fast Fact** Landscape irrigation, including the watering of lawns, accounts for nearly a third of all residential water use in the United States, according to the Environmental Protection Agency. All told, we pour more than 7 billion gallons per day into our landscapes.

- What type of activities do your kids like to do in their free time?
- How will the kids' activities change in five to ten years?

Gardening or Farming This category has the widest range of size options, from a few square feet for a vegetable garden to acres of farmland. In urban settings you might see a balcony with a few pots of herbs. In suburban settings, you could have a small flower or vegetable garden around part or all of your property. In rural areas, you may want to have horses or raise chickens. Ask yourself these questions:

- Do you want to garden? If so, what type of garden do you want? Herbs, flowers, vegetables? All of the above?
- Do you want to have chickens or horses? If so, how many and what kind? How much space will they take?

Relaxing in Private The privacy needed for full relaxation can be achieved through both distance and design. In urban settings look for buildings with balconies strategically designed to block views between apartments. You will be visible from the street and other buildings, but as long as you are far enough away from others that you can't make eye contact, you will feel a sense of privacy. In suburban areas, the distance between homes helps to create privacy. But don't fall into the trap of making the distance do all of the work. How the houses are laid out in a neighborhood will have more to do with the sense of privacy you get in the backyard than the physical distance between homes (see page 225).

Seeking Views There's nothing nicer than sitting inside your home and having something pleasant to look at outside the window, especially later in life, when we tend to be less actively engaged with our surroundings. Think about what views offer the most appeal. Some people prefer an active streetscape, where they can watch the world go by and interact with passersby. Others are soothed and satisfied by nature, whether it's a beautifully landscaped garden, birds at a bird feeder, or simply a well-placed tree.

CONSIDERING CARE AND MAINTENANCE

How much time and money do you want to allocate for care and maintenance of the property? This is a crucial question to consider before making any decisions about the type and size of property you select.

A lush, weed-free lawn, the scene of backyard barbecues and bare-footed children running through sprinklers, is part of many people's dream home. That's all well and good (though I might balk at how much water some species of American grass require). But before you commit to the idea of a lawn, it's important to understand the maintenance costs. If you plan to do the work yourself, you'll have to invest a few hundred bucks in a lawn mower or, for larger lawns, a few

WORDS OF WISDOM

"When I first saw the house, I loved the large backyard with a lush green lawn and an in-ground pool—great for my son and his friends. I figured the expense of upkeep wouldn't be too bad. Well, the first month's bill was over $700! And my son's school activities meant he was rarely home to enjoy the yard. Luckily I was renting, and was able to move out as soon as my lease was up." Irina W., Vero Beach, FL

"Living in a neighborhood with smaller homes and smaller yards has really added to our sense of community. While the big kids are playing soccer in one yard, the little kids are using chalk on another's drive while the parents visit on the front porch." Deborah S., Glenside, PA

thousand bucks in a tractor. Fuel and service costs, including having the blades sharpened, will set you back another hundred dollars or so each year. Mowing frequency varies by season and region, but you're probably looking at a couple of weekend mornings per month on average. Alternatively, you could pay a landscaping company or neighborhood kid to do the work, saving time but adding to your costs. Consider also the cost to water your lawn. A large yard might also add $500 or more to your water bill monthly.

A swimming pool is another major expense that people often overlook, especially if they've never had one before. Pool-service companies charge between $50 and $100 a month to keep the water clean. Then there are the energy costs, which might be $75 per month to operate the pumps, and several hundred dollars more if the pool is heated.

Pocket Neighborhoods

One of the most interesting trends in community development in the United States is the emergence of so-called pocket neighborhoods, clusters of freestanding homes arranged around a common landscaped area. They've actually been around for centuries—a Methodist camp community founded in 1835 in Oak Bluffs, on Martha's Vineyard in Massachusetts, is an early example—but new ones are popping up all over the country.

In his 2011 book *Pocket Neighborhoods: Creating Small-Scale Community in a Large-Scale World,* architect Ross Chapin walks the reader through various examples, including many that cater to a mix of homeowners, including young families, elderly couples, and single residents. The homes are typically smaller in scale, in reaction to the megahouses of the recent McMansion era.

If you like the idea of being part of a close-knit community, without the demands of maintaining a huge yard all by yourself, it's worth seeing if there are any pocket neighborhoods in your area.

ALTERNATIVES TO PRIVATE YARDS

So what if you want the benefits of outdoor living without the cost or time associated with care and maintenance? Here are a few alternatives to consider:

Passive Engagement Look for homes that are within walking distance of cafés, coffee shops, and restaurants with outdoor dining.

Active Engagement Parks are a great outlet for younger, active kids. Keep in mind that you will be more likely to take your kids to the park if it is a safe, short walk from your house. As your kids get older, look for schools that allow kids to play on the ball fields or playgrounds after school and on weekends. Other options are community pools, soccer fields, ice rinks, or tennis courts. Finding places for kids to play and exercise away from your property provides a physical outlet while also encouraging social engagement. Check to see if you can grill at the park: This is a great way to entertain outdoors without everyone coming over to your house!

Gardening or Farming If you are planning to live in an apartment or condo but still want to garden, look in your area for community gardens or garden plots. Ask around or search online at communitygarden.org to find one in your area. Be warned though: Community gardens are widely popular and often have a waiting list of more than a year. If you are considering this, sign up early.

Seeking Views Some people, including myself, love the outdoors best when it's enjoyed from indoors. If visuals are more important to you than participation, consider moving into a community with beautiful common grounds that are maintained by an association.

Around Your Property

FIVE ELEMENTS TO LOOK FOR WHEN WALKING THE PROPERTY

Ideally, your property will be a positive extension of the home. Look for these five elements when assessing a potential property. Note, these elements are not just for single-family homes; they are important regardless of building type.

1. An Outdoor Room

The key for a successful outdoor room is to look for a sense of privacy from your neighbors. Look for definition of space and a place where you can go outside and not feel like your neighbors are looking over at you. Ideally the property around your house will create the feeling of an outdoor room.

For a single-family home, the front yard is a welcoming semipublic zone and the backyard is a private-living zone, ideally with a gathering area close to the home for casual dining and entertaining and a getaway space farther away, perhaps with a hammock and a tree. It's always nice if one or more of these outdoor gathering areas are covered, especially in southern climates where protection from the sun is critical. In attached housing types, look for how the buildings frame courtyards or gardens. Is there somewhere you can sit outside to read a book or eat a meal?

Mature landscapes don't happen overnight, and might even take decades to reach full splendor, but if you walk to the back of a house or urban courtyard and find nothing but a barren stretch of lawn, realize that you may not spend a lot of time there. At the same time, remember that you can give a lawn visual interest pretty quickly with a few flowering bushes and some perennials if you are prepared to invest the time.

2. Angle of the Sun

The character of your outdoor space will be defined partially by how and when the sunlight hits the spaces. Look for your primary outdoor areas—the lawn, garden, and patio—to be on the south side of the house, where it will be sunny for much of the day. When these spaces face north, the shadows make it difficult for anything to grow and make it less desirable to spend time there. Carry a compass with you when looking at homes. This is the best way to determine if a house is situated such that its outdoor spaces will get a lot of sun. Luckily, today most smartphones come equipped with a compass feature, so you don't have to call on a local Boy Scout to help you out.

3. Connection to the Indoors

As you tour the exterior of a potential property, look for connections between the outdoors and indoors. Is there an easy flow between inside and out? Can you actually see yourself using these outdoor areas? Look for clear pathways and well-positioned doors. If there is not a strong connection, is this something that could be fixed with a minor renovation? Sometimes you will find an awkward set of treated wood steps leading down to an undefined patio. It might be possible to transform the blah patio into an inviting terrace, replace the rickety steps, and even add French doors or a glass wall that slides open and closed.

4. Car Connection

Where is the parking? Does the connection into the house facilitate the loading and unloading of groceries, luggage, sports equipment, and other items, even on a rainy day? Although it is not desirable to have the garage as the primary design element of a home, the car is an essential component of our daily lives, and you will want to make sure your parking setup fits your needs. Ask yourself these questions:

- Will you be using the garage for a car or for storage?
- If for storage, is there enough room outside to park?
- How many cars will you have to accommodate?
- When will each car come and go?
- Can you meet your parking needs subtly without turning your property into a parking lot?

5. Trees and Landscaping

When trees are planted between the sidewalk and street, they help create a protective buffer between pedestrians and vehicles. In the yard, they're a much-coveted source of beauty and shade. In fact, a property with plenty of mature trees is worth 20 to 30 percent more than one without, according to the National Association of Home Builders. Native species are best, since they will fit in with the surrounding landscape and require the least care and attention. Invasive species, meanwhile, often require additional nutrients, and they can take over a property.

When trees are properly placed in relation to the house, ideally on the west and southwest sides of the property, they can reduce a home's heating and cooling costs by hundreds of dollars each year. On the other hand, trees can end up costing you dearly if one should fall on your house or your neighbor's. So be on the lookout for diseased or otherwise unsound trees that could end up causing more harm than good. If you have any question about the condition of any existing trees, bring in an arborist to assess the situation and offer solutions.

CHAPTER CHEAT SHEET

Gut Check

What is your ideal outdoor space? A large lawn, farm, paved terrace, or somewhere in between?

Reality Check

Have you taken into account the amount of care and maintenance you are able to invest in both time and money to keep up your outdoor space?

Balancing Act

Function—What type of spaces work best for your outdoor needs? *Cost*—How much can you afford to maintain? *Delight*—How do you want to engage with the outdoors?

Key points to remember

- There are four primary ways to engage with the outdoors: passively, actively, gardening/farming, and visually. Assess your needs now and consider how these needs might change in the future.

- Depending on your exact needs, you might find alternatives to a large suburban yard that better fit your preferred lifestyle.

- Design, not distance, creates privacy between homes.

Chapter 13

Inside Your Home: Beyond Square Feet and Number of Bedrooms

To pick up the matchmaking analogy from Chapter 11, in which viewing homes was likened to a round of speed dating, you're now ready for an actual rendezvous—maybe not a hot and heavy weekend in the country, but at least dinner and a movie. Whereas assessing a home's exterior is mostly a gut check (that is, either you like the way it looks or you don't), evaluating a home's inside needs more time and commitment. That's because longtime happiness is driven by the interior, where you'll spend the majority of your time. That new love interest might be super cute, but the relationship is doomed to fail if there's nothing going on inside. So it is with choosing a home.

Think back over the many homes you've experienced throughout your life—not just the ones you've lived in, but also the residences of close friends and relatives you visited often, and the vacation properties you got to know on a short-term basis. You may have stronger, fonder memories of some of these places than of others. Of course, those feelings have a lot to do with people and relationships, but the physical aspects of a space also affect our psychological impression of it. In short, some homes simply work and feel better than others, and it has nothing to do with grandeur, fond memories, or how much money was poured into their fixtures and finishes.

Finding the right home is, above all, a balancing act. Chances are you'll be checking out different neighborhoods and housing types at various price points. It's good to dream, drool, even aspire. But it is equally important to be realistic about your situation and your needs. First-time home buyers often make the mistake of viewing properties that are way out of their price range. Maybe they'll be looking at a modest one-bedroom in an apartment building and notice a sign for another open house several flights up, with a second bedroom, multiple balconies, and a tricked-out kitchen. Resist the urge to overreach, and don't feel like you are settling for second best. Remember David Brooks's line about Buyers lie, and how the house many people describe at the beginning of their search is nothing like the one they actually prefer and buy. This self-deception was a big part of the housing boom and bust that happened during the first decade of the twenty-first century. Many people bought a home they couldn't afford (and in many cases that didn't meet their needs) because they wanted it to be right for them, even though it really wasn't.

Keep this in mind as you read these next two chapters. You want your home to inspire you. But to genuinely do so, it has to work on all levels—not just in terms of the square footage, character, and counter surfaces, but also its budget and other practical concerns. Unless you are building new with unlimited financing, you'll likely have to compromise on some of the elements discussed. The key is homing in on the two or three things that matter most to you and your family. If you can do that, you'll almost certainly find a home that fits your needs, one where the trade-offs feel like the right fit.

Determining Your Housing Needs

Chapter 4 introduced the idea of the housing profile, or a snapshot of the basic criteria for your housing search: your budget, house type/number of rooms, and neighborhood. Most people expect that their housing profile will change over time, but you might be surprised to find you have several housing profiles at any one moment. The home you select in a walkable neighborhood might be very different from the one you pick out in a car-dependent area. At the same time, if you can meet most of your needs for half the price, you might consider sacrificing a few elements to save money.

Determining your right home across a range of housing profiles requires understanding how you live in a home and occupy the space. Only then can you start to look at the specific rooms or details of any given home. Here is a series of questions to help you determine the needs that will best fit your lifestyle, now and in the future. Some questions will be simple, and others will require a little reflection. Be as honest as possible to get the most accurate picture. And keep an open mind, remembering that your ideal housing profile might look quite different from where you currently live.

QUIZ: INSIDE YOUR JUST RIGHT HOME

Understanding Your Basic Needs

1. How many people are in your household now? How could this change in the future? If you have children, do you plan on having more, will they be moving out in the near future, or will an adult child be moving home? Do you have plans to have parents or other family members move in with you? If your household size will be fluctuating in the next few years, look for homes that can be adaptable over time or properties with the options for a granny flat. (See page 201 for more details.)

2. How many bedrooms do you need? Most housing searches start with the number of bedrooms. Building on the previous question, give some thought to how many bedrooms you need now and how a home might be adapted in the future to meet changing needs, including the possibility for a home office.

Assessing Your Current and Previous Homes

1. What do you love most about your current home? What elements, characteristics, or details of your current home do you love the most? This could be the connection between certain rooms, sunlight in the morning, a compelling view, or something practical like a large basement with shelves for storage. It might also be the specific materials or appliances. If you could have three elements or details from your current home in your new home, what would they be?

2. What spaces or rooms do you use most in your current home? Especially in larger homes, it's common to use only a small fraction of the space. What areas of your house do you use most? Those would be the ones you might want bigger or more centrally located (the kitchen or family room) versus those you rarely use at all (the formal dining room or overscaled entry foyer).

3. What do you love most about homes you have previously lived in or visited? Think back to previous places you have lived. Are there any elements that stand out most that you would love to have back?

4. What do you dislike the most about your current home? What elements, characteristics, or details of your current home really aren't working? It might be rooms that are hard to furnish, finishes that are past their prime, or closets that are impossible to organize. What three things will you be happiest to leave behind?

5. What spaces or rooms do you use least in your current home? Are there areas of your home that you use only once a year, if ever? Do you feel like you must have those rooms even for such infrequent use, or could you live without them?

How You Live In Your Home

1. Where do you plan to eat your meals? Do you eat as a family or individually? Do you prefer formal or informal dining? (See page 255 for more on dining options.)

2. Where do your kids do their homework? Do your kids do their homework at the kitchen table, in their bedrooms, at a computer nook, or elsewhere?

3. Do you work from home? Do your housing needs include space for a home office? Will you be working from home or do you just need a spot to pay the bills? Will it work to tuck your office into the corner of another room or do you need a dedicated room? (See page 258 for more on home offices.)

4. What do you do after dinner? Do you watch TV, go straight to bed, go for a walk? How would you like to spend your evenings?

5. What do you do on weekends? Are you at home or out and about? Do you snuggle in to watch movies, work in the garden, or bring work from the office home?

6. How, when, and whom do you entertain? Think about the type of entertaining you currently do and how you might host in a new home. Consider the types of activities your kids do with their friends now and how that might change in the coming years. What types of space would best accommodate these activities?

7. Do you have guests over often? Do your kids bring friends over to play?

8. Warm climate or cold? Consider the number of people in your household and the amount of outdoor weather gear you will need to accommodate, especially if you are in a cold climate. (More on planning for this space on page 258.)

BOTTOM-LINE QUESTIONS

Of all the questions above, what are the five most important character-istics or elements that stand out? They could be activities you want your home to support, design of a space that works really well, or a material selection. What five characteristics mean the most to you in your life?

Of all the questions above, what are the three least important ele-ments? Now, think about the least important items from the questions asked above. Which ones don't matter to your life at all?

Determining your housing profile involves some give and take. The first step in answering the questions above is to focus in on how you want to live in a home and the elements that mean the most to you.

WORDS OF WISDOM

"Drive all necessary vehicles into the garage to make sure they fit comfortably! Yes, we made this mistake by not doing so. After purchasing our house, we found that we couldn't fit our truck in the garage. Thank goodness for remote starters for cold winter mornings!" Joe D., Atlanta, GA

"In 2007, when we bought our home, the thought of a 5,200-square-foot home with 'oversized everything' seemed like a great investment. Now, five years later, the 'investment' is not at all what we once thought it was and may never be. We now want less space, less clutter, and generally less stuff. With daughters approach-ing their teens, we want our family to be closer together and not spread out over three floors of bedrooms, bonus rooms, and game rooms. I want a nice home in a package that is more comfortable, less expensive to own and maintain, and better matches the size of our family." Lance H., Maryville, TN

The next step is to look at the big-picture flow of a home and how the design elements work together. Once you can start to articulate your lifestyle needs and understand the design characteristics of successful home design, you can tour potential properties armed with the knowledge needed to find the best fit possible. Throughout the process, revisit this list of questions periodically to make sure your potential homes will meet your needs.

Not All Square Feet Are Created Equal

Square footage, number of rooms, and materials alone do not make great homes. Design makes a home great. Great design is the difference between a home that sings and one that falls flat. Here is what you need to know.

ELEVEN ELEMENTS THAT DIFFERENTIATE DESIGNS

Fifty or sixty years ago, people didn't pay square footage much mind. A roof over their heads and a quarter-acre lot was enough for that generation of new families who were pouring into the unfurling American suburbs. But as the average home size swelled from around 983 square feet in 1950 to upward of 2,500 square feet at the height of the latest housing boom, square footage became part of the popular perception of value. The assumption was that more must be better, with little attention paid to how the space was used.

In fact, not all square feet are created equal, which is why some homes live much larger than others, even though on paper they should feel a lot smaller. Sarah Susanka, architect and author of the influential *Not So Big House* books, illustrates that a well-designed house will need one third less space than you think it does. In other words, a 2,000-square-foot home with an efficient, functional floor plan will do the job of a poorly designed home measuring 3,000 square feet.

Like everything else in your decision-making process, one size doesn't fit all. Here are the elements that make a house live large, regardless of its actual dimensions. Some of the elements below will be more important to you than others. It is good to keep them all in mind to some degree, though, and then focus on the ones that are most important in your life.

1. Sense of Arrival

The experience of arrival, including where you enter on a daily basis and where your guests enter, says a lot about the general form and function of a home. Look for a positive flow and a place to put your keys down. When you walk in, what is in your line of sight? Watch out for homes with a direct line of sight into the master bedroom, or worse, the master bathroom, from the front door.

2. Sequence of Space Between Rooms

The arrangement of rooms determines whether there is a natural flow or if you are winding around through narrow hallways. The ease with which you can move throughout a home will have a huge effect on your overall comfort. If you are looking at a smaller home, watch out for long corridors. The more space that is taken up with circulation, the less space there will be for living. If there are long hallways in a house, see if they are wide enough to furnish with shelves, cabinets, or even a small desk. This will activate the space and make it usable square footage.

3. Open Yet Defined Rooms

Open-plan living is a positive development from the smaller, chopped-up floor plans of older architecture, such as ranch homes and split-levels. But it is possible for an interior to get so wide open that it becomes impossible to furnish and use. Look for floor plans that breathe well while retaining some definition. For example, there might be a cased opening or dropped beam separating the kitchen from the living and dining rooms, allowing the rooms to connect while maintaining their own identity. This gives the best of both worlds: You'll feel like you're in a larger room, but you'll also get the sensation of walking between rooms, which makes the house as a whole feel larger.

4. Clearly Defined Public and Private Areas of the House

Although open plans help a house live large, one drawback is that sounds easily transfer throughout the house—in some cases making it impossible to have a private conversation. It is not uncommon for parents to have to step outdoors to have a conversation out of earshot of the kids. If the public areas of the house are open, make sure there are private areas where everyone can get a moment of quiet. Bedrooms that share walls are another privacy killer. Ideally, the floor plan will create a buffer between bedrooms, for example with strategically located closets or bathrooms.

How many square feet do I really need?

There's no hard and fast formula for figuring out how much square footage you need. Does a family of six require six times the space of a single person? Probably not. Indeed, people who live in massive homes often use only a small portion of the space. That's how we ended up with sprawling McMansions in which entire wings go unused, even unfurnished.

Regardless of family size, three main factors play a role in determining the amount of space you will need: proximity to walkable amenities, the type of connection to the outdoors, and the design of the rooms inside the house. A home connected to a walkable public realm requires less square footage than a home in an auto-dependent community. If you can walk to amenities such as cafés and movie theaters, your home does not have to provide these elements as well. Additionally, homes live larger if they are seamlessly connected to the outdoors. If you activate your yard to become living space, you can double the effective size of your home. The design of the interiors is a vital element too. A 2,000-square-foot house with eight-foot ceilings and a small number of four-foot-high windows will feel smaller than a 1,500-square-foot house with ten-foot ceilings and a generous number of six-foot-high windows.

5. Furnishable Floor Plans

This is one of the most important points in this section. Consider whether you can comfortably furnish the home, find a place for the TV, have a bed wall in each bedroom, and make sure that when lying in the master bed, you don't have a view of the toilet. As homes got larger during the boom, plans tended to get dumber. It is not uncommon to walk into a giant home and have no comfortable place to sit and read a book. Think about where your furniture will go and how the rooms will work. If visualizing space is hard for you, consider hiring a decorator or designer to give you a couple of sketches of how the rooms will feel when furnished.

6. Clutter Control

Nothing makes a house feel smaller than uncontrolled clutter. Everyone accumulates stuff, some more than others. Great designs will absorb our treasures and get them out of sight. Storage is something that can be retrofitted in most homes. If it is not there already, make sure there is an opportunity to add it in. Closet space is critical. Note how many closets there are and if there are built-in shelves and cabinetry. If closet space is limited, look for walls that could fit shelves or cabinets and to see if there are places to install hooks.

> **" Homes hold their value best when there is a strong visual and physical connection with the outdoors. "**

7. Abundant Natural Light and Cross Ventilation

Four-sided architecture is important not just for the look and feel of the home's exterior, but for the function of the inside too. Windows on multiple walls of a room add substantially to the live-in value of a home. Side windows also allow cross ventilation in temperate months, reducing your dependency on mechanical systems. But perhaps most important, side windows provide balanced natural light, ensuring sun exposure through a significant portion of the day while reducing glare in the room. As you walk through a house, take note of the time

Find Your Inspiration

Finding the right home requires reflection on how you live, but there's only so far your imagination can go in conjuring up the perfect living situation. Seeing examples of how others live is also essential to the process. Keep a clippings file of both printed and digital images. As the clippings grow, your preferences for certain styles and design type will come into sharper focus. Here are four sources to consider:

Pinterest.com: An online pin board designed to help organize images of things you love. You can use Pinterest to browse the collections that others post or create your own board to keep all of your inspirations in one place. The best part of the site is that it includes links back to the original source, so if you like a product or a designer, you are able to go directly to their site to find more information.

Houzz.com Described by *The New York Times* as the ultimate house porn website, Houzz.com is a well-organized database of images relating to home design. They have hundreds of thousands of interior, product, and exterior images as well. You can search by style or specific element. Like Pinterest, images are linked back to the original source so you can find out more details.

Interiors Books and Shelter Magazines Besides making great coffee table accessories, interiors books and magazines are loaded with inspiring images. The main magazines to look for are *Architectural Digest, Better Homes and Gardens, Country Living, Elle Décor, Dwell, House Beautiful, This Old House,* and *Veranda.*

BHG.com Better Homes and Gardens has an easy-to-use, comprehensive online library of images categorized by room as well as subject. This site also offers design tips and content from their magazine.

of day and position of the sun in the sky. It's best to view a home in the middle of the day, when the sun is high in the sky and the light is most plentiful. If the home is dark at this time of day, it's never going to get lighter. (See "Let There Be Light," page 248.)

8. Connection to the Outdoors

In Chapter 12 we looked at the connection between indoors and outdoors from an exterior viewpoint. Now let's consider it from the inside. Homes hold their value best when there is a strong visual and physical connection with the outdoors. A visual connection can be as simple as a well-placed window that frames a beautiful tree in the backyard or living room windows overlooking a nice streetscape. Visual connections to the outdoors make a home feel larger, by borrowing space from outside and bringing it into the house.

A physical connection to the outdoors is one of the most-valued design elements in a home today. This connection can be in the form of a front porch or a garden terrace easily accessed through French doors or retracting glass walls. As you look at potential homes, note the flow between inside and out. If it isn't currently there, and everything else is right about the house, consider if this is something you might want to change later.

9. Tall Ceilings, Within Reason

As energy prices soar, ceilings are coming down. Double-height ceilings in foyers and great rooms are among the least likely features that builders are including in new homes. Look for more modest nine- and ten-foot ceilings in public rooms in the home's first floor, such as the living and dining rooms, and the kitchen. This gives good height while being reasonable to heat and cool and eliminates the need for a giant ladder to clean the cobwebs from those upper corners. Nine-foot ceilings on the second floor are best, if available, since eight feet in bedrooms can feel very low. Smaller rooms, alcoves, and nooks feel cozy if they have lower ceilings—eight feet, or even seven—to make the spaces feel a little more intimate. These areas might include powder rooms, dining alcoves, and reading nooks. Varied ceiling heights can help define and reinforce the hierarchy of rooms.

Note that you can lower ceilings as part of a remodeling project. Dropped ceilings have negative connotations in many people's minds, probably because they imagine drab foam tiles. But dropped ceilings can take many forms, including beams to define rooms or a lowered drywall ceiling in a corridor to visually expand the two rooms on either end.

10. Overall Character—Use Common Sense

Like beauty, character is often in the eye of the beholder. The ornamental moldings that appear elegant to one person may seem excessive to another. This subjectivity becomes even more pronounced with color. The beige and taupe tones that some people find so refined are downright dull to others. As I introduced in Chapter 11, architecture is a language, and with it comes a few dos and don'ts. Here are a couple to consider for the inside of the house.

Common sense should prevail. As you take in the architectural elements of a home, always ask yourself, Could that work? I gave the example earlier of window shutters that could never close, or if they did, would not actually cover the windows. This type of grammatical error can occur indoors as well, for example in the form of columns that are too slight for the opening that they're supposedly supporting, which gives the impression that they could snap at any moment. In both examples, the result is a design that gives the home a lack of genuineness.

Keep it simple. Less really is more when it comes to cultivating character. Well-placed moldings and trim work can add incredible value to a home. But take care with moldings, since it's easy for them to get a little out of hand. Unless you are looking at a home on the Historic Register, moldings for the sake of moldings can date a house quickly.

11. Flexibility to Adapt

The changing makeup of American households puts a premium on adaptability. Some will need to house a grown child or elderly parent. Others might rent out a room to offset the mortgage. Adaptable features of a home include a suite that can be included in or cut off from the flow of the house, depending on needs, or a basement apartment that has private access.

The physical makeup of your household is just one variable that might require your home to adapt. In other cases, you may need your home to adapt to the physical conditions of someone in your family. As our population ages, there is a good chance that you, someone in your household, or a visiting guest will be confronted

> ❝ **The changing makeup of American households puts a premium on adaptability.** ❞

with some sort of physical disability. Although this may be a temporary need for some, for others, especially those aging in place, these adjustments will be permanent. If you are planning to grow old in this home or have an elderly parent who will visit, look for convertible spaces that can take on more than one role, such as a home office with a full bath that could be converted into a guest room or even a caregiver's room. (See more advice and tips for Universal Design Checklist on the next page.)

Let There Be Light, and Lots of It

HOW A HOME'S PHYSICAL ORIENTATION AFFECTS NATURAL LGHT

Sunlight is an essential feature of any home. Everything else might work on paper, but if the house is dark and gloomy, your live-in value will be compromised. Proper orientation of the home is vital, because it determines the quantity and quality of natural light entering the home. If you're building a new home, you'll be able to work with your architect and builder to capture the right balance of light and shadow through site planning, room placement, and window design. They can even create computer renderings showing how the sunlight will interact with a home on any given day of the year.

If you're buying or renting an existing home, it's a matter of knowing what to look for. The best way to assess a home's solar orientation is to visit it at various times throughout the day, preferably when it's sunny out. The rising and setting sun will help you quickly determine the east- and west-facing elevations. I also recommend carrying a compass (most smartphones are equipped with one) in case it's cloudy out or you arrive in the middle of the day.

Universal Design Checklist

If you are aging or have a physical disability, you might need to adjust your home to accommodate special needs. Here are some steps to consider:

• Put down floors with a nonslip surface, such as textured stone or linoleum, to prevent the risk of falls, which goes way up with age.

• Create counters at multiple heights in the kitchen so that you have the option to sit or stand when preparing meals.

• Change doorknobs to lever-style handles, and swap out knobs for handles on kitchen and bathroom cabinets.

• Increase the amount of light in the home, including task lighting and general room illumination.

• Install comfort-height toilets, which are seventeen to nineteen inches off the ground. The extra few inches of height puts less stress on the back and knees when you're getting on and off.

• Put grab bars in the shower during a bathroom renovation, or at least include the framing necessary for installation, which you can do at a later date.

• Make the doors at least thirty-four inches wide and eliminate thresholds between rooms to eliminate trip hazards and facilitate movement with a wheelchair or walker.

• Install remote controls for blinds and window coverings, as well as lights.

• Look for a clear five-foot-wide area in the kitchen big enough for a wheelchair to turn around in.

• Look for at least twelve to eighteen inches of clearance next to the handle side of doors to make them easier to open.

• Plan for showers with a curbless entry (*zero threshold* is the technical term) to minimize tripping or to make accessible in a wheelchair.

Once you've established the orientation of the home from the exterior, you'll be able to determine if the interior rooms are placed in such a way that each space receives ample light at the appropriate time for the activities that occur there. Here's a quick checklist of what to look for:

East-facing bedrooms and breakfast area. Even if you don't get up at the crack of dawn, it's nice if the bedrooms face east, since our body clocks function best when they're in tune with the circadian rhythms of night and day. A sun-filled breakfast room will allow you to start your day in the early-morning warmth.

South-facing living areas. By noon, the midday sun will be striking the south face of the home. Rooms that will see activity at this time, such as family and living rooms, are ideal to have oriented in this direction. Protect windows in warmer climates with deep overhangs or awnings to minimize heat gain while still allowing natural light to filter in.

North-facing service areas. This side of the house is always dark, cool, and damp, so it's best suited to utility spaces, such as bathrooms, mudrooms, and laundry rooms.

West-facing views. The west side of the house is often the hardest to design, since the buildup of heat is often intense. If the home has a pleasant view, adding a porch (open or screened-in) on the west-facing elevation is one solution. A dining room that will be used mostly in the evening is another option.

CHAPTER CHEAT SHEET

Gut Check

Have you focused on the experience this home will provide, rather than going strictly by numbers like square feet and number of bedrooms?

Reality Check

Are your housing desires realistic? How do you balance the available options with your preferences?

Balancing Act

Function—What needs does your home need to accommodate now and in the future? Additional or fewer people? Physical disabilities? *Cost*—Will you be able to furnish the home with your current collection? Will you need to part with some pieces? Will you need to invest in several more pieces? *Delight*—Have you experienced the home at various times of the day, ensuring that natural light is entering the right rooms at the right times of day, such as eastern light in the majority of bedrooms and breakfast area?

Key points to remember

• Moving to a new house is the ideal time to take stock of your life and see if you have negative habits that you've fallen into because of the design of your home, such as eating in the living room because there's no comfortable eating area in the kitchen.

• Not all square feet are created equal, meaning a home that measures several thousand square feet might feel smaller than a home that's half the size but smartly designed.

• Natural light is essential to a positive living experience, but ideally you want the home to be oriented in such a way that the light pours into the right rooms at the right time of day. East-facing bedrooms and south-facing living areas are best.

Chapter 14

The Rooms and Finishes of Your Home

Most people start their search for a new home based on the number of rooms and the quality of the countertops, floors, and other surfaces. But there is a reason why, in a book about deciding where to live, I thought there were thirteen chapters that needed to come first. The layout of your home, the type and configuration of rooms, and the materials and finishes are elements you will encounter daily. But to find the home that fits your needs, you need to look at and prioritize all of life's variables, including budget, commute, and neighborhood.

I do encourage jumping around in this book, but if you've flipped right to this chapter, I would strongly suggest taking the time to read Chapter 4 about understanding your preferences and Chapter 13, which helps you assess how you want to use the spaces in a home. Remember, the number of rooms in a house is less important than how well you use the ones you have.

All right, now for the fun part! Let's take the tour and look at the finishes!

Your Room-by-Room Tour

TAKING THE GUIDED ROOM-BY-ROOM HOME TOUR

By the time you reach this point in the process, you will already be balancing a number of variables, including neighborhood and street selections. Every home is different, and our individual needs vary too. As you read this section, look for the elements that matter most to you. It will probably not be possible to get everything you want in a house. The key always is to identify the one or two things that really matter and make those your priority.

The Foyer As you pass through the front door, look for a feeling of arrival. This doesn't mean a double-height foyer centered on a grand Scarlett O'Hara staircase (see the section on tall ceilings in Chapter 13 for the reason why). It just means you want to feel like you are home. If you are in a colder climate, you will want to enter into a foyer or vestibule that creates a weather block from the main living areas. In warmer southern climates, it is common to enter directly into the living room.

The front door may not be your everyday entrance, but it's where guests come and go, so a few simple appointments will go a long way toward making them feel welcome, say a mirror to check themselves (and yourself of course!) and a shelf or small table on which to set a bag. Of course, you can add these later, but make sure there's room to accommodate them. In terms of space, four to five feet is the ideal diameter in which people can comfortably remove their coats.

As I mentioned in Chapter 13, pay attention to what is in the direct line of sight upon entering the house. You don't want to walk in the front door and look straight down the hall to the head of the master bed. Make sure there is a clear division between public and private in case you forget to make your bed one morning.

Living Areas: Living Rooms, Family Rooms, and Great Rooms In older homes, you might find a formal living room to one side of the foyer and a formal dining room to the other. This subdivided floor plan survived into the 1980s, when a backlash against chopped-up living spaces gave rise to the great room, which put the kitchen, dining, and living areas in one large space. Open is great; just watch out for rooms that are awkward to furnish or that lack definition altogether. If you are watching TV in the evening, can you do so without having a direct line of sight to the dishes waiting for you in the sink? If possible, look for open yet defined plans.

Key Recommendation: Look for living areas that have a direct connection to the outdoors, either visible or physical. In a traditional neighborhood, this will create the eyes-on-the-street effect that makes streets safer. It also makes an interior space live much larger, maximizing live-in value.

Your First Walk-Through

Don't think too much during your first walk-through of a home. Let yourself feel the space and react positively or negatively to it. If you really don't like it, don't even bother with a second look, since that kind of negative sentiment seldom reverses course. But if your feelings run anywhere from lukewarm to absolute love, you should do another walk-through while looking in more detail, always keeping in mind your balancing act: function, cost, and delight.

Dining Areas The number and type of required dining areas will vary greatly, depending on the size of your family and your lifestyle. If you are a couple or a larger family, you may want to have at least two places in your home to eat. These include an informal easy-access place for breakfast or low-key dinners, such as a nook or kitchen island, and a more formal area for entertaining and larger gatherings. When looking at the dining areas in a home, think about how you eat most meals. Do you eat as a family, and if so, how many are eating together? How often do you entertain? Remember, a dining room table can be used as a homework station or desk on a daily basis if you don't have big meals every night. This is a great example of a part of the house that can serve double duty.

The Kitchen The kitchen is the heart of the home and, short of a sci-fi world where people get their nourishment from little pills, it always will be. Even if you don't like to cook, you'll probably gravitate first to a potential home's kitchen. It's the room that sells the house, more than any other. But it's also one of the hardest to properly assess, because it's a complicated space with many moving parts. There's also a lot of status symbolization happening in this space, such that if you see a Sub-Zero fridge or granite counters, you might assume you're in a top-tier kitchen, when in fact there might be all sorts of problems. Here are a few tips to help you judge a kitchen's potential.

Focus first on a functional layout. That starts with an efficient floor plan in which the refrigerator, sink, and range form the three points of the work triangle. Can you reach the sink from the stove (with a full pot of boiling water) without taking more than a couple of steps? An island or peninsula countertop is a huge bonus, since it provides additional work surface, storage space, and room for seating. Ample cabinetry is another essential, especially in homes where the kitchen opens onto an adjacent living space, since that means one less wall to line with cabinets. A walk-in pantry (even a smaller closet variety) is an excellent source of auxiliary storage space. It is ideal to have some sort of informal eating area, such as a couple of seats at a peninsula or island.

Check out the appliances. As I alluded to above, it's easy to be blinded by the high shine of a suite of professional-grade, stainless-steel appliances. But many conventional models perform just as well, if

> **Fast Fact** A major kitchen remodel, including replacing the major appliances, cabinets, countertops, and flooring, as well as adding a new island counter, will cost an average of $60,000, and could run much higher if you opt for custom cabinetry and high-end fixtures and finishes. You can do the project for $20,000 or less if you refinish rather than replace the cabinets, choose midpriced appliances, and keep the existing floors and floor plan.

not better. The key is to ensure that the appliances are arranged in an efficient layout and that they're in good working order. Check the manufacturer's label inside the appliance to determine when the unit was built and if it's reaching the end of its life (see Kitchen Appliance Life Expectancies below). You can also take down the model numbers and see how the appliances are reviewed on consumer websites.

Kitchen Appliance Life Expectancies

Appliance	Life Expectancy in Years
Compactors	6
Dishwashers	9
Disposals, Food Waste	12
Freezers	11
Microwave Ovens	9
Ranges, Electric	13
Ranges, Gas	15
Range/Oven Hoods	14
Refrigerators, Standard	13

Consider the style. Reconfiguring the layout and upgrading the appliances are major projects that together could take months and cost tens of thousands of dollars, especially if you're moving walls and relocating plumbing lines. But a fairly simple and inexpensive cosmetic makeover can give a kitchen a brand-new look. As you tour the kitchen, think about how the walls might be repainted to bring in a different color. You might also be able to refinish the cabinets, lay down new floors, or swap out the countertops—a simple remodel. Just about any surface in the kitchen will be fair game, provided the layout is sound and all the major parts are in good shape.

Key Recommendation: There needs to be at least forty-two inches between the island and surrounding cabinets and appliances to maintain traffic flow in the kitchen. This is especially important if you're in a two-cook household. I've been told about couples whose marriage was practically pushed to the brink by too many run-ins in the kitchen.

Home Offices and Charging Centers Once upon a time, the library or study provided an elegant retreat from the hustle and bustle of the rest of the house. Over time as more and more people began telecommuting, the home office evolved to house large desktop computers and printers attached with cords. Today, laptops and tablets are revolutionizing how we live in our homes. It is no longer necessary to have a room dedicated as the home office since today's technology allows us to work from any room in the house. As you consider the type of space—whether room, alcove, or desk—determine how much storage is required for paper files and office supplies. Consider a location for your printer and a charging center to manage cords. Are there areas of the house that can support these needs without having to dedicate a private room for them?

The Mudroom–Drop Zone The importance of a mudroom will vary by region, but regardless of where you live, you'll want to plan for where you drop your keys when you come in and out of your house. In four-season climates, where mud, ice, snow, and other elements are a fact of life, a dedicated room is a nice luxury, but not a necessity if the design of the home accommodates this need in other ways, such as a hallway with shelves and cubbies. Often this area is a transition zone from the side or back entrance that you'll likely use most frequently. You often hear mudrooms referred to as "owner's entries" for that reason.

Whatever the name or the exact location, the success of this space is all about its appointments. Look for hard-wearing flooring. Stone tile and textured rubber are two good options. Storage is also key. In a large household with lots of active kids, cubbies and bins are useful. Look for a place for hooks for coats, keys, pet leashes, and the like, as well as for shoes and boots. Lastly, if you are in a colder climate, it is nice to have a sturdy bench or stool to sit on while putting on and pulling off shoes.

Although it is nice when a house comes fitted out with built-ins and cabinets in the mudroom, don't pass up a home because they are missing. During your walk-through, look at the area by the back door or coming in from the garage and see if there is room to add these features. IKEA offers affordable cabinets that you can install easily after you move in.

The Master Bedroom Traditionally, viewing the master bedroom during a home tour would have meant a trip upstairs. But the master bedroom on the main floor, also known as "master-on-main," is one of the features most likely to be included in new homes in 2015, according to a National Association of Home Builders' survey. The ground-floor location has obvious advantages for older people who may experience trouble climbing stairs. Many younger families still prefer a second-floor master bedroom that's closer to the kids' rooms and away from the main living area.

> **Regardless of its location in the house, look for a master bedroom that feels separate from the public parts of the house.**

Regardless of its location in the house, look for a master bedroom that feels separate from the public parts of the house. Pay particular attention to this with homes where the entrance into the master is off one of the public rooms. In these cases, look for homes with clever doorway arrangements that limit the visibility. Especially take care to limit lines of sight from public rooms to the master closet and of course the master bathroom. I recently walked through a spec house that a builder was having trouble selling. When I arrived at the kitchen island, I was looking directly into the master closet. This was a massive violation of the public-to-private divide. The kitchen island is the single most-trafficked part of your home, especially when you have guests. No matter how organized and tidy you might be, you don't want your guests looking at your dirty laundry.

Large bedrooms are a luxury, but not a necessity for most. Some of the most successful master suites are actually quite modest in size: twelve by fourteen feet is a good base dimension, enough to fit a king-size bed, dresser, and chair, perhaps with alcoves off to the side for a sitting area or small office.

Key Recommendation: Make sure that you can identify at least the bed wall in your potential master bedroom. Try to avoid bed locations on walls shared with children's bedrooms. It is ideal to have room for a dresser opposite the bed. And most important, stand where the master bed will go and make sure that you don't have a direct line of sight to the master toilet. In most cases you will have a line of sight into at least some part of the bathroom, but you don't want it to be the toilet.

The Master Closet An ample, organized closet can make the difference between a cluttered mess and peace of mind. It's one of those spaces that you'll interact with every day. Besides helping to preserve your clothes by keeping them off the floor or backs of chairs, a well-appointed closet will prevent daily frustrations as you search for misplaced garments and accessories. If you have the means, hiring a professional to install a closet system is money well spent. I know people who make this their very first order when they move into a new home.

> **If a full built-in closet is not in the cards, you can greatly enhance the single rod that's found in most closets with store-bought storage systems.**

If a full built-in closet is not in the cards, you can greatly enhance the single rod that's found in most closets with store-bought storage systems. For example, installing a second shelf above the existing rod-and-shelf activates otherwise wasted airspace, and can serve as a place to store off-season apparel. This

The Rise and Fall of the Roman ~~Empire~~ Tub

Inspired by Roman baths of old, the Roman tub was supposed to be the ultimate luxury, a spacious vessel with massaging jets delivering a total, spalike experience. Builders started making it a default option in just about every master bathroom (even in starter-sized homes), and in an oddly forced evolution, real estate agents turned it into a necessity. The Roman tub is a symbol of the hostage standoff I mentioned earlier in the book. Builders were told they had to include it to make a sale, homeowners thought they had to have it to make the house worth a resale, and real estate agents were in the middle of the mix, keeping it going. Yet, despite all of this effort, most of these tubs are rarely, if ever, used and spend most of the time filled with damp towels and dirty laundry. The Roman tub can easily add $5,000 to the cost of a home, so determine if this amenity is worth it to you or if you'd like to spend your money elsewhere in the house. Bottom line: Buy the house that you want to buy. Have in your home the things that you want. Don't allow yourself to be pressured into something just because you "need it to resell."

advice applies to owners and renters alike, given the minimal costs. If you are renting, you might still ask your landlord to chip in a few bucks, since the improvements will help attract future tenants.

The Master Bathroom Master baths are one area where we are seeing a major shift in consumer preference in recent years as people downsize into smaller homes. Less space with nice finishes has become more important than palatial elements such as columns. Although one size doesn't fit all, most people are happy with a three-by-five-foot shower fitted with a powerful showerhead (be sure to turn on fixtures when touring a home). Most people prefer that the toilet be tucked away for as much privacy as possible. A double vanity is also nice for couples, but depending on the available space, consider trading a double vanity for a single vanity with more counter space.

Space for linens in the bathroom is a nice luxury, though if the room isn't well ventilated with a ceiling fan, you may find that towels take on a mildew smell.

If you are looking at a home with old fixtures or that is badly planned, you can learn to live with it or consider a bathroom remodel. Prices range from a couple of thousand for a new vanity to around $15,000 for the entire bathroom.

Secondary Bedrooms The number and size of secondary bedrooms depends on the size of your household. But even if you're single or child-free, it is nice to have a guest room or home office if space allows. If the secondary bedroom will be occupied full time by children, try to make sure they're separated from the master suite by some other space, be it a hallway, a second bathroom, or even a closet. This physical separation is important to maintain privacy for everyone in the home. If you cannot have a private conversation with the door shut, you'll never feel comfortable in that home. You might even consider soundproofing the bedrooms with insulation.

Although ten by twelve feet is the rule of thumb for secondary bedrooms, most kids will be happy with any space that they can call their own. Even an eight-foot-wide room might suffice, provided there's room to fit a bed and dresser.

Secondary Bathrooms If you have kids, you will most likely find that a second bathroom is a necessity, not a luxury. It is nice to have a direct connection between the secondary bedrooms and the bathroom when possible so you don't have to go out in the hall to go to the bathroom. There should be a standard bathtub somewhere in the home, and the secondary bathroom is usually the best candidate.

Powder Room The powder room is the half bath on your main living floor for guests. In homes where all the bedrooms are on the same floor, the guest bath can be shared with one of the bedrooms, but you will want to have an entrance from the hall so your guests don't have to pass through someone's private space. Nor should a guest bath be accessed directly off the living and dining rooms. It's too exposed while entertaining, and it feels unsanitary if it's located directly off the kitchen.

What's In, What's Out

We are witnessing a changing of the guard in terms of standard design elements most commonly found in new homes. If you are considering a home built before 1995, you might find that many of the "new" trends are actually already included! Here is a list of what is "in" and what is "out."

Out	In
Pro-style appliances	Double-duty appliances like double oven ranges
Roman tubs	Large showers
Three-car garages	Two-car and one-car garages—even detached garages are making a comeback.
Dark iron or rubbed bronze hardware and fixtures	Polished chrome or nickel finishes for hardware and fixtures
Granite	Any number of alternatives such as laminate, which is more affordable, as well as solid surfaces or quartz, which are more durable
Outdoor fireplaces and outdoor kitchens	Connection to the outdoors from inside the house
Light-stained oak kitchen cabinets	Painted cabinets, often white, or dark stained
Front-loaded washers	Top-loaded washers, without the agitator

WORDS OF WISDOM

"It's easy to get swept up in the romantic aspects of a house (the tub! the beautiful entryway! three fireplaces!). It's far more important to focus on the practical needs of a home. Good use of space (bed fits in bedroom), layout (laundry room upstairs where most of the laundry is generated), well-insulated (heating bills manageable), good water pressure (ability to run dishwasher while kids shower), etc. All of these things are so much more important and can so easily be overlooked." Amy P., Colorado Springs, CO

Laundry Room The ideal location of the laundry depends on the overall layout of the home. When the master bedroom is on the first floor, many people like the laundry to be there as well, so they don't have to carry clothes up and down the stairs. When the home houses a larger family with children, a second-floor laundry room is advantageous. In homes with a basement, the laundry room can be there to free up space in the main house, but this can be a hassle because you have to carry the clothes up and down the stairs (unless there's a laundry chute, which helps get the clothes down).

Regardless of the location, walk-in laundry rooms are ideal since they create room for folding and hanging clothes. As with kitchen appliances, check the age and condition of the home's washer and dryer. It could cost you more than $1,000 to replace the pair, though you'll benefit from a lot of new technologies, including high-efficiency washers that use less water and energy. Washing machines have a life expectancy of about ten years, dryers about thirteen. The newest development in washers are large top-loaded washers without the central agitator. This allows the full drum size of a front-load machine, but it is much easier to transfer clothes to the dryer. It also provides a lower top surface to be available for folding.

Materials and Finishes

ASSESSING THE MATERIALS AND FINISHES

This book is not meant to be a guide to the latest and greatest materials and finishes in a home. There are plenty of interior design magazines on the rack to satisfy that itch. But I do want to go over a few of the basics, since a home's surfaces fall into that category of features you'll interact with on a daily basis. Whether it's the softness underfoot of the proper kitchen flooring or the implied permanence of a stone countertop, the right materials can make a big difference in the overall form and function of a home.

The slant of this section assumes some measure of tabula rasa, since surfaces are fairly easy to replace as part of a cosmetic remodel, but use it also as you assess the existing materials in any potential new home. Before going over some of the most common options, let me share three rules of thumb to keep you on track.

Follow the hierarchy of importance. Always strive for the best surfaces you can afford. Wall-to-wall hardwood or natural stone might be out of your budget, but that doesn't mean you should settle for a home filled with vinyl. The trick is to balance your budget smartly, spending more in rooms that have a strong visual presence (the open dining-living area, for example) and less in secondary spaces (say the guest bedroom).

Forget about trend spotting—stainless steel is tomorrow's harvest gold. If you're old enough to remember avocado and harvest gold, you know that every appliance finish has its day in the sun. We're in the midst of a prolonged age of stainless steel, which is starting to show signs of abating. Don't rule out white or black appliances, if they better suit the style and color scheme of the kitchen. Similarly, granite countertops have been de rigueur for the last decade or more, but there are other materials that may be more appropriate to your budget and aesthetics.

Keep a clippings folder. Between floors, countertops, and finishes for fixtures and appliances, there are dozens upon dozens of surface options out there. That's why it's really important to keep a folder of ones you like. Divide it by rooms, and stock each section with pictures from magazines and websites as well as actual samples when possible. It's likely to grow pretty thick over time, so you may want to go with a three-ring binder or other expandable system. Open a Pinterest account or download Houzz's free smartphone app to maintain a digital clippings folder of inspiring images.

MATERIALS CHEAT SHEET

Here's a rundown of the most common surfaces in the home, including pros and cons.

Flooring

Solid Wood This all-natural material conveys warmth and beauty. It comes in a variety of species, from open-grained oak to tight-grained mahogany and can be sanded and refinished. It can be expensive and is prone to denting. From $5 to $10 per square foot, installed.

Engineered or Laminate Wood Consisting of a veneer of natural wood over a manufactured substrate, this flooring is easier to install than solid wood and often less expensive, though it can't be refinished over and over. There is a wide range of prices and quality. Watch out for the lower grades of laminate flooring, which can have a hollow sound when walked on. From $3 to $9 per square foot, installed.

Natural Stone Available in marble, slate, limestone, travertine, and more, natural stone is beautiful and long lasting, though it's also the most expensive option in flooring. Take into account that stone can be hard on the legs and back in locations where you do a lot of standing, like the kitchen. From $10 to $50 per square foot, installed.

Ceramic Tile Comes in a wide range of styles, colors, and price points, most of which stand up well to most forms of abuse in kitchens and other busy areas. The downside is that it can crack if heavy items are dropped on it, and you can get grout stains. Look for the tightest joints possible. From $8 to $15 per square foot, installed.

Vinyl This synthetic material is inexpensive, easy to install, fairly hard-wearing, and soft underfoot. It can have a shiny sheen and smell like plastic. It will never look as good as natural stone or wood, though some of the newest products come close. From $2 to $6 per square foot, installed.

Linoleum Made from linseed oil, resins, cork, and other organic materials, linoleum is a natural product that has much of the resilience of vinyl with lots of design choices, though it's not quite as hard-wearing. From $4 to $9 per square foot, installed.

Carpet The softest of all flooring materials, especially if you choose a plush fiber. Prone to dirt and stains. If your budget is limited, you might carpet the bedrooms and use engineered wood in the public rooms of the house. From $4 to $7 per square foot, installed.

Countertops

Granite Still the favorite in high-end kitchens, granite is stain- and heat-resistant and comes in a wide range of colors and patterns. But it's pricey, and most varieties need to be resealed to prevent staining. From $40 to $100 per square foot, installed.

Natural Stone Soapstone and marble are also popular stone countertops for kitchen and bathrooms. But they need to be cared for properly, including sealing regularly. From $50 to $150 per square foot, installed.

Quartz Technically an engineered product made with quartz and some synthetic resins, quartz can look like natural stone, though it also comes in vibrant colors. It's as durable as granite without the need for sealing, though it will never look totally natural. From $50 to $100 per square, foot installed.

Laminate Think Formica, with its wide variety of colors and patterns, all at an affordable price. New versions are available that scratch and stain less, also without the black seams. From $10 to $30 per square foot, installed. You won't want to put a hot pan down on your laminate counter, but if budget is a major issue, you can work around this with the purchase of some hot pads.

Tile Whether ceramic or porcelain, countertop tile comes in a variety of sizes, styles, and colors, and it's heat-resistant, making it a good option near stoves. The biggest problem is the staining that inevitably mars its grout lines. From $10 to $30 per square foot, installed.

Solid Surfacing This synthetic material is available in any style, and it's seamless. Dupont's Corian is the best-known brand, though there are other manufacturers. The material scratches easily, one reason why you see it in bathrooms more than kitchens. From $35 to $100 per square foot, installed.

Wood Typically in the form of butcher block, wood confers a country feel, and it's great for cutting up produce and other germ-free foods (i.e., not meat). It will definitely show marks though, so you have to be okay with that. From $30 to $60 per square foot, installed.

Concrete This poured-in-place material can be dyed any color and has a uniqueness that can be quite visually compelling. But it must be installed properly or serious cracking can occur, and sealing is required. From $80 to $120 per square foot, installed.

CHAPTER CHEAT SHEET

Gut Check

What are the three visual components that you can't compromise on?

Reality Check

Are you clear about which rooms in a home you absolutely need, which you'd like to have, and which are likely to sit empty or unused? Are the rooms furnishable? Of the elements and finishes that you want, which ones do you really need?

Balancing Act

Function—Does the home live larger than its dimensions suggest by connecting well with the outdoors, not just its immediate yard, but also the neighborhood beyond? *Cost*—Can you afford the home you are considering? Do you need this much home, or would you be happier in a smaller home with smaller monthly expenses? *Delight*—What is the most important element in your potential new home? Have you experienced the home at various times of the day, ensuring that natural light is entering the right rooms at the right times of day, for example eastern light in the majority of bedrooms and the breakfast area?

Key points to remember

• The features that sell a home are often different from the ones that make it a pleasing and positive place to live over the long haul.

• Logic and spatial hierarchy, which make it easy to move from one room to the next, are the guiding forces of any successful floor plan.

• Look for value in the elements of the home that you will interact with on a daily basis, such as those surfaces you can touch and feel.

Part 3: Deciding and Moving In

Chapter 15

Making Your Decision

I love waking up the first morning in a new home. Exhausted by the move and surrounded by boxes, I am filled with anticipation and relief. I can't wait to see how the sunlight will enter my new bedroom. Sometimes, I'm a little nervous about starting a new routine, but I am always relieved to be finished with the uncertainties of searching and the stress of physically moving. Getting to this first morning is no small accomplishment, regardless of whether you are moving down the hall or across the country: It feels great.

If you are entering the decision phase of your search, you might feel overwhelmed, wondering if that first morning will ever arrive. The good news is that anxiety evaporates when you have a clear understanding of your priorities and your range of options. The goal of this book is to help you assess how you want to live, learn all of the options, and know how to search, so that you will have confidence when the time comes to decide.

In Parts 1 and 2 we explored preparing and searching for where you want to live. Now, in Part 3, we will look at the variables you need to consider when making your final decision and beyond. We will explore the condition of the home, energy efficiency, renovating options, and how to work with professionals to make it all happen.

Narrowing Down the Finalists

The best decisions in life result from a balance of education and instinct. Essentially, you need to be as informed as you can, but in the end you should follow your gut. As we discussed in Chapter 4, very often our decisions are guided by the presentation of options or assumed default mind-sets. Don't let perceptions or the need to impress "the Joneses" derail your decision-making process. Make sure your decisions meet your needs.

In the searching phase, you want to look at every viable option, even if they aren't all perfect. This will give you a good understanding of comparable properties and the full range of choices. You will be naturally drawn to some homes and easily eliminate others. Now, as you enter the deciding phase, it is time to assess your short list and narrow it down to a finalist by frequently checking back in with your *priorities* and listening to your *instincts*.

QUIZ: DECIDING ON YOUR PRIORITIES

Your Priorities

Throughout Part 2 you were asked to consider a series of questions about how and where you want to live. Each chapter looked at these questions through the lens of its content: regions, city, neighborhood, street, building type, property type, outside your house, and inside your house. Now it's time to pull everything together and look at these questions in the context of one another.

1. What are the three most important elements inside your home?

2. What are the three most important elements of a neighborhood and community?

3. What are the visuals you want to see daily? What do you want to see when you look out of your house? What do you want to see when you travel to and from work?

4. What are your proximity priorities?

5. Of all the priorities you are balancing, which are the three most important?

6. Of all the priorities you are balancing, which are the three least important?

Your Family Unit

1. How does each member of your family feel about the questions above?

2. Are there elements that everyone agrees on?

3. Are there elements that you disagree on?

4. How might you balance trade-offs to meet everyone's needs?

Your Short List

1. How do the homes on your short list meet your top priorities?

2. Do these homes fit into your long-term financial plan?

Gut Check

Listen to your instincts. Your priorities will create your road map and streamline the available options into a short list. The best way to narrow down your short list to one or two finalists is to follow your instincts. When you really listen to your gut, you will always make the right decisions. Consider these questions:

1. Which option feels right?

2. Can you see yourself living here? If so, for how long?

3. What are the pros and cons?

4. Does this home meet both short-term and long-term needs?

5. How does each member of the family feel?

6. Are you choosing this option for you or to impress your friends/family/colleagues?

Reality Check

Understanding your priorities, wants, and needs is crucial, but so is being honest with your realities. Consider these questions:

1. Can you afford this home and still afford to both live a comfortable life and save for the future?

2. How secure is your job? If you lose your job, can you find work in this city and maintain this home?

3. Is the value of the home worth what you are about to pay?

4. If the value of the home dropped, would you be happy and able to continue to live here for the foreseeable future?

5. Is your financial plan sustainable?

WORDS OF WISDOM

"I was stuck, didn't know where to go after downsizing from our big family home. A cousin suggested a small bucolic village closer to family and surrounded by gorgeous farmland. I wanted to find a tiny piece of land and build a very green modern house, but ended up falling for a vintage charmer right in the village. Now I can walk daily to get the newspaper and coffee, go to a Pilates studio, hit the library, and just see friendly faces. It was a huge gamble but has brought big rewards. I love living in a little village for the first time in my life; the biggest problem is that so many want to come and visit—and stay!" Barbara E., Rhinebeck, NY

> **Fast Fact** Days on Market, or DOM, refers to the number of days between the day a property is first listed and the day a sales contract is signed. A market is generally considered strong if the DOM is less than 50 and weak if it is 100 or higher. Keep in mind that the DOM for an individual property will typically reset if the owner decides to list it with a different real estate agent.

THE FINALIST(S)

How is your list looking? Remember that narrowing your search is a back-and-forth process. As you take a closer look at your options, you might find that none of them are right, forcing you to start over. Try not to get discouraged if that happens. The housing market is fluid. New options come on the market every day, so if you have the time, waiting for the right fit is better than settling. At the same time, if you have your eye on something that could be right, know that someone else might be considering it too. How you balance a fluid market will depend on how hot the real estate is in your area. Check online to see how long the property in question has been listed. See if the price has been dropped, and look at the average time on the market for comparable homes. In a slow market, you have all the time in the world, but hot markets require faster action.

Vetting the Finalists

As you develop your list of finalists, you need to get a firm handle on how much your prospective new home will cost to operate and maintain. This covers four basic categories:

Durability: The condition of the home and the cost to maintain it.

Energy Efficiency: How much the home will cost to operate.

Safety: What health-related concerns might be lurking in the home?

Assessing Potential Changes: Move in as is, cosmetic changes, or renovations?

UNDERSTANDING THE CONDITION AND PERFORMANCE

Chapters 16 and 17 explore in depth the questions you need to ask and red flags to look for when determining the condition and performance of a prospective home. Don't make a move without reading these chapters first. Just about anything is manageable and fixable, but you'll want to go in with your eyes wide open and a clear understanding of the time, energy, and budget needed to operate, maintain, and live in any home.

PLANNING FOR CHANGES

As you get a full picture of the condition of a potential home, you might consider simple cosmetic changes or even a larger renovation. Chapter 18 discusses tips and suggestions for renovating your home. If you are looking at a home that will require a lot of changes to fit your needs, give careful consideration to the time and money it will take to upgrade. This could be the best way to make the ideal out of the available, but if you aren't realistic about your means and capabilities, you can easily get in over your head.

Fast Fact Between the years 1997 and 2007, nearly two thirds of sellers over the age of seventy-five had been living in their home for twenty years or more, and the figure for those sixty-five to seventy-four was 39 percent, according to Harvard University's Joint Center for Housing Studies. Not surprisingly, remodeling costs are higher on homes bought from older owners, though it's also true that the older the seller, the lower the value of the home. Bottom line: You can probably get a good deal on a home being sold by an older owner, though you'll need to be willing to take on some serious renovations.

CONSIDERING STAYING PUT?

Sometimes you can search and search for the perfect home only to realize you were living there all along. Or perhaps you are dreaming of a new home, but the realities of life mean a move is not in the cards right now. If you decide to stay put, this isn't the end of your decision-making process. Consider the changes and renovation suggestions in Chapter 18. Your dream home might be a lot closer to home than you think.

COMMUNITY RENOVATIONS

Changing cabinets and adding a room are two types of renovations, but so are adding sidewalks and planting street trees. Renovations don't have to end at your property line. If you love your home but wish your neighborhood were better, look at the suggestions outlined in Chapter 18 for renovating your community.

CHAPTER CHEAT SHEET

Gut Check

Does the home you are deciding on feel right?

Reality Check

Does it work for your life and budget?

Balancing Act

Function—Does this home balance proximities and livability? *Cost*—Can you afford this home, both to purchase (or rent) and to maintain over time? *Delight*—Do you like this home?

Key point to remember

- Keep the big picture (city, neighborhood, and street) and details (house and yard) in mind while deciding on a home. And always keep your realistic budget in mind.

Chapter 16

Understanding the Condition of a Home

We require from buildings two kinds of goodness: first, doing their practical duty well: then that they be graceful and pleasing in doing it.
—John Ruskin

This book so far has largely been about a search for a graceful and pleasing home, one that balances your many needs. Before finalizing your decision, however, you also need to understand the overall condition of your potential home so that you can tell, to paraphrase John Ruskin, if the building will fulfill its practical duty.

The age of a home is not necessarily an indication of condition. A renovated and well-maintained house from 1920 might be in better shape, and more in keeping with current styles, than one from 2005 when, at the height of the construction boom, homes were being sold faster than they could be built and sometimes with shoddy products. As you narrow your list of potential finalists, taking the time to assess the condition of the home will give you a clear picture of how much it will cost to maintain and allow you to anticipate major replacements or renovations on the horizon.

Six Questions to Help Assess the Condition of a Home

Before you purchase a home, it's essential to have a professional inspection of the property. This will give you a detailed description of the home's condition. (See page 290.) Unfortunately, the home inspection happens pretty late in the process, meaning you could invest a lot of time and emotional energy falling in love with a home, only to be blindsided by the need for extensive repairs.

In advance of a professional inspection, here are six questions that will guide you in gaining an understanding of the condition of a potential home.

1. WHEN WAS THE HOUSE BUILT?

As noted previously, old doesn't necessarily mean poor condition, and new may not guarantee that everything is in sound working order. Having said that, it's nonetheless important to establish the age of the home as a baseline.

Here are a few red flags that will indicate the need for additional work if they have not already been updated:

Old wiring and electrical systems (especially pre-1970 homes) Oftentimes, the wiring in older homes isn't able to handle the electricity loads of modern appliances and electronic devices. That raises the risk of fires. Dimming lights and discolored electrical outlets are two sure signs that a home's system is ready for an upgrade. The project is not cheap, sometimes costing several thousand dollars or more, depending on the size of the house, but it's absolutely critical to making a home safe.

Lead paint (especially pre-1978 homes) The federal government banned lead-based paints in 1978, but it's still in more than 20 million housing units, according to the Centers for Disease Control and Prevention. Breathing lead dust, for example after it's been kicked up during renovation work, can cause damage to the brain and nervous system, especially in children. If you're considering an older home, you might want to make lead detection part of the inspection process.

Asbestos (especially in pre-1989 homes) This is a mineral fiber that was once used to provide heat insulation and fire resistance in various products, such as roof shingles, floor tiles, and siding materials. It was officially banned in 1989, though it was beginning to be phased out earlier. If you're looking at a home built between 1930 and 1950, there is a good chance asbestos was used as insulation. You should have this checked by a professional or ask if it has been fixed. In most cases, the materials can be encapsulated, rather than removed, keeping costs down, though it's still an expense of several hundred dollars.

Mold (all homes) An outbreak of mold spores in the home can trigger allergic reactions, asthma, and other respiratory complaints. Mold is often found in damp basements or other humid environments where spores can thrive. The use of exhaust fans and dehumidifiers can be enough to control the problem, though major outbreaks will require fairly intensive and costly remediation, especially if the mold has gotten into the walls of a home. Be cautious if you smell moldy odors or see water stains or discoloration on ceilings, walls, floors, or windowsills.

Boom-era homes (2000-2005) Homes built during the housing boom from 2000 to 2005 often suffer from very poor craftsmanship, leaks, and material failures. Make sure to check for signs of leaks. And pay close attention to the energy requirements to heat and cool these homes. (See more on this in Chapter 17.)

The Fifteen-Year Rule: Warranties, Life Cycle, and Aesthetics

A good rule of thumb to use when projecting potential renovation costs is the fifteen-year rule. Warranties for most major components in a home will last anywhere from ten to thirty years, and aesthetic styles cycle every fifteen years. That makes fifteen years a good rough estimate of when systems, appliances, and components will need upgrading.

2. HAS THE HOUSE BEEN RENOVATED, AND IF SO, WHEN?

Remodeled homes have both pros and cons. On the positive side, if you are looking at a home built before 1950 that hasn't been remodeled, it's almost guaranteed that you will need to invest substantial money in the coming years to update any number of components. In this case, finding a house with the renovations already complete can save you time and money. On the other hand, if you are looking at a home recently renovated and you don't like the renovations, you will be paying extra for work you might end up wanting to tear out and redo. Take note of when the renovations were completed and remember the fifteen-year rule when making plans. (See page 283.)

Additionally, give a little extra attention to the quality of the workmanship, especially if you are looking at a "fix and flip" job, where investors purchase a home at a low price, make minor repairs, and try to sell it for a profit. A red flag should go up immediately if the current owner who did the remodeling never actually lived in the house. Besides relying on inferior materials and workmanship, flip remodeling can also carry legal pitfalls if the investors didn't get all the necessary permits. You could be on the hook if these unsanctioned changes are discovered at a later date, say during a building inspection of a subsequent remodeling project.

3. WHAT IS THE TYPE AND THE CONDITION OF MATERIALS USED IN THE HOUSE?

In Chapters 11 and 14, we looked at the spectrum of materials common to most residences, inside and out. Take a moment to review these sections against the home you are considering. Look closely at the exterior materials and their condition, especially the type of roof and the year it was installed. Look at the interior finishes and consider if you will want to keep them; if not, start thinking of a budget for replacements.

As you look at the materials, keep in mind that there is a difference between low-maintenance and no-maintenance materials. Zero-maintenance materials are best the day they are installed. Every day after that is one day closer to replacement. As we enter an era of staying in our homes longer, remember, the long-term durability of your home matters more than ever.

4. IS IT A FIXER-UPPER OR A MONEY PIT?

If you're buying a home, chances are you'll need or want to do some work on it, either before you move in or soon afterward. On average, new homeowners spend between $4,000 and $7,500 in the first two years on home improvements, furnishings, and other upgrades. If the home needs more repairs, the expenses will go way up. But there is a huge difference between a fixer-upper and a money pit, so you need to know what you're up against. It is *very* easy to underestimate the amount of time, money, and effort that will be needed to update a home (see "Project Costs and Returns at a Glance," page 309), especially if it has other things going for it, like being in a great neighborhood and on a terrific block. A thorough home inspection (see page 290) should steer you away from potential money pits. But here are four general tips to ensure you don't fall for a home that will cost you much more than anticipated.

Distinguish between patent and latent defects. Patent defects are right out in the open, like large cracks in the walls and water stains on the ceiling. Latent defects are lurking beneath the surface, and might include termite damage, faulty wiring, or the presence of lead-based paint. A home can have one without the other, meaning all might appear well when in reality there are some very costly latent issues waiting to wreak havoc on your remodeling budget and schedule. An experienced home inspector will be able to catch both patent and latent defects.

> **On average, new homeowners spend between $4,000 and $7,500 in the first two years on home improvements, furnishings, and other upgrades.**

> **WORDS OF WISDOM**
>
> "We are not the fixer-upper types, but we ended up in a bidding war over a total wreck of a home because of its relatively low price and our fast-talking real estate agent, who had my husband believing he was the next Bob Vila. Thank God we didn't get it. Our marriage never would have survived!" Rebecca P., Brooklyn, NY

Assume that estimates are low. Your real estate agent might be able to provide a ballpark sense of how much work a home requires. But if you're serious about a residence, bring in a professional to discuss actual figures for improvements. Remember, even when a trained architect or remodeling contractor gives an estimate for a remodeling project, you need to tack on 15 to 20 percent for unforeseen issues.

Be willing to live with certain features. This rule applies particularly to older homes. If you can't live with squeaky floors, for example, you should probably consider newer construction. Similarly, although it's possible to reconfigure an outdated floor plan, that type of renovation can easily run to six figures. If you can make the separate kitchen and other old-fashioned elements work, you'll save yourself enormous trouble and expense.

If you are looking at a condo or co-op, understand your maintenance responsibilities. Most buildings charge a maintenance fee, which covers things like the façade, roof, hallways, lobby, common areas, and heating system. But you will likely be responsible for everything inside the walls of your home, such as leaky faucets and issues with the electrical system.

5. IS THE HOUSE PREPARED FOR NATURAL DISASTER?

If you are moving to a region that is prone to natural disaster, you need to make sure that the home has all the necessary safeguards in place. You should also be prepared to pay extra insurance premiums that come with living in a high-risk area. Here are the major natural disasters and what to look for:

Hurricanes States along the Gulf Coast and Eastern Seaboard are most hurricane prone, everywhere from Texas to Maine. The most secure homes will be built with hurricane-proof glass and special strappings on the foundation and roof that keep the house and roof from being blown away. Make sure your insurance covers flooding as well as wind.

Tornadoes So-called Tornado Alley sweeps up the middle of the country and includes Texas, Oklahoma, Kansas, Colorado, Nebraska, and South Dakota. Given the intensity of the wind, look for a home with a basement or storm cellar, or consider fortifying a safe room in your home.

Flooding Anywhere there's water, be it from a river, lake, creek, or snowcaps, there's a chance of flooding. Many Midwest states are prone to flash flooding, from North Dakota to Mississippi. Check the FEMA Map Service Center (www.fema.gov) to see if your prospective home is in the flood zone. If so, you can buy federally sponsored protection through the National Flood Insurance Program (FloodSmart.gov). You may not be by a body of water, but if your house is at the bottom of a hill, you may get flooding from rainstorms.

Fires Many states, especially in the Southwest, are at risk of wildfires, with some of the most dangerous recent outbreaks happening in California, Arizona, and Nevada. In addition to fire insurance, it's ideal to have noncombustible materials on the entire home, including the eaves, roof, and even gutters.

Earthquakes The most vulnerable fault lines are on the West Coast, in particular California but also Oregon and Washington. Hawaii and Alaska also see a lot of seismic activity. If you are looking at taller structures or ones with a lot of glass, research to see if they have been designed and engineered to accommodate seismic forces. Retrofits for seismic activity are common in most major cities. If you are looking at a high-rise in one of these areas, you should be able to get the information you need by asking around.

6. HOW IS THE INDOOR AIR QUALITY?

One of the dilemmas of new home construction is that although tight construction improves energy efficiency by preventing the escape of conditioned air (heated in the winter, cooled in the summer), it also prevents fresh air from getting into the home. This can result in indoor air pollution stemming from a variety of sources, including wet carpet, pressed-wood cabinets that contain formaldehyde, and even regular household cleaners. If the home was built before 1978, when lead was banned in paint, this toxin may also be present. Radon, a colorless, odorless radioactive gas that results from the natural decay of uranium in soil and rock, is yet another concern.

These pollutants can trigger short-term health problems such as irritation of the eyes, nose, and throat, as well as serious long-term ones like respiratory ailments, heart disease, and cancer. Indoor air pollution can often be corrected, usually through source control—that is, removing the objects or systems that are causing the pollution in the first place. Improved ventilation, through the installation of exhaust fans, for example, is another option. A whole-house air-exchange system, which constantly filters the air in your home, is another effective system.

Although these fixes don't have to be prohibitively expensive, they could come at a time when you're being hit with many other expenses, from closing costs to new furnishings. So it pays to sniff out any major indoor air quality issues before you commit to a home.

Consider Hiring an Indoor Air Quality Consultant If there are signs of indoor air pollution in a home, such as the presence of mold or peeling paint in older homes, you may want to consider hiring an indoor air quality consultant. That's especially true if your household contains small children, an elderly person, or anyone with an existing condition such as asthma or allergies. Indoor air quality consulting is a fairly specialized field, with various levels of training and experience. Some consultants are industrial hygienists, some are mechanical engineers, and some are architects with special training in preventing indoor air quality problems. Be sure to check their credentials and references. And be extremely wary of duct-cleaning

Eight Warning Signs to Watch For

Although magazines often get a little carried away with their "How Your House Can Kill You" type of articles, some issues can be serious. The following red flags needn't necessarily be deal breakers, but they're signs that a home may need serious reconditioning, sooner rather than later.

Damp basement A sign that moisture is penetrating the foundation. Possible fixes include installing a sump pump and adding gutters and downspouts.

Cracked foundation walls Small fissures are no problem, but if they're wider than ³⁄₁₆ inch, you may need to call in a structural engineer.

Water stains in the ceiling This probably means water is getting in through the roof, maybe as a result of ice damming. Repairs to the roof will likely be required.

Wobbly decks A sign that the structure was not adequately secured to the house and/or the concrete footings. It will need to be braced or even rebuilt.

Pest infestations Termites and carpenter ants can wreak havoc on a home, especially if you plan to renovate, in which case any infiltrated framing will need to be replaced.

Mold and mildew This indicates poor indoor air quality that will need to be corrected with ventilation.

Soggy patches in lawn The home may have a septic tank that is overfilled or failing. The system may need to be replaced.

Cracks at upper corners of windows and doors Some settling is normal, but severe cracks are a sign of problems with the foundation. A structural engineer will need to do an inspection.

contractors who claim to be experts in indoor air quality, since this is often a scam. Prices vary, depending on the nature of the problem. A simple radon test may cost as little as $100, whereas a whole-house assessment could run many times that.

Professional Inspection

Before you purchase a home, you need to determine its exact condition. A home inspection, which typically costs between $200 and $600, provides the most comprehensive analysis of the home's condition. Inspections usually happen pretty far into the process, after the purchase contract is in place. But the contract should have a contingency allowing you to back out of the deal if the inspection turns up costly problems, such as a crumbling foundation wall or major mold outbreak. For big and small issues alike, you might be able to ask the seller to cover some or all of the costs (and to have problems remedied before you move in).

HOW DO YOU FIND A HOME INSPECTOR?

When choosing a home inspector, make sure they're affiliated with a professional organization, such as the American Society of Home Inspectors (ASHI). The organization's website, www.ashi.org, offers a search tool for finding inspectors by zip code or metropolitan area. You can also do an advanced search for inspectors by specialty, such as historic homes, high-end residences, or those in disaster-prone regions.

Any inspector you find through ASHI will have undergone rigorous training and they'll have to keep up with mandatory continuing education. Certified inspectors must also follow the ASHI Standards of Practice and Code of Ethics, which prohibits engaging in conflict-of-interest activities that might compromise their objectivity. See page 330 for questions to ask a potential inspector.

BEYOND THE GENERAL INSPECTION

A general inspection will cover the house's physical and structural components, spotting things like leaky roofs, shoddy electrical wiring, and missing smoke alarms. But there are things it probably won't cover, including termite or pest infestations, which can be an issue in many regions of the country. If you're in a known danger zone, plan on spending another $150 to $300 for a specialized pest inspection.

Other specialized inspections may be needed based on the results of the initial general inspection. For example, you may be advised to hire a structural engineer to assess the house's foundation. If the property has specialty features, such as a swimming pool or septic tank, they could also warrant an additional inspection. The American Society of Home Inspectors (www.ashi.org) can direct you to specialized professionals.

CHAPTER CHEAT SHEET

Gut Check

Do you have a clear understanding of the condition of this home?

Reality Check

Are you prepared to spend the time and money necessary to operate, maintain, and potentially renovate this home?

Balancing Act

Function—Will the house be easy to maintain? Cost—Can you afford to maintain the house? Delight—Will you enjoy working on your home?

Chapter 17

Energy Assessments and Improvements

Homes today that are solidly built and tout features that save effort, energy, and dollars—such as low-maintenance materials, good insulation, and high-efficiency appliances—are starting to attract more buyers than residences that rely on bells and whistles like a media room, home spa, or cook's kitchen with commercial-grade cooking appliances.

Homes still have to provide for entertainment, grooming, and home-cooked meals, but these lifestyle-based luxuries are more about a home's accessories than its bones. After all, you can always add a six-burner range, massage table, or sixty-inch plasma TV. Factors like durability, efficiency, and sustainability, on the other hand, are inherent to the home. Either the building saves energy dollars or it lets them fly out leaky windows and an uninsulated attic. As live-in value replaces resale value, people are taking a longer view of their homes, and these notions that used to be for the fussy few are entering the mainstream.

Fortunately, the understanding of building science and performance is better than ever. Some experts predict that by 2020, so-called home performance professionals who specialize in energy-related building assessments and remediation will be as common as remodeling contractors. In fact, the awareness is already growing. This chapter outlines how to assess the energy consumption of a home and offers suggestions, both easy and in depth, to enhance performance.

Assessing Energy Efficiency

The performance of your home directly affects your bottom line. By assessing its current condition, you not only will be able to plan accurately for your monthly expenses but will also have an idea of the big-picture improvements that might be on the horizon. Here are the two steps to assessing the energy efficiency of a potential home.

DETERMINE MONTHLY ENERGY BILLS

Before seriously considering any home, either to rent or to own, get a full understanding of its monthly expenses. If you move in expecting to pay $150 a month and end up with bills in excess of $700, your monthly budget will take a huge hit.

This is especially important for people who are moving to a home that's heated with oil from one that ran on a cheaper fuel, such as natural gas. For example, during the 2011–2012 heating season, households in the Northeast that used oil paid upward of $2,500, whereas those in the Midwest that used natural gas paid around $750. That nearly $2,000 swing will make a big difference in a household's annual budget. And it doesn't even take into account the costs of electricity, which also vary widely (see "Electricity Rates by State," next page).

Determining the type of fuel used to heat and cool the home is your first step. But you should also ask to see the last year's worth of utility bills for the home. If you're working with a real estate agent, they can work with the seller to get this for you. Or you may be able to call the utility company and get the information yourself, especially for rental properties. That might seem a little invasive, but once you explain your rationale, the owner should understand the request, and if they don't, it may be because they're hiding their home's serious inefficiencies. As you examine the utility bills, don't be surprised if there are dramatic spikes throughout the year, such as a surge in electricity costs during warmer months because of air-conditioning. Just make sure the total tally for the year is in line with what your household budget can handle, and consider improvements you could do to lower the costs.

Electricity Rates by State in Cents per Kilowatt Hour

Most Expensive	Least Expensive
Hawaii 28.10 cents	Idaho 7.99 cents
Connecticut 19.25 cents	Washington 8.04 cents
New York 18.74 cents	North Dakota 8.13 cents
New Jersey 16.57 cents	Kentucky 8.57 cents
New Hampshire 16.32 cents	Utah 8.71 cents
Alaska 16.26 cents	Wyoming 8.77 cents
Rhode Island 15.92 cents	Arkansas 8.86 cents
Maine 15.71 cents	Oregon 8.87 cents
Vermont 15.57 cents	Nebraska 8.94 cents
California 14.75 cents	South Dakota 8.97 cents

HIRE AN ENERGY INSPECTOR

Seriously consider getting an energy assessment of the home. The technical term for these pros has been *energy auditor,* though the industry is now moving toward *energy inspector,* which conjures up the image of a friendly doctor rather than a forbidding tax man.

The service includes a comprehensive assessment of the home's heating, cooling, and distribution systems, a check for insulation and air leaks, and a review of recent energy bills. An energy checkup might cost anywhere from $300 to $800, depending on the age and size of the home and the complexity of its systems. Some local utility companies offer the service for free, though you have to be the owner to make the request. You could always ask the seller to have the checkup done and share the results with you. Otherwise, you can find a professional through one of the two industry organizations: the Building Performance Institute (BPI) and the Residential Energy Services Network (RESNET).

Energy Upgrades

Energy enhancements and adjustments can save you hundreds, if not thousands, of dollars each year. And over several years, these savings can be substantial. Knowing where to start is easier than you might think. Minnesota Power developed a very helpful graphic tool called the Pyramid of Conservation, pictured on the facing page. It organizes actions based on the cost, complexity, and potential return.

The base of the pyramid consists of the affordable options that offer the most return on investment. Do these first to maximize the benefits of the items higher on the chart. A common misconception about energy retrofits is that you have to replace your windows or HVAC—short for heating, ventilation, and air-conditioning—system to make your home more energy efficient. In actuality, you might save more on energy bills by doing the cheaper job of fixing leaking ducts. Although there's no clear dividing line between each step, actions fall into three basic categories: behavioral changes, weatherization, and deep energy retrofits.

BEHAVIORAL CHANGES

This category includes the no- or low-cost changes that, when added up, can lead to significant energy savings. Here are some examples:

Pyramid of Conservation

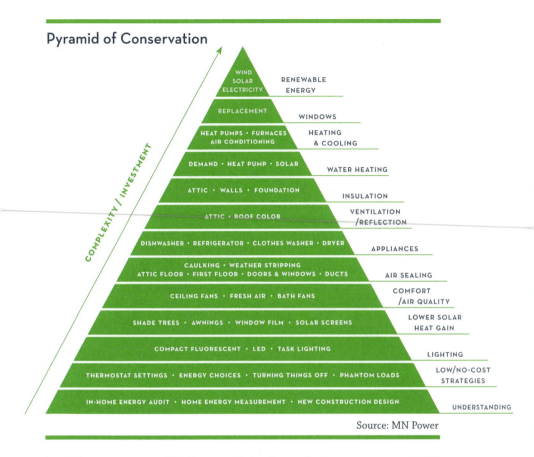

Source: MN Power

Install a programmable thermostat. These devices cost around $75 and you can install them by yourself, without hiring a contractor. They can lower a home's annual energy bills by as much as 10 percent by automatically turning the thermostat down 10 to 15 percent during the sleeping hours. It's important to find a model with clear controls. Some models on the market are so confusing that you could program them incorrectly. Indeed, a 2011 study by Lawrence Berkeley National Laboratory found that half of homes surveyed had their thermostats set in such a way that they were inadvertently overriding any programmed temperature adjustments. But there are models on the market that make it easy to save—look for larger screens and easy-to-follow instructions and controls with arrows and clear prompts, rather than vague symbols.

Manage electricity use. There are a lot of little ways to lower your electric bill that can add up to significant savings. Switching from standard incandescent lightbulbs to energy-efficient compact fluorescent lightbulbs (CFLs) or light-emitting diodes (LEDs) could save you hundreds of dollars over the life of the bulb. Activating the sleep mode on computers and unplugging electronic devices that aren't in use can also help chip away at your bill. Power strips are an easy way to turn off a lot at once. With regard to hot water, simply lowering your water heater's temperature to 120 degrees from 130 and insulating your home's hot-water pipes can trim up to 5 percent off your energy bills.

WEATHERIZATION

This is the practice of making a building more energy efficient by sealing its exterior against the elements and protecting its interior from heat and cold. Here are three key components you should consider with any prospective home. Although some are DIY friendly, you'll need a professional to deal with faulty HVAC systems. If you're working with an energy inspector, that person will be able to make referrals. Otherwise, you can find a professional through the Air Conditioning Contractors of America (ACCA.org).

Insulate the attic. In most parts of the country, there should be at least eleven inches of fiberglass or rock wool or eight inches of

WORDS OF WISDOM

"Several years ago, we had an energy audit performed on our 3,000-square-foot single-story home. Ten items were listed for improvement. We had our air leaks and air conditioning ducts sealed and added insulation. These measures improved our comfort and health and decreased our power bills. Over the years, we have made further improvements and have reduced our power consumption by more than half. We're going to keep at it so that by the time we retire our house should be paid for and have virtually no utility bills." Farrow S., Las Vegas, NV

cellulose insulation. This will prevent heated air from escaping through the roof during the winter, which can result in a so-called stack effect, whereby cold air is pulled in through gaps in the basement or foundation slab and up through the roof. It can save you $200 per year or more.

Seal air leaks. The attic is the big one, but there can also be leaks in a home's envelope around windows, doors, and even electrical outlets. In some cases, the cumulative effect of these leaks is equal to an open window. Along with laying attic insulation, plugging these leaks with a combination of weather stripping, caulk, foam board, and expandable sealant could lower the average home's annual heating and cooling bills by $500.

Correct ductwork. The ducts that run through homes that use forced-air heating and cooling are often leaky and poorly insulated. When the ducts run through crawl spaces and other unconditioned parts of the home, the hot air escapes during the winter and cool air escapes during the summer. By spending about $500 to fix the ducts, you could save about $400 per year in energy costs, according to the Energy Efficient Rehab Advisor (rehabadvisor.pathnet.org), an online calculator developed by the U.S. Department of Housing and Urban Development. So after fifteen months, you'll have an extra $400 every year to put in your pocket (or somewhere else in your house).

DEEP ENERGY RETROFIT

As you near the top of the pyramid, projects become increasingly complex with a longer payback time. Most experts consider a deep energy retrofit as one that reduces a home's energy consumption by at least 50 percent.

HVAC. If the home is heated with a furnace or boiler that's more than fifteen years old, you will probably be able to upgrade to a more efficient system. For example, a new furnace with an annual fuel utilization efficiency rating of 90 percent or greater will be 15 percent more efficient than a standard model. Go to energystar .gov to learn more about the latest high-efficiency heating and cooling systems for the home.

Upgrading to energy-efficient windows. It can take up to twenty years to recoup the investment on new windows, so you might think twice before replacing them only for the sake of energy savings. But if the units are dilapidated, or you're replacing them as part of a larger renovation, be sure to take advantage of modern energy-saving innovations. That includes double-glazed windows, which often

Home Energy Saver

A typical U.S. family spends about $1,900 per year on energy bills, according to the Lawrence Berkeley National Laboratory, which created the Home Energy Saver website (hes.lbl.gov) to show how much of that expense can be cut.

Visit HomeEnergySaver.lbl.gov, enter your zip code and the Home Energy Saver will show you how your utility bills and energy-related carbon dioxide emissions compare with an energy-efficient home in your area. You can then answer a set of basic questions about your house, including its floor area, the number of occupants, type of heating and air-conditioning equipment, and fuel prices, to get a custom-tailored energy bill breakdown.

Here's an example of the potential savings for a family of five living in a 3,000-square-foot home built in 1980 in Omaha, Nebraska. In addition to the financial savings, the upgrades would lower this home's greenhouse gas emissions by 12,872 pounds, equivalent to taking one car off the road.

	Total Utilities	Heating	Cooling	Hot Water	Appliances	Lighting
Existing home	$2,164	$1,416	$115	$209	$210	$113
With upgrades	$1,207	$631	$84	$173	$178	$40
Savings	$957	$785	$31	$36	$32	$73

have insulating argon gas between the two panes that makes them extremely efficient. Low-emissivity (low-E) coatings, meanwhile, prevent solar heat gain in the summer but let it through during the winter, helping to trim your energy bills by as much as 25 percent. In places with extremes between hot and cold, triple-glazed windows provide extra comfort (and savings).

Installing renewable energy equipment. This includes such items as photovoltaic systems and residential wind turbines. Although these systems can generate power for the home, and in some cases will even send electricity back to the grid, they are unlikely to save you money for many years, up to twenty in some cases. But they are essential for zero-energy building, which describes a home that generates at least as much, if not more, energy than it consumes.

POLICY POINT: EVERY HOME IN AMERICA SHOULD HAVE AN ENERGY RATING

In the future, the process of assessing the energy efficiency of a home ideally will be as easy as checking the fuel-efficiency sticker on a new car or the EnergyGuide label on an appliance. Other countries have taken sizable steps in this direction, including England and Denmark, which require home sellers to share the result of an energy audit with prospective buyers.

In the United States, we've made good progress with new construction. For example, the Energy Star program identifies homes that are at least 15 percent more energy efficient than homes built to the 2004 International Residential Code (IRC). These homes typically include additional energy-saving features that make them 20 to 30 percent more efficient than standard homes. But we have a ways to go with existing homes, despite the extensive network of energy auditors and various standards and certifications developed by BPI (Building Performance Institute) and RESNET (Residential Energy Services Network). A handful of cities, including Austin and San Francisco, require some sort of audit during the home-selling process. For every home to reach its maximum level of efficiency, however, policies must be adopted at the federal level.

This idea gets plenty of pushback from those who want to see less government regulation, not more. Many are also opposed to mandatory energy audits, since it's another piece of paperwork to deal with, plus it would highlight the fact that most homes aren't as efficient as they could and should be. For example, it's estimated that approximately 80 percent of homes in the country lack proper insulation in the attic, which is driving up their annual energy costs.

Despite the resistance, the U.S. Department of Energy is in the process of developing something called the Home Energy Score. Under the program, specially trained contractors (call them "the green team") would walk through homes and use a standardized assessment tool to score a home's efficiency on a scale of 1 to 10. They would also indicate how the home stacks up against others in the area, and suggest smart energy upgrades, like adding insulation or replacing an inefficient heating system.

The big question is who should foot the bill. Studies have shown that energy-efficient homes sell for a few percentage points more than their less-efficient counterparts, so there's an argument to be made for putting the onus on home sellers, since they'll recoup the cost. But it's also in the interest of the government to provide incentives for homeowners to make energy retrofits part of our national effort to use fewer fossil fuels and be energy independent. Several bills have been proposed, including the so-called Cash for Caulkers bill, which would provide $5 billion in rebates to homeowners who make energy-efficient upgrades. Despite bipartisan support, the

Defining *Sustainable* and *Green*

Sustainability and *green* are nuanced terms, because like the word *natural*, they have many applications but few actual parameters. Everything from lumber to coffee to neighborhood developments is now branded as sustainable and green, but what that means exactly varies from one category to the next. When it comes to homes, I like to say that the most sustainable home is the one you care enough about to want to maintain over time.

bill has not been able to get through Congress. It is in all of our best interests for the federal government to pass some version of Cash for Caulkers. In the meantime, you need to realize that home energy costs vary wildly. Do what you can to figure out where your next potential home falls on that spectrum.

CHAPTER CHEAT SHEET

Gut Check

There is a wide range of options for energy efficiency. It all comes down to your available budget and the time you have to make it all happen. What level of efficiency makes the most sense for you at this time?

Reality Check

What are you willing to invest to get that level of energy efficiency?

Balancing Act

Function—Are there simple upgrades that will make the home more energy efficient, such as adding insulation, installing a programmable thermostat, and sealing air leaks? *Cost*—Do you have a clear understanding of how much this home will cost to heat and cool? *Delight*—Do you love this home enough to want to take care of it over time?

Key points to remember

- Energy expenses, namely heating and cooling bills, are a commonly overlooked cost of ownership that can take a sizable bite out of a household budget. In extreme cases, you could have to spend $500 or more each month to heat your home.

- The three types of energy upgrades are behavioral changes, weatherization, and deep energy retrofits. Before jumping into a deep energy retrofit, make sure you have addressed small moves like fixing leaking ducts. This can have a huge effect on the efficiency of a home and give you the best return on investment.

Chapter 18

New Rules of Renovation for Home and Community

As you go through the process of articulating how and where you want to live, you may come to realize where you want to live. As you go through the process, you may come to realize that with only a few changes, the home that best fits your needs is the one you're living in now. Alternatively, you may want to move, but after assessing your realities, you might determine that it isn't in the cards at the moment. Don't worry. Staying put doesn't mean you can't transform your home—or even your community—to better fit your dreams. That is what this chapter is about.

Perhaps you have found the perfect community, but the available homes need work. Or you have found a great home, but the community is missing key elements of your housing profile.

These are all paths that bring you to the same point: a discussion on renovating not only your home, but also your community. Should you stay or go, rent or own, buy existing or build new, renovate or leave as is? In Chapter 2 we looked at the possible paths your move might take. Your journey will be unique, depending on your individual needs, but in the end, once you have a place selected, even if it is your current home, you will have three main choices:

Leave As Is If moving, send in the cleaning crew and movers. If you are staying, do nothing.

Make Cosmetic Changes New paint, new flooring, new hardware

Renovate Light or deep; includes kitchen renovations, moving walls, adding on, and energy retrofits

The path you choose will be driven largely by the condition of the home and by how much money and effort you're able to put toward upgrades and improvements. Especially if you've never taken on a home improvement project, don't underestimate the costs and complexities that can quickly creep in. Always assume that both the budget and schedule will go over by 20 percent. Giving yourself a very soft cushion will reduce the anxiety that comes with home remodeling, and if you come in under budget, you can put the windfall toward your emergency fund—or even reward yourself with a new luxury item for your new home.

Updating Your Home

COSMETIC CHANGES TO YOUR HOME

Cosmetic changes are skin deep: new paint, new carpet, refinishing existing floors, new hardware, new cabinets, and more. The project costs can range from a few hundred dollars into the thousands, depending on your scope and the materials you select. Putting on a fresh coat or two of paint is the most common cosmetic change, either inside or out. Anyone can do it, and the materials are relatively cheap (figure on a few hundred dollars to cover the cost of paint, brushes, rollers, tape, drop cloths, and so on for a good-size project including several rooms).

Cosmetic Changes Outside You've heard the term *curb appeal*. That's what these changes are all about—sprucing up the exterior of

WORDS OF WISDOM

"We decided to remodel the house we had rather than move. Our house has great 'bones' and our lot is wonderful. We also have exceptional neighbors. For the amount of money it took to remodel we have a customized home that works for our family. Granted, it's not as big as many houses out there, but it is designed to suit us, and our mortgage is still affordable." Carolyn B., Anchorage, AK

your home so that it looks better from the curb. That might include repainting the exterior, installing a new roof, adding or updating the landscaping, or replacing windows. Tidy up the yard. Wash the windows. Trim your bushes. These measures will make you feel better while improving your home's appearance.

Clean Up the Clutter Nothing makes the walls close in faster than piles of clutter. The messiest spots in the home are typically the result of poorly designed or insufficient storage. Invest in shelving and storage systems for your closets to rein in clutter throughout your house. Options in the marketplace are plentiful, including do-it-yourself systems from IKEA and the Container Store or custom jobs by California Closets.

Install New Hardware Upgrade doorknobs and cabinet hardware throughout your house. Replacing the lightweight knobs you engage with every time you walk through a door or open and close a cabinet adds value that you can touch and feel. Avoid bright brass or dark finishes like rubbed bronze, both of which are dated looks. Opt for nickel or chrome or, if you select brass, look for finishes that are unlacquered or antiqued. For doors, consider egg-shaped or crystal knobs to give a unique look. Knobs are available from Home Depot or other big-box chains. Nice ones range in price from $75 to $125 per set. If you want a higher-end product, Baldwin Hardware offers a wide range of stock and customizable combinations. Prices start at around $150 per set (BaldwinHardware.com).

Change the Blinds Replace cracked, warped, and bent horizontal or vertical blinds with Roman shades or fitted window treatments. Bed, Bath & Beyond offers Roman shades starting from $40 to $100 an opening, depending on style and size. You can also work with a custom blind company to match window treatments exactly to your openings and décor.

Kitchen Cabinets You have several upgrade options, depending on the condition of your cabinets, the cabinet material, and your budget. The easiest and most affordable, as noted above, is to replace the cabinet knobs ($2 to $15 each). If you want the look of new cabinets without the price, you can replace the doors (IKEA's start at $25 to $100 per door). If you have solid wood cabinets, you can sand them down and varnish or paint them.

Add a Backsplash The wall space above the counter and below the upper cabinets is visually prominent but small enough not to need much material. Redoing it can change the entire look and feel of a kitchen. Paint is the simplest and cheapest option. Tile—ceramic, colored glass, or stone—costs $10 to $40 per square foot installed. Or use stainless steel, $100 to $150 per square foot installed, for a mirrored finish that might complement stainless-steel appliances.

Hire a Decorator We've all seen those amazing before-and-after images on TV when an überdecorator takes a sad room with no personality and transforms it into a personal oasis. If you are struggling to add flair to your home, wondering what colors might look best, or looking for ways to reimagine your interiors, call a decorator. Prices start at a few thousand dollars and go up from there, depending on the number of rooms the person works on and the number of items he or she specifies. See more details about hiring a decorator in Chapter 19, page 334.

RENOVATING AND REMODELING

Chances are you'll want to make some changes if you buy a home, even if it's just to put your personal stamp on the interior style. The widespread changes that have affected the housing industry since the

Project Costs and Returns at a Glance (2011–2012 *Remodeling* Magazine "Cost vs. Value Report")

Project	Midrange Cost	Recouped	Upscale Cost	Recouped
Major kitchen remodel	$58,000	66%	$111,000	57%
Bathroom remodel	$17,000	63%	$52,000	56%
Bathroom addition	$40,000	51%	$76,000	53%
Roof replacement	$21,000	58%	$37,000	55%
Siding replacement	$12,000	70%	$14,000	70%
New windows	$11,000	68%	$19,000	69%
New deck	$10,000	70%	$38,000	55%
Master suite addition	$106,000	59%	$227,000	50%
Garage addition	$58,000	57%	$86,000	52%

collapse are also changing the way we remodel. First and foremost, you can't expect the same return on investment that was commonplace during the housing boom. This point is made clear by the annual "Cost vs. Value Report" that is put out each year by *Remodeling* magazine. As the chart above illustrates, at most you'll get back seventy cents on the dollar, and the return could be as little as fifty cents. Search for the costs in your area for thirty-five common remodeling and replacement projects at CostVsValue.com.

Translation? Just as you need to choose a home based on live-in value, as opposed to resale value, so should you remodel to get the home you want, not the home that's going to get the highest sale price somewhere down the line. Here are some tips to keep in mind to make sure you make positive changes:

Don't Increase the Value of Your Home Too Much It doesn't pay to have the most expensive house on the block, since your home's value is directly related to that of your neighbors. As a result, you'll make their homes more valuable while they bring yours down. Also, it's important for homes on the block to be of a similar scale to preserve the feeling of a streetscape, as discussed in Chapter 9, so you don't want to put on a massive addition that will upset the neighborhood harmony.

Build in Adaptability Is there a place in your home that can be separated out to be an income-producing suite, a home for an elderly parent, or an apartment for guests or a boomerang child? With the increase in multigenerational families and need for supplemental income, one of the highest value-added renovations you can make is to either add an accessory dwelling unit on your property or carve out part of your house as an adaptable suite. (See more on page 201.)

Improve Your Home's Efficiency Replacing dilapidated windows, insulating the attic, and switching to Energy Star appliances will improve your home's performance, lower its monthly bills, and

Rule of Thumb

For kitchen projects, you should plan to spend between 10 and 15 percent of the value of your home. So if your home is worth $200,000, expect to spend between $20,000 and $30,000 on the job, including labor and materials.

> ## Staying Put
>
> If you do decide to stay in your current home instead of making a move, it's worth checking out a book by Duo Dickinson—*Staying Put: Remodel Your House to Get the Home You Want.* Dickinson is a Connecticut-based architect who has written extensively about remodeling and design. The book is brimming with helpful insights and advice organized around the various rooms of the house.

increase its resale value if the time does come to put it on the market. Chapter 17 outlines your energy retrofitting options.

Create a Connection to the Outdoors Homes are often closed off from the exterior, with yards visible only through small windows that rattle every time the wind blows. Consider glass wall systems, which open up entire walls to the outdoors.

WHEN DO YOU NEED A BUILDING PERMIT?

Although the answer to that question depends on the local building codes where you live, generally speaking a building permit is required anytime you alter the structure of a house. That includes adding or removing interior walls, building an addition, installing new windows or replacing the existing ones, and building a masonry or retaining wall. Electrical and plumbing permits are separate, and apply to such projects as updating a home's electrical wiring or repairing water and gas lines.

Permits are not required for minor remodeling projects, such as replacing appliances, painting, or laying carpet or other types of flooring onto the subfloor.

If you're hiring a contractor, it will be their responsibility to get the permits from the local building inspection department. Make sure this stipulation is written into your contract. And think twice about working with a contractor who asks you to get the permits for them, since this is a good sign that they're not in good standing with the building inspector.

The Dos and Don'ts of Upgrading a Rental

It might sound crazy to pour a lot of time and money into a property that belongs to someone else. But as more people choose renting over owning, renter-directed remodeling is becoming more common. *The New York Times* reported an extreme example from 2009, around the height of the flight from homeownership, of a couple in Brooklyn, New York, who did more than $20,000 worth of work on a two-bedroom apartment in exchange for a four-year lease with a $400 monthly discount, which would enable them to recoup their investment over the life of the agreement. That level of commitment, financial and otherwise, is beyond the pale for most people, especially highly transient renters who aren't thinking past a one-year lease. But if you're part of the new breed of renters who are anchored in their community but not willing or able to own, you might think about investing more than a fresh coat of paint in your rental, in particular if you've signed a multiyear lease. There is, however, a right way and a wrong way to personalize a temporary living space. Here are my rental renovation dos and don'ts.

DO

Get It in Writing. If your landlord is willing to help out with some or all of the cost of the work, whether with money up front or a discount on future rents, you need to write the terms of the agreement into your signed lease. Never enter into a handshake agreement where real estate is concerned.

Keep the Work Cosmetic. Even if you're a handy and intrepid DIYer, there's no sense in tackling structural work with a rental. There are too many surprises lurking behind walls and under floorboards, from termite damage to outdated electrical wiring. Focus on surface upgrades, such as laying new floors or replacing the countertops.

Look for Everyday Life-Enhancers. Earlier in this chapter, I mentioned closet systems as a perfect rental project, since they have an overnight (or maybe over-weekend) effect on quality of life. Look for other small-scale, big-effect upgrades, such as installing cabinet organizers in the kitchen if you cook a lot, or putting in a high-powered showerhead.

DON'T

Bite Off More Than You Can Chew. This rule goes for any remodeling project, but it's particularly true when you're not the property owner. Staying on budget means planning every phase of the project ahead of time and avoiding any "while we're at it" add-ons.

Ignore Codes and Permits. Even if your landlord okays the project, you still need to make sure you follow local building laws. In most cities, the remodeler (i.e., you under the contract you signed with your landlord) is responsible for correcting any code violations, which could mean having to undo the finished work.

Make It Too Personal. You might love neon-orange floor tiles in the kitchen, but the next renter down the line may feel differently. To maintain good working relations with your landlord, stay neutral with the design of any permanent or semipermanent upgrades, saving pops of color for paint and accessories.

Renovating Your Community

As with your individual home, communities can be enhanced and improved with both cosmetic changes and deeper renovations. Making changes at a community level often seems daunting and bigger than what we as individuals can achieve, but this doesn't have to be the case if you know the steps for making things happen.

It is a pure coincidence, but I happen to be writing this section on Jane Jacobs's birthday. Jacobs was the author of several books, most famously *The Death and Life of Great American Cities*. She was also a community activist. Through her tireless efforts, Jacobs led a grassroots movement that stopped construction of the Lower Manhattan Expressway planned by Robert Moses, a developer in New York City who at the time was extremely powerful. If built, the expressway would have destroyed much of the urban fabric and cobblestone streets of Greenwich Village and Lower Manhattan. Jacobs is a reminder of what a single individual can achieve on behalf of an entire community.

Although it is unlikely you will personally be taking on freeway removals, there are many things large and small you can do locally to enhance your community.

COSMETIC COMMUNITY CHANGES

Simple changes can make a huge difference in not only the look and feel of a community, but also the likelihood of it being walkable. It has been proved that great-looking, walkable communities hold value longer than their auto-dependent counterparts. Here are a few things that can be done to increase the value of your community.

> Simple changes can make a huge difference in not only the look and feel of a community, but also the likelihood of it being walkable.

Add Sidewalks and Street Trees Take advantage of large setbacks in residential areas to add street trees and sidewalks. Not only is this proven to add value to all the homes in the community (see page 232), but it will also make the streets safer to walk on, promoting safe routes to school and fostering community interaction. Often cities will reimburse homeowners the cost of the tree and plant it. In other cases, community groups raise funds for weekend planting events. The Alliance for Community Trees (actrees.org) is a national organization dedicated to urban and community tree planting, care, conservation, and education. Visit their website to find a member organization in your area. One example is TREEmendous Miami, a member organization of the Alliance for Community Trees. Since the organization started in 1999, it has planted more than 10,000 trees in Miami-Dade County with the help of more than 6,000 volunteers through fund-raising and donations.

Allow On-Street Parking On-street parking is a natural traffic-calming device that adds another layer of safety for pedestrians on sidewalks. (See page 181.)

Bike Lanes Support local initiatives to add dedicated bike lanes to support safe biking alternatives. Remember, every car off the road means your trip is that much easier. Learn more at BicyclingInfo.org.

Complete Streets Complete Streets is an organization that pulls together all of the points above to transform auto-dominated streets to "complete streets" where pedestrians, bikers, and cars can coexist safely and with purpose. The coalition's website includes a map pinpointing locations where "complete streets" are being implemented as well as advice for getting them adopted in your community. More than 300 jurisdictions nationwide have adopted Complete Street policies. Learn more about complete-street initiatives in your area at CompleteStreets.org.

REMODELING YOUR COMMUNITY

If you are looking for a single-family home, you will most likely be touched in some way by suburban sprawl. Sprawl is low-density, single-use development that has resulted in auto-dependent communities. (I discuss sprawl in more detail in Appendix 1.) Although sprawl can make finding a walkable community difficult, the good news is that a lot of very smart people are working hard to address these issues, including planners, architects, activists, developers, and city officials, so that over time, any community can be reimagined and transformed for the better. Here is a brief snapshot of some of your options.

Sprawl Repair and Retrofitting Suburbs Sometimes it might not be an option to live in a walkable community. The housing stock in older neighborhoods is often one of two extremes: either prohibitively expensive or run-down. Or perhaps the housing options are great, but the school system in an older neighborhood is lacking. One option is to look for communities open to sprawl repair.

Additional Resources

Sprawl Repair Manual by Galina Tachieva
Don't believe existing suburban sprawl can be fixed? This book will convince you otherwise. Urban planner Galina Tachieva lays out a comprehensive methodology for transforming failing suburbs into thriving communities. Her book shows how to turn auto-dependent subdivisions into walkable neighborhoods, and shopping centers and malls into town centers. "The primary tactic of sprawl repair is to insert needed elements—buildings, density, public space, additional connections—to complete and diversify the mono-culture agglomerations of sprawl," she says.

Retrofitting Suburbia: Urban Design Solutions for Redesigning Suburbs by Ellen Dunham-Jones and June Williamson
An excellent companion to *Sprawl Repair Manual,* this comprehensive guide profiles three dozen real-world projects to illustrate how existing suburbs—especially places like abandoned big-box stores—can be redesigned and redeveloped.

The Smart Growth Manual by Andres Duany, Jeff Speck, and Mike Lydon
The definitive guide to smart-growth development, this book breaks down the building blocks of proper city planning. Professional planners and developers will definitely benefit from reading it, but if you're a layperson looking

"Sprawl repair is the transformation of failing single-use, car-dominated developments into complete communities that promise to perform economically, socially, and environmentally," according to Galina Tachieva, author of *Sprawl Repair Manual*. Examples of sprawl repair include reclaiming parking lots of failed malls to create town centers, carving through the ends of cul-de-sacs to connect streets, and building apartments and stores in low-density areas. Parks replace berms. Empty space is replaced with a walkable public realm. See "Additional Resources," above, for more details on Tachieva's teachings.

to live in a traditional neighborhood, the manual will tell you exactly what to look for, right down to the material used on the sidewalks and the location of the parking lots.

Sustainable Transportation Planning by Jeffrey Tumlin
This book considers the topic of urban planning from the perspective of how we get around. Tumlin's argument is that transportation planning is stuck in a 1950s mind-set where everyone is happy to hop in their cars to fulfill their daily needs. He calls for including biking, walking, and mass transit in transportation and city economic development plans, rather than considering only cars. In laying out his argument, Tumlin considers success stories from all over the country.

CNU.org Congress for the New Urbanism (CNU) is the leading organization promoting walkable, mixed-use development, sustainable communities, and more healthful living conditions. The movement's complete mission is laid out in its Charter of the New Urbanism, available on the website. Now in its third decade, the CNU has chapters all over the United States, as well as around the world. Find out if there's a chapter in your area by visiting the website. If there isn't one, learn how to start your own.

What Can You Do? Gauge potential and get involved. Unless you are a developer or planner, many of the details will probably be handled by others. What you can do, though, is seek out areas that are already enacting sprawl repair or are at least open to the idea. It is easier than you might think to assess the future growth plans for a potential community. One option is to read your local newspaper for reports on new "mixed-use" or "walkable" developments. Or you can visit the website of your city's planning department. (Google your city together with "planning commission" or "planning department" and "city plan.") Once on the site, look for any mention of "a comprehensive growth plan" or "studies." Skim through these reports for mention of "mixed-use development." Look also for plans to support accommodations for pedestrians and bikes. If you have questions about what you are finding, call the planning department. Then, get out and be heard. Support positive growth in city council and planning board meetings.

Infill or Greyfield Development Infill development is development that fills in empty lots in cities and urban neighborhoods. Cheap land, cheap oil, and a tolerance for endless commutes once drove development farther and farther away from city centers. It was cheaper and easier to move out to build in farm fields than to repurpose land in the city. Today, everything has changed, and the value of this abandoned land is understood again—saving forests, grasslands, and farmland outside of cities, and saving tax dollars by not requiring new roads, sewers, or other infrastructure. Greyfield and brownfield developments repurpose failed strip malls, abandoned grocery stores, and dilapidated factory complexes into new mixed-use, walkable communities. These neighborhoods are often more affordable than historic neighborhoods in your city and offer many of the same features.

What can you do? Ask around to see if there are new residential infill projects or redeveloped grey- and brownfield sites in your city. And, as with sprawl repair, get out and be heard; attend city council and planning board meetings to speak out in support of positive growth.

Support Form-Based Codes Form-based codes are an alternative to conventional zoning codes. Conventional zoning codes focus on use and statistics (units per acre, parking ratios, and so forth), and as a result, the built structures often do not work together to create a greater whole. Form-based codes, on the other hand, focus first on the creation of a public realm. Density and parking are still addressed, but in the context of a whole area. Form-based codes are being adopted in municipalities nationwide to combat and repair suburban sprawl. To learn more about form-based codes and your community, visit the website of the Form Based Code Institute at FormBasedCodes.org.

NIMBYS AND BANANAS

Density is a word that scares a lot of people, typically because they don't really know what it means. Density in and of itself is not the problem. Poorly designed density is the problem. When done well, density increases property values, is beautiful to look at, and allows for multiple options for transportation, including walking. Unfortunately, the sad

> **Density in and of itself is not the problem. Poorly designed density is the problem. When done right, density increases property value.**

reality of our recent building history is that rather than contributing to the public realm, new high density development more likely will simply be an eyesore that you have to look at while sitting in the traffic congestion that it causes. As a result, the kneejerk reaction by many is to fight all density, regardless of its merits.

What are NIMBYs and BANANAs? NIMBYs (not in my backyard) and BANANAs (build absolutely nothing anywhere near anything) work hard as activists at city council meetings and planning board sessions to stop new development. I get it. I really do. But not all development is equal.

Here's the challenge: Cities need development to grow and keep a strong tax base. Development in and of itself does not create traffic. Poorly designed development creates traffic. Density does not have to mean apartment complexes with treated wood balconies set around amoeba-shaped berms. Instead, density can be a row of town houses linking up with a main street and public square. Mixed use doesn't mean that your neighbor is going to start an auto repair shop next to your house. It means living down the street from a dry cleaner, coffee shop, or corner store.

"But Wasn't Jane Jacobs a NIMBY?" It's one thing for Jane Jacobs to rally against a multilane expressway that would have plowed through Lower Manhattan. But it's another to oppose growth just for the sake of opposition, especially when it comes to infill development that turns vacant parts of a neighborhood into homes, offices, and stores so that population growth can be accommodated without building new roads or consuming more natural land and resources.

How to Determine Which Developments to Support Unfortunately, so much of the growth that's taken place in recent decades has been harmful that it is hard to differentiate between positive and negative. What is important to realize, though, is that mixed-use, high-density development can be a very good thing for a neighborhood. More buildings mean an increase in retail space, bringing shops and services closer to home. More homes mean an increase in tax base, which pumps revenue back into the community. So how do you distinguish between positive infill development and NIMBY-justified negative growth? Here are four questions to ask:

1. Is the density used to create a public realm and define an outdoor room?
2. Is parking accessible, yet hidden (tucked behind a building rather than in front)?
3. Is there potential for connecting to a mass transit system to accommodate the increase in population over time?
4. Is there a mix of uses (commercial and residential) on streets designed to be walkable such that residents aren't required to get in the car to meet all their needs?

If you are fighting sprawl, by all means, fight the good fight. But if you are fighting for the sake of fighting, please stop. Development can be a good thing for you and your community. It is worth your time to differentiate between positive and negative growth.

CHAPTER CHEAT SHEET

Gut Check

Do you want to make changes to your home or community, and if so, do you want to make cosmetic or deeper renovations?

Reality Check

Do you have the time, budget, and patience to make these changes?

Balancing Act

Function—What changes would be necessary to get your home or community to meet your needs? *Cost*—What is the price for making these changes? *Delight*—Will these changes really make a difference?

Key points to remember

• If you can't find the right home to move into or are unable to move because of finances, consider making changes, either cosmetic or with deeper renovations, to make your current home your dream home.

• Renovations aren't just for homes. Look for ways to enhance your neighborhood through either cosmetic or deeper renovations.

• If you are a renter, consider cosmetic changes, but avoid deeper renovations.

Chapter 19

Working with the Pros

Although online research is an essential component of your search, finding a new place to live, especially for those who are buying, requires working with a group of professionals. This chapter is devoted to helping you assemble a real estate team that has the necessary expertise. No matter how well intentioned, not all professionals are created equal, nor does everyone match your personal style. And so, for the key professionals who will aid you in the process of your search, purchase, and beyond, I'll tell you their basic role and what fees, if any, that they're likely to charge, and provide you with a list of questions to ask as well as the answers you want to hear. Although each relationship is unique, and you'll work far more closely with some than others, they should all share the goal of helping you find the best home on the best possible terms.

Real Estate, Mortgage, and Legal Professionals

REAL ESTATE PROFESSIONAL

Think of this person as your lead liaison. He or she is with you from the start of the process until the keys are handed to you at closing.

You'll spend a lot of time together, either in person or on the phone and via email, so it's important to have chemistry, trust, and excellent communication. In Chapter 1, we looked at some of the default real estate jargon you might encounter: "Location, location, location," "You'll need it to resell," "But if you look for just a little more, you can have . . . ," all of which roughly translate to purchasing more house than you can afford, filled with things you don't want, in a "great" location, even if that location isn't anywhere near where you need to go daily. As you start to meet with real estate professionals, look for ones open to shedding these default statements in favor of these three crucial points:

Proximity trumps location.

Live-in value trumps resale value.

It's not a great deal if you can't afford it.

Before Your First Meeting Go into your first meeting with a firm understanding of your budget, proximity priorities, and housing needs and wants. Although you might adjust these during your search as you tour the available options, your search will be more informed because you are prepared up front.

Real estate professionals go by different names, depending on their level of training and experience. Here are the three main types:

Agents If you visit RE/MAX or Century 21 or any of the big, nation-wide real estate agencies, you'll most likely end up with a real estate agent, the most common type of professional. They must be licensed in the state where they work, which typically involves classroom instruction, passing an exam, and renewing their credentials every few years.

Brokers A step up from an agent, brokers have more training, education, and experience. Brokers often serve as supervisors in large agencies, overseeing the work of agents in the field. In smaller offices, brokers may still work directly with clients. That's the advantage of working with a smaller agency—hands-on treatment from an experienced pro.

Realtors Though this term has become synonymous with real estate professional, it actually refers only to members of the National Association of Realtors. That means they must comply with the association's standards of practice and code of ethics, and they must renew their license every few years. Realtors are also likely to be well-connected, with a deep knowledge of listings in an area, and they're often up on the latest industry news and happenings. Both agents and brokers can be Realtors.

No matter which type you choose, your real estate pro is there to work for you. He or she will have access to the Multiple Listing Service (MLS), a database of available homes for sale from many real estate agencies. This does not include homes for sale by owner. Although the big real estate offices offer more services and probably know about the greatest number of listings through their extensive network of offices, you may get more personalized treatment and deeper knowledge of local markets by going with a boutique agency.

Most real estate professionals work with buyers as well as sellers. A buyer's agent works to find the best property and get the best deal for the buyer. A seller's agent works to get the highest price for the seller. There is also such a thing as a dual agent, who represents both the buyer and the seller on the same transaction. That can be a serious conflict of interest, which is why most states require written consent by both parties in this type of transaction. Your best bet is getting a buyer's agent who is contractually bound to represent your interests only. For good measure, ask the agent if they will ever represent you in dual agency. The right answer is "Not a chance." Here are six other questions to ask, and the types of answers you want to hear:

> **" Go into your first meeting with a firm understanding of your budget, proximity priorities, and housing needs and wants. "**

Is this your full-time job? Yes, I've been in this profession for many years, long enough to have watched the last boom-and-bust cycle and others like it.

What are your bona fides? In addition to my state's license and general membership card from the National Association of Realtors, I have my Accredited Buyer Representative designation, which means I have special skills and training working with buyers.

How many transactions do you handle in a typical year? Unfortunately, given all the volatility in the recent housing market, there haven't been too many typical years lately. But I always have at least ten transactions, and the majority of them are in your price range and geographic area, so I'm confident that I'll be able to present you with many good options as we begin the search together.

How do you get paid? Like all real estate professionals, I work for commission. The good news for homebuyers is that it's the seller who pays my entire fee. Commissions are usually around 6 percent of the sales price of the home. So on a $200,000 transaction, the commission will be $12,000. This payment usually ends up split between the buyer and seller agent.

Can you give me references of recent clients? I would be happy to provide you with as many names as you like, including three names from the last year. I hope that will give you an understanding of how I've been dealing with the current market challenges.

What's the best way to reach you? My cell phone is always turned on, though I prefer that you try to call me during office hours. But if it's an emergency, or you're feeling particularly anxious about something, don't hesitate to call. Remember, I work for you.

> **Fast Fact** By the end of 2011, the National Association of Realtors had just over 1 million active members, down roughly 25 percent from its 2007 peak.

MORTGAGE PROFESSIONAL

Unless you plan to pay cash for your next home, there will be a mortgage professional in your not-so-distant future. Given the mortgage meltdown in the recent housing collapse, the mortgage industry is still trying to recover its reputation. The good news is that most of the hucksters who were just in it to make a quick buck have been weeded out. But you still need to do your due diligence to find the right fit. As with real estate professionals, there are multiple options.

Mortgage broker A middleman between you and the bank or lender whose job is to sort through all the options and find the best deal for you, given your financial situation and long-term goals. They make money by marking up the cost of the loan, usually in the form of points, with one point equaling 1 percent of the loan value.

Mortgage banker You can also get a home loan directly from a lender by using a mortgage banker. You avoid the broker fees, though you have to shop around for the best loan, which can be a time-consuming and confusing process.

It's always best to secure a mortgage pro before you find your home. That way you won't rush into a relationship without proper vetting. If you go the broker route, you should still call a few lenders directly—say your local community bank, a larger national bank, and a credit union—to get a sense of the going rates. It pays to get a crystal-clear understanding of your financial situation before shopping around for a mortgage. Remember these key points from Chapter 3:

When buying a home, you need to consider the total costs of homeownership. In addition to the mortgage payments, insurance, and taxes, four big costs to think about are transportation, operating costs, maintenance, and any remodeling expenses that you'll need to incur before moving in. Your mortgage lender will likely not ask these questions, so it is up to you to consider all the costs of your new home. It is also a good idea to learn your credit score before meeting with a mortgage professional. If you use a mortgage broker, be sure to ask these questions:

Do you work full time as a mortgage broker? Yes, this is my sole profession, and it has been for many years. I work almost exclusively on residential properties.

What other services do you offer that I can't do on my own? My certification from the National Association of Mortgage Brokers shows that I have the experience and knowledge of today's market to give you the best possible financial advice. Once we settle on the right loan, I'll help you assemble all the necessary documents, coordinate the property appraisal, and help you navigate any bumps that come up on the way to closing.

> **Fast Fact** Approximately 4.5 million existing homes were sold in 2012, compared with a record 7 million homes in 2005. Tougher rules by mortgage lenders contributed to the decline. For example, the share of mortgages given to people with credit scores below 600 dropped from 9.0 percent in 2006 to just 0.5 percent in 2010, and the share given to people with scores of 740 or higher increased from about 34 percent to about 44 percent.

How do you get paid? My fee will either be a fixed dollar amount, a percentage of the loan amount, or a combination of both. But once the fee is set, you'll have it in writing, and there's no way it will change. I can guarantee this because I'm a member of the Upfront Mortgage Brokers Association, a consumer advocacy group whose mission is to ensure total transparency in all mortgage transactions.

Will I be preapproved by you or just prequalified? The process starts with prequalification, where I tell you what size mortgage I think you can afford based on such factors as your income, credit report, and savings. If you decide to actually apply for a mortgage, we'll then go through the preapproval process, which is more thorough and requires you to compile a lot of paperwork, including pay stubs, W-2 forms, and bank statements. Although you will have to pay a credit report fee, I do not charge any sort of application fee, which is a common practice among predatory lenders.

Can I check your references? Absolutely. I'll give you three names of clients I've worked with in the past year and others from before the housing crash so you can see the consistency of my standards and practices.

ATTORNEY

Many states require an attorney for real estate transactions. Even if yours doesn't, it's worth hiring one to structure the deal. Don't expect the seller's attorney to have your legal interests in mind. There's a lot to keep track of in real estate, including reviewing the sales contract, ensuring compliance with terms and conditions, doing a title search and going over its commitment, negotiating any disputes with the seller, and being there with you at the closing. These three questions will help you land the best lawyer:

Do you practice many types of law? No, I'm strictly a real estate attorney. I've been practicing for many years, and I have a lot of experience in residential real estate transactions, so I'm very familiar with contracts, titles, and so on.

How do you charge? I charge by the hour, but because I've been doing this for so long, I don't waste time getting up to speed with local real estate laws. I'll write up a fee agreement that will outline what I do and when you'll pay me. And I'll let you know anytime the number of hours and corresponding fee start to go over the amount in the original agreement.

Can I check your references? Because of the confidential nature of my work, I can't give out names. But if you really want to speak with a former client, I can ask one of them to contact you.

CLOSING AGENT

You may not meet your closing agent until the actual closing day, but he or she will have been working behind the scenes to get all the paperwork together. That includes arranging your title insurance, coordinating with your lender and the seller to make sure the latter is paid in full before the property changes hands, and establishing an escrow or trust account to keep your deposit or any monies the seller has agreed to deposit for repairs.

The closing agent's fee is typically included in the closing costs. Sometimes it's split between the buyer and seller, though it may also be charged in full to one of the parties. Unlike with a home inspector, it's usually okay to go with a closing agent who's recommended by your real estate agent, especially if you have an attorney who is reviewing all the terms and conditions of the transaction. There's certainly no harm in asking for references and speaking to a couple of past clients. You also want to make sure the closing agent is conveniently located, since you'll have to get there for the closing.

Inspectors and Contractors

PROPERTY INSPECTOR

Paying for a thorough inspection before you sign on the dotted line could be the best $200 to $600 you spend on your home. A trained eye will pick up on latent defects you could easily miss, such as termite tracks in the sill plate or soggy ground around the septic tank. In newer homes, lack of ventilation and moisture intrusion are two invisible concerns that can lead to serious mold problems down the line. Although most property inspectors are ethical, it's one of those professions with a lot of opportunity for corruption. An important rule of thumb: Think twice if your inspector offers to repair the problems he or she spots. This scenario creates too much conflict of interest. For tips on finding a property inspector, see page 290. Here are three questions to ask during the vetting process:

What are your credentials? I've been a member of the American Society of Home Inspectors for many years, so I have the latest training and I follow the code of ethics. Before I became a home inspector, I worked as a residential contractor. That means I understand home construction and can determine pretty quickly if a home was well built or not, and which systems are coming to the end of their life cycles. Depending on the market, I'll do between 200 and 400 inspections a year.

What's covered in your inspection report? All the property's major structural and mechanical systems. That includes a close inspection of the foundation, where I'll be looking for serious cracks or buckling walls; the siding and roof, where I'll check for leaks and general wear; the plumbing and electrical wiring, which need to be up to code; and the heating system, which should be properly sized and in good working condition. Those are just a few examples. I'll provide a full written report that goes over every last detail of the inspection. The one thing that won't be included in my general inspection is pest control, since that has to be handled by a separate inspector.

Can I tag along on the inspection? Absolutely. In fact, I prefer that clients be present during my inspections. You don't have to climb into the crawl spaces with me, but I want you to be close by in case I come across major issues that need explaining.

ENERGY INSPECTOR AND INDOOR AIR QUALITY CONSULTANT

I discussed these two professionals at length in Chapters 16 and 17, where their specialties of home efficiency and safety were most applicable. But I'm including them again here because they belong on any complete roster of the real estate team. An energy inspector will typically charge a few hundred dollars to perform a soup-to-nuts assessment of a home's efficiency, including an inspection of the insulation and the heating and cooling equipment. An indoor air quality consultant may charge more or less, depending on the number of pollutants he or she is testing for, with lead and radon being common targets.

REMODELING CONTRACTOR

If you plan to remodel the home, it's important to get a contractor early in the process. But do so after the home inspection so that the contractor can figure those findings into his or her estimate of the remodeling project. If you plan to work with an architect, get that person's early buy-in as well. Word of mouth is typically the best way to find a good contractor, though you can also try online services like Angie's List and Service Magic. Be sure to meet with at least three contractors and ask them the following questions:

Will you provide a written contract? Yes, my contract will spell out every phase of the project, including the targeted start and end dates and every product, down to the model number on any appliances and the choice of finish on the fixtures. I try to limit the number of allowances in a contract, since these blank lines are where a lot of the unexpected costs can come in. Of course, it's up to you to make sure you don't keep changing your mind on the project, since that's by far the costliest overrun.

Do you have your license and insurance? Yes, I am licensed to do business in this state and I carry general liability insurance and workers' compensation. That means that if one of my guys gets hurt during the project, you won't be liable.

Can I check your references? I'll give you three names of recent clients, including ones whose project was about the same size and scale of what you're planning. I recommend you go inspect the work in person if possible, since that will let you see the quality of my craftsmanship and you can also hear firsthand how the project went.

How much do you charge? It depends on the scale of the project, of course, but as a general rule, the labor and project management comes in at around 40 percent of the total project cost. In other words, if we're doing a $50,000 kitchen, this breaks down to $30,000 for materials and $20,000 for time and labor.

Design Professionals

"Minimizing the importance of good design is the biggest mistake people make when remodeling," says Bruce Irving, a renovation consultant and longtime producer of the PBS show *This Old House.* I couldn't agree more, and the point is true for interior design and renovations as well as new construction. The alignment of openings, the proportion of space, and even the selection of complementary colors can make a small room live large or blah space feel fantastic. As with finding a contractor, word of mouth is usually the best way to find design help, though each of the professions below has its own organizational backing that can help you find names in your area.

ARCHITECT

If you are planning a major renovation or new construction, consider hiring an architect. Although stock house plans are available online, nothing beats living in a home that was custom designed for you. Some architects charge a flat rate, and others charge by the hour or by a percentage of the total construction costs, so it's important to establish up front how the fee will be structured. The American Institute of Architects (aia.org) is the national association.

DESIGNER

The word *designer* covers many specialties. For renovations as well as new custom home design, consider hiring a residential building designer. (It is a little-known fact that most homes are not designed by architects but rather by residential building designers. Architects typically focus more on commercial projects.) Like architects, the fee will vary, depending on the scope of work, and will be either a flat rate, an hourly rate, or a percentage of the cost of construction. The American Institute for Building Designers (www.aibd.org) is the professional organization for residential building designers. Designers can also specialize in single room remodels, namely the kitchen or bathroom. The National Kitchen and Bath Association (nkba.org) has a national directory. According to the organization, design fees typically work out to about 5 percent of the total cost of the project, though some designers may choose to charge an hourly rate.

INTERIOR DECORATOR

If you're paralyzed by paint color, flummoxed by furnishings, or simply uninterested in sifting through catalogs of bathroom fixtures, hiring an interior decorator (or designer, as they're also called) could be money well spent. Fees are either hourly or a percentage of the items purchased. An added benefit of hiring a decorator is that not only do you get great advice, but some of the cost will be offset by the discounts pros get on furniture and other big-ticket items. The American Society of Interior Designers' website (asid.org) has an online referral service that can lead you to professionals in your area.

LANDSCAPE ARCHITECT/DESIGNER

These professionals can help you create the "outdoor room" effect discussed at length in Chapter 8. This includes creating zones throughout the property, such as a welcoming zone in the front yard and a private-living zone behind the house. Learn more and find a local professional through the American Society of Landscape Architects (asla.org) or the Association of Professional Landscape Designers (apld.com).

ORGANIZER

Professional organizers are often called in after years of clutter have collected in closets, hallways, and more. But they can be useful before you've moved a single item into your home, helping you come up with organizational strategies that will prevent clutter issues in the future. Even if they only help you come up with a system for the various storage closets, it can be worth the cost, which might amount to a few hundred dollars. To find a professional organizer in your area, check the website of the National Association of Professional Organizers (napo.net).

Changing Local Codes

Throughout the book, I have talked about the power of individuals to make a difference in their community, whether it's arguing for the benefits of granny flats (page 202), cautioning against material ordinances (page 217), or offering suggestions for renovating your neighborhood (page 313). If you are interested in getting involved locally to change codes and ordinances to support positive growth in your community, here are the professionals you might encounter.

City Councils The city council is typically made up of the mayor and a board of elected officials. They meet once or twice a month to conduct the business of the city and to hear concerns from citizens. The city council votes on the codes, ordinances, and zoning rules of a municipality. Agendas are posted in advance of meetings so you can plan your attendance to speak in support of or against developments and policies.

City Planning Board Most cities have a planning board that will meet monthly to discuss new projects. You can attend and speak out for or against proposed developments. The planning board is typically limited to following the codes and ordinances put in place by the city council, but it has the power to approve or deny projects.

REAL ESTATE PROFESSIONAL PREP WORKSHEET

Seasoned real estate professionals will guide you through the process of making a move, but the more you can articulate about yourself, the better they will be able to help you. Take serious stock of he following questions before your first meeting.

Your basic stats:

1. Why are you searching for a new home?
2. What is working or not working about where you live now?
3. When would you like to move?
4. Do you want to rent or own?
5. What price range is most comfortable for you?

Your wants and needs:

1. What are the most important elements in a neighborhood?
2. What are the essentials for your new home?
3. What have you looked at so far?
4. What do you like and dislike about what you have seen so far in your search?

Your realities:

1. Will you pay cash or will you be taking out a mortgage?
2. Are you pre-qualified for a mortgage? How much?
3. Do you need to sell an existing home to move forward?
4. Do you have the funds to make a deposit?
5. Do you have to consult anyone else before making a decision?
6. What other factors could impact the decision to move forward? (Example: a new job or promotion)

CHAPTER CHEAT SHEET

Gut Check

Do you feel comfortable with and trust your team of professionals?

Reality Check

Are you on the same page with your real estate professional about your wants, needs, and financial realities? Have you checked references, especially for contractors, to make sure your team can deliver what has been agreed upon?

Balancing Act

Function—Have you done your homework so that you can come to meetings prepared? *Cost*—Can you afford the decisions you are making? *Delight*—You don't have to be friends with your team of professionals (in fact it is better if you are not friends), but it is necessary to have a good rapport and working relationship. Do you?

Key point to remember

All professionals offer a range of skills, expertise, and personalities. The first people you meet with might not be the exact right fit. Spend the time to assemble a team whom you trust and with whom you believe you can work well.

Appendices

APPENDIX 1 Navigating the Landscape

CRASH COURSE: A BRIEF HISTORY OF SUBURBAN SPRAWL AND WHY IT MATTERS TO YOU

If you are in the process of deciding where to live, most likely many, if not all, of the places you consider will be part of, or touched by, suburban sprawl. *To make the best possible decision about where you want to live, you need to understand what suburban sprawl is and how it works.* Although it can be argued that this content is technical in nature, explaining these details is crucial so you will have an insider's advantage when searching for a new place to live. We are living in a time where the formulas for how, where, and what we build have been turned upside down. The givens of yesterday are no longer true today. Only by understanding what has come before can you make a truly informed decision about where and how you want to live tomorrow.

NOT ALL DEVELOPMENT IS CREATED EQUAL

Think of quaint places you have visited, vibrant neighborhoods with streets rich in character—the places that you love the most. What stands out in your mind? Perhaps it was a sidewalk café, maybe a pocket park or a canopy of trees. There is a better chance than not that the places you're visualizing were built before World War II, or were modeled on prewar patterns of development. These communities were built with stores, libraries, churches, schools, and so on close to homes and apartments. This mix of uses and walkable streets has been proven over time to hold value longer, promote more healthful lifestyles, and consume fewer natural resources than places like strip malls and suburban tracts that are dependent on cars. These are places where you want to spend time.

Now think about the neighborhood where you live or are looking at in your search. If the neighborhood was built after the war, there is a good chance it is auto dependent, where the streets are conduits for cars rather than places shared between cars, pedestrians, and retail. There is a good chance you live in or are looking at moving to suburban sprawl.

WHAT IS SUBURBAN SPRAWL?

The Suburban Dream It began as the iconic image of the American Dream Home after World War II: the house with the white picket fence and a car in the driveway. Auto independence allowed you to get in a car and go anywhere you wanted to go at any time. The suburban dream provided relief from overcrowded and polluted cities.

The Sprawl Nightmare Over time, with the rise of the automobile and shifting zoning codes, the positive patterns of suburban growth as seen in streetcar suburbs and bungalow neighborhoods gave way to uncontrolled, low-density development known today as suburban sprawl. In areas of sprawl, building types and uses are completely separated from each other—with grocery stores and movie theaters often miles from residences—and accessible only by car. Sprawl is primarily auto dependent, offering residents little or no opportunity to walk or bike and with limited, if any, access to mass transit.

The Takeaway It is hard to argue with the desire for clean, convenient, and easy living. The vision for our suburbs was strong, but in the end, the pattern of growth did not deliver on the promise. The dream of auto independence turned into the reality of auto dependence. Cities that were once overcrowded and polluted are now clean and easy to navigate, and the roads of sprawling suburbs are overcrowded and polluted.

For decades, living in sprawling suburbs has been the default setting for most of the American middle class. This is a lifestyle that has come at a great cost to many people. In most cases, we accepted sprawl as a given, because as an individual, it's hard to change how our streets or cities are made. Luckily, today we have a chance to reset the default and you can be first in line. You might find that your only option is to live in some part of sprawl, but not all sprawl is created equal, so with a little savvy, you can navigate through to find the best possible fit.

THE COST OF SPRAWL

The environmental, economic, and social cost of sprawl and uncontrolled growth has been, and will continue to be, enormous. The dream of auto independence has turned into complete dependence. Not only is the car required for every trip outside most homes, but gridlock and congestion are accepted as normal. Here are some of the costs of sprawl:

- Nearly two thirds of the petroleum used in the United States is consumed by transportation, primarily individual cars.

- Transportation contributes to 85 percent of greenhouse gas emissions, and an estimated 46 percent of vehicles in the United States leak hazardous fluids, contributing to water pollution.

- More than one third of adults (35.7 percent) and approximately 17 percent (or 12.5 million) of children in the United States are obese, according to the Centers for Disease Control and Prevention.

- A 2011 study by Umea University in Sweden found that couples in which one partner commutes for longer than forty-five minutes are 40 percent likelier to divorce. In the United States, roughly one in six workers commutes for more than ninety minutes each day, and a Gallup survey found that one in three of them has recurrent neck or back problems.

- Over a five-year period, the costs of owning, operating, and maintaining a car, assuming you drive 15,000 miles a year, can add up to $25,000 for a compact sedan or more than $100,000 for a luxury sedan, according to Kelly Blue Book. Multiply these expenses times the number of cars in your household, often one for every member of your family over the age of sixteen.

STRATEGIES FOR NAVIGATING SPRAWL

Avoid Sprawl Altogether If you are interested in living a lifestyle where you can spend more time out of the car, look for communities with sidewalks, access to transit, and a way to walk to work, school, stores, and recreation. This might take the form of moving into a city center or a neighborhood adjacent to a downtown. You can also look at streetcar suburbs and bungalow neighborhoods (see pages 167 and 168).

Action Item: Your best go-to resource will be WalkScore.com. Plug in the city name that you are looking at, and the site will give you a list of the top ten most walkable areas. From WalkScore.com, you will also be able to calculate your projected commute time from any of these neighborhoods to your place of work.

Balance Your Proximity Priorities So, what do you do when the housing options in your city's walkable communities don't meet your needs and/or budget realities? For you, I would recommend making it a priority to have at least one place near your home that you want to walk to. Perhaps you can find a home near a good school. Even if you have to drive to all of your other needs, at least your kids can walk to school—and you will save more than ten car trips a week. Maybe you can find a house near a convenience store or coffee shop or a couple of blocks from a park. You would be commuting long distances, but at least when you got home, there would a viable reason to park your car and walk.

Action Item: As you look for homes, try to make sure that there is at least one amenity (such as a school, shop, restaurant, beach, or park) within a safe and viable walking distance from your home. Safe and viable means not only being a short distance but also that the route is designed in such a way that you would actually walk to this amenity.

Look for Communities Open to Sprawl Repair Municipalities and communities across the country are beginning to embrace the idea of converting sprawling suburbs into walkable mixed-use neighborhoods—places with homes, stores, apartments, and offices. In Chapter 18, I cover this concept in more detail, explaining examples of sprawl repair as well as outlining how you can find communities open to embracing the concepts.

BACK TO THE FUTURE: THE RISE OF NEW URBANISM

New Urban or Traditional Neighborhood Developments (TNDs) and smart-growth policies create sustainable, walkable, and mixed-use communities where people can walk to work, school, and other places to meet a variety of their daily needs. These developments combine the best of traditional planning principles of walkability, connectivity, and mixed use with the benefits of modern technology, from smart transportation to solar-powered heating and cooling systems.

Since the New Urbanism movement started in 1988, more than 4,000 TNDs have either sprung up or are in the works throughout the United States. A 2007 study by real estate professors Mark Eppli and Charles Tu, found that the prices of single-family homes in two New Urban communities, Kentlands and Lakelands in Maryland, were 16.1 and 6.5 percent higher, respectively, than comparable homes in surrounding suburbs with conventional subdivisions.

> **These developments combine the best of traditional planning principles of walkability, connectivity, and mixed use with the benefits of modern technology, from smart transportation to solar-powered heating and cooling systems.**

In 2011, the federal government conducted a similar study comparing eighteen smart-growth developments and eighteen conventional developments across the country. In ten of the comparisons, higher resale appreciation was recorded for the smart-growth developments. The study concluded that "housing units in these developments not only hold their value over time, but in more cases than not, buyers are willing to pay a premium to live in these projects over other competitive suburban housing units in the same market."

Andres Duany, a founding principal of the architecture and planning firm Duany Plater-Zyberk and widely recognized as the leader

Suburban Nation

Suburban Nation: The Rise of Sprawl and the Decline of the American Dream **by Andres Duany, Elizabeth Plater-Zyberk, and Jeff Speck.** Want to dive deeper into how sprawl happened and what can be done to reverse the trend? If so, this book is an essential read. *Suburban Nation* unpacks the nuanced history of sprawl while explaining how we can make changes that will improve the health and wealth of our cities, neighborhoods, and homes.

of the New Urbanism, attributes the success of New Urbanism to the role of the public realm in encouraging social interaction. He explains that the private realm of sprawl—i.e., the inside of your home or your office—is usually pretty nice. But the minute you enter into public, everything changes. The process of getting to your next destination becomes a negative experience. As you sit in your car, every person you encounter is also in a car. Not only does this eliminate positive social encounters, but it actually creates stressful exchanges as you compete with the other drivers for the precious commodity called asphalt. Duany explains that New Urbanism, by contrast, uses the designs of communities to form the backdrop for an active public realm, one in which the journey between destinations while walking on sidewalks becomes an opportunity to run into acquaintances and even meet potential new friends.

"But isn't that only for rich people?" Despite the high quality of life TNDs afford, there are a fair number of New Urbanism critics, including those who say the communities feel contrived. Critics of New Urbanism contend that the communities lack ethnic and economic diversity by catering too heavily to white, affluent homeowners. Although yes, the prices in these communities are often higher than conventional developments in neighboring areas, this is a result of supply and demand. When you build a community with an identity, people want to live there. Often prices start low and shoot up, as the example above of Kentlands in Maryland shows. This is why New Urban communities can be a great place to purchase a home.

"Nice idea, but you can't build like that anymore." In some respects, no, you can't. But not because the design skill or construction knowledge isn't available. Often it is illegal to build mixed-use walkable communities because building and zoning codes don't allow it. The codes are often focused on ensuring that single-family residences are separate from offices, multifamily buildings, or other land uses.

On August 29, 2005, the storm surge from Hurricane Katrina literally swept away large swaths of communities across the Mississippi Gulf Coast. As the rebuilding efforts started, a painful truth emerged: Over the course of the previous sixty years, zoning codes had changed so much that on August 30, 2005, it was illegal to rebuild the neighborhoods that had been standing just forty-eight hours earlier. Luckily in most cases, allowances were made through new planning efforts and grandfathered rights. But it was a very telling moment in the history of planning.

Think about your city. What would happen if your most cherished neighborhoods, the streetcar suburbs and bungalow neighborhoods, were destroyed by a natural disaster? Would you not want to rebuild them? Now think beyond the old: If these places hold so much importance, doesn't it make sense to allow new communities to be built using similar patterns?

Action Item: Search for Traditional Neighborhood Developments in your area by visiting TNDTownPaper.com. Click on the link for "TND Neighborhoods" to see a list of TNDs by state. Each development listed includes a link to the project's website.

APPENDIX 2 Driving Me Crazy

Ever notice that we park in a driveway and drive on a parkway? You might not find the humor in this old planners' joke if you're one of the millions of commuters spending rush hour parked on a freeway. Long commutes and traffic congestion aren't just a hassle and a bore;

they have deep implications for your pocketbook, physical and mental health, and the environment, especially as cheap gas seems to be a thing of the past.

The irony about traffic congestion is that while you are driving one inch per hour on a freeway, traffic is racing like stock cars through your "quiet" residential neighborhood.

So what can you do? Surprisingly, quite a lot.

CUL-DE-SACS CREATE SPEEDING TRAFFIC

No matter how well designed your streets are, if there is only one way to get in and out of a neighborhood, the volume of traffic will be heavy on the streets that connect. This is why if you live in a neighborhood with cul-de-sacs, the cul-de-sac is the preferred location.

It is easy to look at the cul-de-sac as a solution to traffic problems, but in reality, it is a cause of traffic problems. This is an important enough point to repeat: Cul-de-sacs create the very traffic that they are built to avoid. Cul-de-sacs greatly reduce the number of through-streets within a community, resulting in residents being forced to drive long distances on a road for what is actually a short distance as the crow would fly.

If all of the streets in a community were connected in a network with a hierarchy of sizes, there wouldn't be a backlog in any one area. The traffic would be diffused throughout the grid, relieving the pressure on a few small streets to carry the burden for all. That's why some cities and municipalities, including Charlotte, North Carolina; Portland, Oregon; and Austin, Texas, have all but banned cul-de-sacs.

Action Item: When looking for a new place to live, pay careful attention to the flow of traffic on the streets in, out, and around a potential neighborhood. If the neighborhood has a large number of cul-de-sacs, expect the few connecting streets to turn into busy thoroughfares during rush hours.

> **Fast Fact** It is estimated that every shared car results in somewhere between nine and twenty fewer private vehicles on the road.

SPEEDING UP CONGESTED STREETS—HURRY UP, THEN WAIT!

At the other extreme from the speeding traffic in residential neighborhoods is the congestion on larger collector roads and freeways. The best way to reduce traffic congestion is to take cars off the road, which might be easier than you think if you consider that half of all car trips are three miles or less and 28 percent are one mile or less. But even though many of these trips are short, the only way to realistically take cars off the road is to offer viable alternatives that are convenient, safe, and clean.

In his 2012 book *Sustainable Transportation Planning: Tools for Creating Vibrant, Healthy, and Resilient Communities*, Jeffrey Tumlin says that even in the most congested corridor, the difference between gridlock and free-flow traffic is only 10 percent, and he offers several options to reduce traffic congestion. *One of the most important points in the book is that the addition of more lanes to a road does not cure traffic—it creates more of it.*

The easiest way to take cars off the road is to design communities where some, if not all, of your daily needs can be met by walking, biking, or taking mass transit. Although this is the easiest way if you are starting with a blank slate, it does not help those who are in existing communities or looking for a home in a city with a limited range of neighborhood options. There are several things you can do, both for your community and individually.

> **The easiest way to take cars off the road is to design communities where some, if not all, of your daily needs can be met by walking, biking, or taking mass transit.**

Support bike lanes and racks. According to Tumlin, biking is a reasonable option for trips three miles or less (almost half of all car trips). Making biking a viable alternative requires safe, dedicated lanes for bicycle riders as well as accessible bike racks. Even if you don't plan to ride, every person on a bike is one less person on the road with you.

Become an activist. Support initiatives for infill development that provides a mix of uses and higher densities. If more residences are closer to retail and offices, that means fewer cars will be on the roads. (See more in Chapter 18.)

Give priority to high-frequency transit (bus, light rail, and so on). If taking the bus takes twice as long as commuting by car, more people are going to hop behind the wheel. But if taking transit is faster and easier than driving, more people will take transit. Some cities are giving buses priority at traffic signals so they don't have to wait at stoplights.

Consider car sharing. In the absence of options at a community scale, Tumlin offers other creative options such as car sharing, a paid service that provides 24/7 access to vehicles in city neighborhoods. It is ideal for anyone who occasionally needs a car but doesn't need day-to-day access to one. Zipcar, the biggest car-sharing service in the world, now operates in about a dozen U.S. cities. Rentals are available for as little as one hour at a time. Members sign up online and pay an annual fee of about $60. This gets them a special card that unlocks cars reserved through their computer or smartphone. Rates are about $10 per hour or $80 for the day.

The city of Austin passed a resolution that creates free parking spaces for car-sharing vehicles and exempts them from parking meter charges. An active car-sharing community is a good sign that a city has a healthy transportation ecosystem.

APPENDIX 3 McMansions: What You Need to Know

"They've been called McMansions, Starter Castles, Garage Mahals, and Faux Chateaus, but here's the latest thing you can call them— History," declared a 2010 CNBC feature. So what are McMansions, how did they happen, and are they really finished? And most important, what do you need to know about them when making your housing decisions? This section will answer these questions.

McMansions come in all shapes and sizes, from "Happy Meal" snout houses to larger Hummer Homes with multigabled roofs and rocket-ship entries. To understand where they ended and what comes next, first we need to understand how they evolved.

THE AUTOPSY OF THE MCMANSION

Let's begin by going back to 1980, to a hypothetical half-acre lot in a converted cornfield where an up-and-coming luxury-home builder has just broken ground on a new project. The blueprint calls for a formidable 4,000 square feet—not the biggest house in town, but a good deal bigger than its neighbors. More complicated too, with half a dozen gables on its front elevation and a mishmash of materials, including brick, stone veneer, and clapboards. When folks inquire about the style, they get a variety of answers: It's neoclassical, it's neocolonial, it's eclectic. It's different, they say, and drive on.

They were right. It was different. And that was the point. After years of bland, uninspired residential architecture, marked by split-levels and ranch-house designs, people were looking for homes with more presence and pop, open floor plans, and tall ceilings. A little extra space wouldn't hurt either, what with all the new stuff houses were having to contain, including desktop computers, big-screened tube TVs, overstuffed sofas, and more. As the emerging pop icon Madonna would intone a few years later, we were living in a material world. Here was our material home.

What it was, we now know, was the first of the McMansions, a style of architecture that would slowly dominate the decade. If only McMansions had gone the way of junk bonds, gauzy headbands, and other epitomes of the era, they might seem quaint today. But the 1980s were just the beginning. As the U.S. economy roared through the '90s, the McMansion's hold on American home building only tightened. The fin-de-siecle dot-com crash and September 11 attacks might have halted its progress temporarily, but a historic housing boom during the first decade of the new millennium quickly regained any lost momentum.

KEEPING UP WITH THE JONESES

The Alpine Roof Line tells you that budget was spent to "differentiate" this house from the neighbors rather than creating usable places to engage with the outdoors, like a porch or garden terrace.

HIGH ENERGY BILLS

Double-height entry tells you that behind this window is an expensive room to heat and cool, yet most likely a space you will never enter (see note below for the reason why).

WE RAN OUT OF MONEY

The material mash-up of brick and stucco combined in vertical strips says "we didn't have quite enough to cover the entire house."

NOBODY ARRIVES AT THIS HOUSE BY FOOT

Without a path, no one will ever walk to this front door.

CARS DOMINATE THIS STREET

Rolling curb without sidewalks tell you that this is an auto-dependent neighborhood. Not only is there nothing to walk to, but traffic will speed on these streets, making it unsafe to walk even if there was a destination.

What is this house telling you? This house is isolated and expensive. Every house has a story. Most can be read from afar and at a glance. This house tells us that a car is required for all trips outside the home. It also indicates it will be expensive to heat and cool.

"TOLL-HOUSE" COOKIE-CUTTER HOMES

Toll Brothers was one of the first builders to catch on to the new business model. Started in 1967 by Robert and Bruce Toll, the Pennsylvania-based company was fairly small potatoes during its start-up years, building thirty or so homes annually. But the brothers understood the public's desire for bigger, more exclusive homes,

LOTS OF LIGHT

Windows on multiple walls will bring light into rooms evenly throughout the day, giving you nice light and making the house easier to heat and cool.

EASY HEAT & COOL

Simple roof lines allow budget to be spent on elements that add value you can touch and feel, like a cupola that brings light into the center of the house. Simple roof massing also reduces heat load in the attic, making the house easier to heat and cool.

ENJOY THE OUTDOORS & CONNECT TO COMMUNITY

A large front porch lets you know that you will be able to enjoy the outdoors easily on your own property. And that you will have a chance to meet your neighbors and connect to a community.

MULTI-GENERATIONAL LIVING

Your car will have a place to live, easily accessible, yet out of view of the street. You will also have an extra room for a boomerang child or aging parent.

ESCAPE THE BUGS!

You will be able to escape from the bugs and even your neighbors, while still enjoying the outdoors.

YOU CAN WALK TO AND FROM THIS HOUSE

Sidewalks make streets walkable. Trees make sidewalks safe. Also, if both are included in a new community, there is a good chance that there is something worth walking to nearby.

Now, what is THIS house telling you? This house is livable and connected. In contrast to the previous example, this house is telling you that you will be able to safely walk to nearby amenities. It also will allow you several options to engage with the outdoors on your own property; it is adaptable over time to meet the changing needs of your family and should be reasonable to heat and cool.

and they spent the 1970s cementing their reputation as builders of "dream homes." Playing off the emerging neo-eclectic vernacular of the day, the company offered clients a menu of customized options, from floor plans to siding materials. In this sense, it brought the efficiencies of cookie-cutter home building to the luxury market. At its core, a McMansion is basically a split-level on steroids.

These efforts, coupled with a savvy marketing strategy and tightly managed construction costs, paid off. Toll Brothers raked in nearly $50 million in 1979, and that was just the beginning. Revenues would surge upward of 300 percent between 1982 and 1987 to $120 million, peaking at $6 billion in 2006. The success of Toll Brothers inspired many imitators. By the end of the decade, the nation's biggest developers had converted over to this model and McMansions had become the established norm, with builders focusing their efforts on producing as many homes as possible. This meant repeating and repeating.

Repeating homes on a street is not a bad thing. In fact, some of the most treasured neighborhoods with the highest property values in the country are on streets where the same home is repeated over and over, such as in parts of San Francisco, Boston, and Georgetown in Washington, D.C. The problem with the repeats of the Toll Brothers and their contemporaries is that they were caught in the rising tide of suburban sprawl with low-density, auto-dependent development where the emphasis was on impressive individual homes rather than the streetscape.

Removing the design of the neighborhood and streetscape from the equation eliminates the glue that holds everything together. Without the outdoor room of the streetscape, the entire focus is on the home, which leads to a game of one-upmanship. Repeating homes isn't a bad thing, but repeating ugly homes without connection to a larger streetscape is a problem.

I'LL SEE YOUR SIX GABLES AND RAISE YOU THREE

We all want to identify with where we live and to feel like our home is special. Traditionally, this process started at the community level. Buildings worked together to form streetscapes. Neighborhoods were composed of a hierarchy of streetscapes with civic, commercial, and residential uses integrated together. Streets were designed to be walkable, and the neighborhoods provided multiple reasons to get out and walk. In this system, it was easy to identify your home. You might live down the street from the city hall. Or around the corner from the local school. The identity of one's home came from its proximity to local landmarks.

As civic and commercial uses were separated from the residential, and streetscapes evaporated into auto-only thoroughfares, it became harder and harder to differentiate individual homes and communities. The first generation of transitional neighborhoods in the '60s and '70s, filled with ranch homes and split-levels, left many feeling the need for more interest in their homes. Rather than turning back to community building, builders addressed the issue by making homes more interesting.

The earliest McMansions relied largely on height to generate interest. After decades of low-slung, horizontal architecture, people wanted to see that second, third, or even fourth story on their home. Unfortunately, adding interest in architecture alone is a game of diminishing returns. Although it addresses one issue—people want to feel a sense of identity of where they live—it treats only the symptom, not the disease.

Soon it wasn't enough for houses just to be tall. They also had to grab attention with increasingly complex rooflines; three gables were better than two, but not as good as four or six or ten. When rooflines could not handle any more 45-degree angles, builders looked to other design elements for differentiation. Enter the patchwork of siding materials you see on many McMansions. A hodgepodge of window designs is another ploy, including the Palladian window, a hallmark of McMansion design. The harder the attempt to differentiate, the more homes look the same. Eventually individual homes contained enough architectural elements for an entire town. In this scenario, not only did every home end up looking the same, but they were often poorly built. And ironically, as more and more effort was poured into the front of these homes, less and less attention and budget were allocated to the sides. In many cases, the resulting homes had little more depth than a stage set.

WHAT TO DO?

The solution is simple. Build communities again where houses and streets work together to create places. Simplify the design of the homes (thus making them more affordable to build), and add details to areas you can touch and feel, such as porches, rather than gratuitous design elements on the roof. Organize streets to work together in such a way that residents identify and take pride in the place. These moves will release the pressure on the individual home to deliver all of the interest on its own.

McMansions resulted from the compensation for the lack of community and a misperception about what was actually being delivered. The dream of open floor plans, "lots of light," and gourmet kitchens resulted in a reality of unfurnishable floor plans with commercial-grade kitchens sized to cater grand parties where only the microwave was used. The dream of a large yard turned into an expensive hassle while the kids stayed inside to watch TV.

So, is the McMansion dead? Perhaps it is too soon to make the call. The only question that matters for you is whether the house you are considering meets your needs. When the perception of what a home "should be" and the desire for what a home "could be" don't align with the realities of how homes (and households) really live, the resident loses. As you look for a new place to live, take serious stock of how you want to live in a home as well as what the street outside that home looks and feels like. McMansions were fueled by a combination of easy money and unrealistic aspirations. Keeping up with the Joneses, enabled by lax lending and artificial home appreciation, resulted in millions of people living in homes that didn't really meet their needs. Take time to examine your true needs with your eyes wide open and you'll end up in the right place.

Notes

Introduction

More than 37 millions (plus) people switch addresses in any given year: *Geographical Mobility: 2010 to 2011*, U.S. Census Bureau, census.gov/hhes/migration/data/cps/cps2011.html

Chapter 1

Millions have defaulted on their mortgages, millions more are underwater (owing more than the property is worth), and credit is all but frozen: "The State of the Nation's Housing 2012." Joint Center for Studies of Harvard University (2012), jchs.harvard.edu/sites/jchs.harvard.edu/files/son2012.pdf

Even people shopping for major purchases don't know what they want: David Brooks, *The Social Animal: The Hidden Sources of Love, Character, and Achievement* (Random House, 2011), page 172.

If you've ever tried to sustain a great-tasting diet on a budget, then you have wrestled with the Decision Balancing Act: Based on teachings of Vitruvius Pollo, first-century Roman engineer who is often referred to as the first architect. In *De Architectura*, he taught that every building must have firmness, commodity, and delight.

Brooks Stevens definition of planned obsolescence: Wisconsin Historical Society, wisconsinhistory.org/topics/stevens/

Echo boomers are increasingly driving less and looking for ways to live in an area where they can walk: *National Household Travel Survey 2009*, U.S. Department of Transportation, http://nhts.ornl.gov/introduction.shtml. Survey found that from 2001 to 2009, the annual number of vehicle-miles traveled by young people (16- to 34-year-olds) decreased 23 percent—from 10,300 miles to 7,900 miles per capita.

Estimated there will be 22 million unwanted large-lot suburban homes by 2025: Patrick C. Doherty and Christopher B. Leinberger, "The Next Real Estate Boom: How Housing (Yes, Housing) Can Turn the Economy Around," *Washington Monthly* (2010), washingtonmonthly.com/features/2010/1011.doherty-leinberger.html

Chapter 2

Single women have been the fastest-growing segment of the real estate market, representing about 20 percent of all buyers. Single men add another 10 percent: "2011 National Association of Realtors Profile of Home Buyers and Sellers," National Association of Realtors (2011), realtor.org/news-releases/2011/11/nar-home-buyer-and-seller-survey-reflects-tight-credit-conditions.

One national survey in 2011 found that 30 percent of households were doubling up: "Housing 360 Survey," Hanley Wood (2012), remodeling.hw.net/remodeling-market-data/housing-360-research-on-attitudes-to-homeownership.aspx

By 2012, the homeownership rate was down to 65.4 percent, almost 5 percent below its 2004 peak, and the lowest level since 1997: Housing Vacancies and Homeownership First Quarter 2012, U.S. Census, census.gov/hhes/www/housing/hvs/qtr112/q112ind.html

The growth in foreign-born households has slowed considerably: "The State of the Nation's Housing 2012," Joint Center for Studies of Harvard University (2012), jchs.harvard.edu/sites/jchs.harvard.edu/files/son2012.pdf

Strongly dependent on fiscally dependent individuals: Eli Beracha and Ken H. Johnson, "Lessons from Over 30 Years of Buy versus Rent Decisions: Is the American Dream Always Wise?" *Real Estate Economics* (2012), fma.org/NY/Papers/Lessons_from_30_years_of_Buy_vs_Rent_Decisions.pdf

Older manufacturing firms, jobs, and industries are being destroyed: Richard Florida, *The Great Reset: How New Ways of Living and Working Drive Post-Crash Prosperity* (HarperCollins, 2010), 174.

Average homeowner consistently derives more pain (but no more joy) from their house and home: Grace W. Bucchianeri, "The American Dream or The American Delusion? The Private and External Benefits of Homeownership," The Wharton School of Business (2011). real.wharton.upenn.edu/~wongg/research/the%20american%20dream.pdf: 4

Consistent findings show that homeownership does make a significant impact on educational achievement: *Social Benefits of Homeownership and Stable Housing,* National Association of Realtors (2010): 7.

Chapter 3

Commuting is one of the least pleasurable activities in life: "Wellbeing Lower Among Workers With Long Commutes," Gallup-Healthways Well-Being Index (2010), gallup.com/poll/142142/Wellbeing-Lower-Among-Workers-Long-Commutes.aspx. "Long-distance commuters get divorced more often," Umea University (2011), umu.se/ViewPage.action?siteNodeId=4510&languageId=1&contentId=160978

More than half of buyers considered purchasing a foreclosure but didn't buy one for a variety of reasons: "2011 National Association of Realtors Profile of Home Buyers and Sellers," National Association of Realtors (2011), realtor.org/news-releases/2011/11/nar-home-buyer-and-seller-survey-reflects-tight-credit-conditions

Chapter 4

We knew that if we could identify them in their second trimester, there's a good chance we could capture them for years: Charles Duhigg, "How Companies Learn Your Secrets," *New York Times* (2012), nytimes.com/2012/02/19/magazine/shopping-habits.html?pagewanted=all

Average American now spends more than $7,600 annually on transportation, more than they spend on food: "A New Economic Analysis of Infrastructure Investment," Department of Treasury with the Council of Economic Advisers (2012), treasury.gov/resource-center/economic-policy/Documents/20120323InfrastructureReport.pdf: 3

Americans were coping with economic hardship by reassessing which home appliances were necessities and which they considered a luxury: "Luxury or Necessity? The Public Makes a U-Turn," Pew Research Center Publications (2009), pewresearch.org/pubs/1199/more-items-seen-as-luxury-not-necessity

Chapter 5

Today, 35 percent of people start their search online: "2011 National Association of Realtors Profile of Home Buyers and Sellers," National Association of Realtors (2011), realtor.org/news-releases/2011/11/nar-home-buyer-and-seller-survey-reflects-tight-credit-conditions

Chapter 6

In the U.S., as elsewhere, it matters where you live. Healthcare is not the same in Massachusetts and Texas: Cynthia Enloe and Joni Seager, *The Real State of America Atlas* (Penguin Books, 2011), 10.

Housing Market Data: Jonathan Smoke, Hanley Wood Market Intelligence, hwmarketintelligence.com/

Chapter 7

The average American moves once every seven years: Richard Florida, *Who's Your City? How the Creative Economy Is Making Where to Live the Most Important Decision of Your Life* (Basic Books, 2008), 6

Asked to name their biggest life decisions, he asserts, most people will say one of two things: career path or spouse: Richard Florida, *Who's Your City? How the Creative Economy Is Making Where to Live the Most Important Decision of Your Life* (Basic Books, 2008), 5–6.

Transportation accounts for 27 percent of greenhouse gas emissions and 72 percent of petroleum use in the United States: Jeffrey Tumlin, *Sustainable Transportation Planning,* (Wiley, 2012), 4.

Chapter 8

Currently we are tied to a 19th-century approach, which isolates the big city unto itself: Marianne Cusato, "Your Home in 2020." *Forbes* (2010), forbes.com/2010/04/08/mortage-foreclosure-2020-technology-data-companies-10-housing.html

Chapter 9

In Boulder, Colorado, for example, two decades' worth of investment in sidewalks, bike paths, and pedestrian crossings has resulted in a 14 percent decline in the number of people who drive to work: *Modal Shift in the Boulder Valley* (National Research Center, Inc.), 4

In 1969, approximately half of all students walked or rode bikes to school: "Background and Statistics," Safe Routes to School National Partnership, saferoutespartnership.org/resourcecenter/quick-facts

The number of overweight children in the United States has tripled, from 5 percent to 15 percent: "Childhood Obesity Facts," Center for Disease Control and Prevention, cdc.gov/healthyyouth/obesity/facts.htm

Chapter 10

Roughly one third of homeowners and one fifth of renters are doubling up: "Housing 360 Survey," Hanley Wood (2012), remodeling.hw.net/remodeling-market-data/housing-360-research-on-attitudes-to-homeownership.aspx

A front porch is an outdoor feature most likely to be included in the average new home built in 2015: "The New Home in 2015," National Association of Home Builders (2011), nahb.org/generic.aspx?sectionID=734&genericContentID=153664&channelID=311

Chapter 11

The percentage of U.S. homes with a three-car garage peaked at 20 percent in 2005: "Characteristics of New Single-Family Houses Completed," U.S. Census (2011), census.gov/construction/chars/pdf/parkingfacility.pdf

Chapter 12

By 1870 separateness had become essential to the identity of the suburban house: Kenneth T. Jackson, *Crabgrass Frontier, The Suburbanization of the United States* (Oxford University Press, 1985), 58

Landscape irrigation, including the watering of lawns, accounts for nearly a third of all residential water use in the United States: "Outdoor Water Use in the United States," Environmental Protection Agency, epa.gov/WaterSense/pubs/outdoor.html

A property with plenty of mature trees is worth 20 to 30 percent more than one without: A. Duany, J. Speck, M. Lydon, *The Smart Growth Manual* (McGraw Hill, 2010), 13.9

Chapter 13

The master bedroom on the main floor is one of the features most likely to be included in new homes in 2015: "The New Home in 2015," National Association of Home Builders (2011), nahb.org/generic.aspx?sectionID=734&genericContentID=153664&channelID=311

Chapter 15

Between the years 1997 and 2007, nearly two thirds of sellers over the age of seventy-five had been living in their home for twenty years or more: George Masnick, Abbe Will, and Kermit Baker. "Housing Turnover by Older Owners: Implications for Home Improvement Spending as Baby Boomers Age into Retirement," Joint Center for Housing Studies of Harvard University (2011), jchs.harvard.edu/sites/jchs.harvard.edu/files/w11-4_masnick_will_baker.pdf

Chapter 18

Galina Tachieva, *Sprawl Repair Manual* (Island Press, 2010), 5

Appendix 1

A 2007 study by Mark Eppli and Charles Tu: "Market Acceptance of Smart Growth," Environmental Protection Agency (2011), epa.gov/dced/pdf/market_acceptance.pdf: 9

A 2011 study by Umea University in Sweden: "Long-Distance Commuters Get Divorced More Often," Umea University (2011), umu.se/ViewPage.action?siteNodeId=4510&languageId=1&contentId=160978

Appendix 2

Some cities and municipalities, including Charlotte, North Carolina; Portland, Oregon; and Austin, Texas, have all but banned cul-de-sacs: "Cul-De-Sac Backlash," Bradford Plumber, *The New Republic* (2010), tnr.com/blog/the-vine/the-cul-de-sac-backlash#.

Index

O

R

S

Photo Credits

Pages 180–181: Images provided by author

Page 224: Photo by author

Page 225: Photo by Rob Karosis Photography, design by Smith & Van Sant Architects PC

Page 350: Photo by Stephen A. Mouzon

Page 351: Photo by Otto Studios, Courtesy of Union Studio Architecture & Community Design

About the Authors

Marianne Cusato is a designer, author, and lecturer in the fields of real estate trends and housing. Her messages speak to the ever-changing needs of homeowners striving to balance the practical requirements of economy and durability with the desire to love where we live.

Ranked the No. 4 most influential person in the home-building industry by *Builder* magazine, Cusato is well known for her work on the Katrina Cottages. In 2006, her 308-square-foot cottage design won the Smithsonian Institution's Cooper-Hewitt Design Museum's People's Design Award. That same year, Congress appropriated $400 million for an alternative emergency housing program based on Cusato's designs. In 2012, Cusato was voted one of the 30 Most Influential Women in the Housing Economy by *HousingWire* magazine.

Cusato is currently developing a new series of designs with Clayton Homes, a Warren Buffett/Berkshire Hathaway company. She is the author of two previous books, is a blogger for Huffington Post, and has been a visiting professor at both the University of Notre Dame and the University of Miami. Cusato is a graduate of the University of Notre Dame School of Architecture and is based in Miami, Florida.

Daniel DiClerico is a senior editor at *Consumer Reports*, where he covers the housing industry and products for the home. He has worked and written for various publications, including *This Old House*, *Martha Stewart Living*, and *Garden Design*. He lives in Brooklyn, New York, with his wife and two children.